THE *CLASH* **OF RIGHTS**

THE *CLASH* OF RIGHTS

LIBERTY, EQUALITY, AND LEGITIMACY IN PLURALIST DEMOCRACY

Paul M. Sniderman

Joseph F. Fletcher

Peter H. Russell

Philip E. Tetlock

Yale University Press New Haven and London

Published with assistance from the Louis Stern Memorial Fund.

Designed by Nancy Ovedovitz and set in Meridien type by The Composing Room of
Michigan, Inc. Printed in the United States of America by BookCrafters, Inc.,
Chelsea, Michigan.

Library of Congress Cataloging-in-Publication Data

The clash of rights : liberty, equality, and legitimacy in pluralist democracy /
Paul M. Sniderman . . . [et al.].
p.   cm.
Includes bibliographical references and index.
ISBN 0-300-06535-3 (cloth : alk. paper). — ISBN 0-300-06981-2 (pbk. : alk. paper)
1. Democracy.   2. Liberty.   3. Equality.   4. Legitimacy of governments.
5. Democracy—Canada.   I. Sniderman, Paul M.
JC423.C59   1997
321.8—dc20   96-12149
CIP

A catalogue record for this book is available from the British Library.

The paper in this book meets the guidelines for permanence and durability of
the Committee on Production Guidelines for Book Longevity of the Council
on Library Resources.
10   9   8   7   6   5   4   3   2   1

Out of a wish to acknowledge the quality of
their scholarship in the service of the value of tolerance,
we dedicate this book to James L. Gibson,
Herbert McClosky, and John L. Sullivan.

CONTENTS

PREFACE

My colleagues have generously allowed me a personal word of introduction to our book, perhaps because, in the course of writing it, each has seen so many of my preconceptions bowled over.

When we started this project, I was quite sure I knew the principal intellectual landmarks, accepting their validity without question so that we could make our way further down the road. On no point was I surer of the truth than the special role of elites, above all, political elites, in providing a bulwark for democratic rights. When I was a graduate student the heart of my training was with Herbert McClosky, and my very first book, *Personality and Democratic Politics,* drew on much that he taught me, setting out for the first time the social learning theory of democratic commitment.

Our book was very much designed with this previous work in mind. I not only took its validity for granted, but even with the data from our surveys in hand, for a year or more read our results as being perfectly in line with it. Only slowly and, if I am to be honest, only reluctantly did I begin to see our findings in a different light. It was not quite that our new results showed our old ideas to be wrong. Rather, when our surveys were analyzed with a fresh eye, they showed that the old account was so partial as to be profoundly misleading. Misleading, moreover, at two different levels: omitting at one level the role of political institutions and, above all, the party system; obscuring at the other the inherent contestability of claims to democratic rights. The result, I gradually realized, was an account of the politics of rights that very largely left politics out.

In this book we have tried to put the politics back in. No doubt some will think we have put in too much, others perhaps too little: and no doubt the strictures of both will have merit. But we should not have made the attempt but for what we have learned from those who have grappled with the problems of political rights and public opinion before us. Without minimizing the work of many others who have made valuable contributions, we want to recognize the contributions of three scholars who in our judgment stand out: John Sullivan, who with his colleagues introduced the most innovative conception of political tolerance over the past quarter century; James Gibson, who both on his own and working with an array of colleagues has done work of genuine originality; and my own teacher, Herbert McClosky. We wound up where we have because we had the benefit of their work.

We could not have undertaken the fieldwork for this book without the generous support of the Social Sciences and Humanities Research Council, for which we are most grateful. But however generous the council's support, we would not have been able to carry out the surveys either of the general public or of elites without the unstinting, skilled, and creative assistance of the staff of the Institute for Social Research at York University. They put together the first networked version of computer-assisted interviewing and played indispensable roles in designing the elite samples, in assembling and pretesting the survey instruments, in conducting the interviews, and in preparing and disseminating the data to interested scholars. It is a pleasure to record our debt to John Tibert, David Bates, Bill Bruce, Tammy Chi, Anne Oram, and—above all—David Northrup.

For many years the Centre for Criminology at the University of Toronto provided a home, both intellectual and administrative, for the Charter of Rights Project. For all four of us it has been a site of support, encouragement, and collegiality, and we thank all of our colleagues there, particularly Anthony Doob, former director of the center, and Rita Donelan, administrator extraordinaire. The Institute of Personality and Social Research of the University of California at Berkeley provided valuable intellectual and logical support. We especially appreciate help above and beyond the call of duty from Helen Ettlinger, the office manager of the institute. In addition, both the Program for Computer-Assisted Survey Methods, under the direction of

Professor J. Merrill Shanks, and the Survey Research Center, then under the direction of Professor Percy Tannenbaum, both of the University of California at Berkeley, generously assisted us and our colleagues at the Institute for Social Research at York University. Beyond the debt that the project as a whole owes to both, I have myself a special debt to Professor J. Merrill Shanks that it gives me pleasure to acknowledge. For a decade now, all of my studies have been predicated on the innovations that computer-assisted interviewing makes possible, and it is my friend and colleague Merrill Shanks who in developing his CASES program has provided means of my doing my work.

A project that has run over many years and in more than one country inevitably owes much to colleagues at many universities. We could not be more appreciative of the assistance that so many have extended to us. In particular, we want to thank Richard Johnston, André Blais, Jean Crete, and Henry Brady, authors of the prizewinning *Letting the People Decide,* for releasing their data to us, and Stanley Feldman, who devised the equality items for the National Election Studies and counseled us in their use. In addition, we were ably assisted by Robert Boyd, Marie-Christine Chalmers, Elizabeth Jollimore, Matthew Kronby, Richard Powers, Kent Roach, Mark Sniderman, and Lyn Turner. John Covell of Yale University Press encouraged us over a number of years and is an advertisement for the distinctive contributions of an academic press. For those who care about clarity and conciseness, Lawrence Kenney, also of Yale University Press, is a godsend.

As for my more immediate colleagues, two require special mention. When so many now talk of the politicization of the university, and not entirely without cause, it gives me pride to point to two of my colleagues—Professor Martin Sanchez-Jankowski at Berkeley and Professor Susan Okin at Stanford—whose encouragement and criticism were altogether independent of the politics of our arguments. Finally, I want to thank Laurel Elms. She prepared all of the figures, and we are in her debt for her technical assistance; we are still more indebted to her for improvements she made to our arguments on page after page through the quality of her mind.

—Paul M. Sniderman

ONE **INTRODUCTION**

This work is an essay in democratic theory, albeit in an empirical key. We have spoken with a few thousand ordinary citizens and with more than a thousand decision makers—parliamentarians, government officials, senior lawyers. In the process, we have tried to elicit their judgments of right and wrong across an array of issues at the center of contemporary democratic politics: How should decisions of what is right and wrong ultimately be made in a democracy? How do the political institutions of liberal democracy sustain such fundamental rights as freedom of speech? What forms does the clash of values—say, between liberty and equality—take in contemporary politics? What rights might members of a group be entitled to by virtue of their membership in the group? How willing are people to give up a claim to a right if confronted with a competing right?

Our concern is thus the tangle of claims put forward on behalf of both individuals and groups that is now at the center of the politics of liberal democracies. Some are long-standing claims, for example, to freedom of expression; others are more modern, for example, to group equity. But ideas about all, we argue, have to be understood as being bound up with the political institutions of liberal democracy, and above all, the party system. Because the nexus between ideas and institutions is so intimate, we want first to set out the political context of our study, then describe its design and relate its principal themes.

Political Context

The immediate impetus for this study, its proximate cause, was Canada's adoption in 1982 of a constitutional charter of rights and freedoms. In making this change in its Constitution, Canada joined a lengthening procession of modern democracies that have adopted the classical American device of codifying fundamental rights and freedoms in constitutional texts.

The watershed in the movement toward codification of fundamental liberal democratic rights was World War II. The fascist tyrannies starkly revealed the evils that flow from a complete denial of basic democratic liberties and from taking theories of racial superiority to their logical conclusion. The founding of the United Nations in 1945 and the proclamation of the Universal Declaration of Rights in 1948 marked the beginning of a process of establishing a worldwide consensus on fundamental human rights. Bills of rights became a prominent feature of the new constitutions adopted in the postwar period by the defeated Axis powers and by decolonized Third World nations. The very form of these instruments fostered the view that democracy depends, above all, on achieving a binding consensus on liberal democratic values.

In this international movement, it was the American Constitution with its emphasis on a judicially enforced constitutional bill of rights that served as the most influential paradigm.[1] This tendency coincided with the United States' position as the most powerful constitutional democracy in the postwar world. In many ways American constitutionalism began to play a role in the world akin to that of Roman law centuries ago. But, as with Roman law, each country put its own spin on the American model, weaving through its statement of fundamental rights something of its own principles derived from its own political tradition and experience. In the Canadian case, the adoption of an American–style bill of rights had a distinctive indigenous rationale: it was the centerpiece of a strategy for resolving the struggle over the future of the Canadian federation, a struggle waged with increasing intensity since the rise of Quebec separatism in the 1960s. The Canadian Charter of Rights and Freedoms was designed by its chief architect, Pierre Trudeau, to serve above all as an instrument for national unity. Trudeau's final speech on the Charter summed up the case for its adoption in these words: "Lest the forces of self-interest tear us apart, we must now define the common thread that binds us together."[2]

This intuition that a political constitution weaves a "common thread that binds us together" has become a staple of political speech, its very familiarity obscuring the paradox lying behind it. A constitution may supply a common thread of beliefs, but increasingly in liberal democracies these beliefs define claims to both individual rights and political identities. The thread of common belief thus comes to define the very terms of political conflict.

It is the idea of political rights and of group identities as bases of political conflict in liberal democracies that interests us. We also examine questions specific to the Canadian context, but not at the outset and not primarily. For though the Canadian Charter contains provisions reflecting the particular circumstances of Canada's long (and seemingly endless) constitutional debate,[3] it also contains the basic rights and freedoms that derive from a more universal democratic tradition going back to the French and American Revolutions. Freedom of speech and assembly, freedom of conscience and religion, freedom from arbitrary detention, the right to due process of law and equal protection of the law, in other words, the standard rights and freedoms found in the bills of rights of most constitutional democracies, are present in Canada's Charter. Thus the data we have assembled about the politics of Canadian Charter rights can be used, and indeed will be used, to pursue more fundamental questions about the politics of liberal democratic rights.

When the issues contested in politics are cast in a discourse of rights, as is increasingly the case in the liberal democracies, normally what is at stake is not the existence of support for a particular democratic right or freedom, but rather the relative weight attached to competing claims by the political actors involved in debating concrete questions of public policy and constitutional politics. It is in the rough and tumble of controversies over such issues as the propagation of racial hatred and the exhibition of pornography that the politics of liberal democratic rights is played out. If we are to understand this politics, what we must have our eye on is how those engaged in these clashes of rights, be they ordinary citizens or political leaders, are influenced and moved by the interplay of values that sometimes complement and sometimes conflict with one another in contested applications of democratic rights. This theme of value pluralism frames the Charter study. So while at one level this work is about how Canadians respond to questions about democratic rights, at a more universal level, it is about the pluralism of values that, in a political era permeated by "rights talk" and a "rights discourse," we believe to be at the very heart of politics in all of the liberal democracies.

Although no country can serve as a paradigmatic model of contemporary democracy, Canada arguably is better placed than most to testify to the complexity of historical traditions and societal conditions that shape the politics of democratic rights. Indeed, Canada provides a more promising site for investigating the politics of rights than does the United States, where most of the research in this field has been done. This may seem ironic, given that the American Constitution is the exemplar for the codification of fundamental rights. But it is precisely the relative ideological purity of the American tradition of constitutional rights—its saturation in a philosophy of liberal individualism—that makes it so idiosyncratic. Canada's engagement with liberal democratic rights and freedoms, by way of contrast, has been mediated by a richer array of ideological forces. Its very lack of a clear national identity or dominant political ideology, though problematic for the country's future as a unified political community, gives it a comparative advantage as an arena in which to study the interplay of values and perspectives in the politics of rights and freedoms.

There is a further advantage in basing an inquiry of this kind in Canada as it takes on the mantle of a constitutional bill of rights. One thing the adoption of such an instrument tends to do, especially when it is joined to a vigorous system of judicial review,[4] is to expose for public discussion questions about democratic rights that had hitherto been latent in the country's political practice. There is a freshness and openness to debates about the balance to be struck between political freedom and public morals, between individual rights and the need for public order, between the claims of liberty and the claims of equality when these questions are posed for the first time as constitutional issues of democratic rights. As problems are being thrashed out, the positions of both citizens and leaders are apt to be less fixed, the arguments less rehearsed, and the interplay of contending players and ideas more visible than in a society in which these questions have long been cast in a framework of constitutional rights.

Although Canada's political culture is well within the mainstream of Western liberal democracy, the ethos of Canada's founding compared with that of the United States was, as S. M. Lipset's *Continental Divide* recently reminded us, distinctly counterrevolutionary.[5] Canada's founding English settlers were loyalists who fled to British North America to escape what they regarded as the democratic excesses of the American Revolution. In establishing the Canadian federation, these English loyalists collaborated with French Canadians reared in a conservative Catholic tradition that abhorred the French Revolution. Canada's founders believed in social hierarchy and strong government. Their watchwords were "peace, order and good government," not "life, liberty and the pursuit of happiness." Government was to be not distrusted but used to carry out the projects of the governing class. Later on, this "tory touch," to use Gad Horowitz's telling phrase, together with the absence of a strong laissez-faire ideology, would provide a more favorable political climate than the United States for British and European immigrants of a socialist persuasion advocating an activist state.[6]

Important as these counterrevolutionary and statist tendencies undoubtedly were in the outlook of Canada's founders, they have never been more than one aspect of the country's political culture. Since the early nineteenth century there has been a strong liberal tradition in Canada. A distinctive tory touch may well have modified Canadian liberalism and made it more open than American liberalism to the challenge of conservatism on the right and socialism on the left. But the point is that a tory touch is just that, a touch, not the dominant political tradition. Canada's founding fathers may have rejected American republicanism, but they did not reject the liberal heritage of the American founders. Their intellectual leaders were influenced much more by Locke, Hume, Blackstone, and Bentham than by proponents of authoritarian or aristocratic government. The lawyers among them were bent on maintaining the rudiments of English liberalism so that governmental authority would be exercised according to laws enforced by an independent judiciary. The monarchy to which these Canadians were loyal was one that had to be fully compatible with representative and responsible government. And, in the realm of political economy, though Canada's founders had a positive view of the state as an economic facilitator and did not worship free enterprise, nonetheless they were strongly committed to capitalism. Indeed, in large measure they supported Confederation as a scheme to provide a stronger infrastructure for Canadian capitalism. The key to understanding Canadian political culture is not the dominance of liberalism, conservatism, or collectivism but the interplay of often competing values derived from these traditions.

A study of contemporary thinking about liberal democratic rights cannot call into question the contrast between the *founding* traditions of Canada and the United States that Lipset and others have so insightfully portrayed. But it is quite another thing to assume the continued potency of these historic traditions over time. In investigating empirically how contemporary Canadians think about democratic rights and comparing their attitudes on crucial points with those of contemporary Americans, we treat the enduring weight of founding traditions as an open question. In an era in which the domestic politics of the democracies are so open to global influences, we and our readers should be prepared to find both convergence and divergence across the "continental divide."

Moreover, historically the most distinctive feature of Canadian politics, the political salience of the ethnic and collective divisions of the country, arguably has become the new fulcrum of the politics of liberal democracies. The divisions run so deep that the very concept of nation is contested. Although there are plenty of Canadian nationalists who yearn for a stronger, more unified Canadian nation, Quebeckers refer to their provincial legislature as a National Assembly. Confederation was possible only when the English abandoned a program of cultural assimilation and agreed to a federation with a province in which the French could be a majority with the power to secure their distinctive identity. This has produced a state that, much more than the United States, privileges ethnic differences and fosters collective identities based on these differences. Most recently this feature of Canadian life has been manifest in the mobilization of ethnic nationalism among Canada's indigenous peoples and the official recognition of the rights of Aboriginal peoples in the Canadian Constitution.[7]

Recognition of group rights in Canada extends beyond ethnicity and language to provincial rights. It is one of the great ironies of history that Canada, whose founders accepted federalism only as an unfortunate compromise, has become and has remained much more federal than the United States, whose founders saw federalism as a way of perfecting the Union. Canada has adhered assiduously to the principles of classical federalism, respecting the division of sovereignty between its two levels of government and living with the divided loyalties of its citizens. Provincial rights, unlike states' rights, were never tainted by slavery. Provinces (and not only the province of Quebec) continue to be primary political actors. In spite of its written Constitution, which is considered to be only quasi-federal,[8] Canada functions as a thoroughly federal society.

All of these features of the Canadian political tradition are manifest in the text of the Canadian Charter of Rights and Freedoms. The Charter certainly includes freedom of speech, religion, and assembly, the right to due process of law, equal protection of laws, and most of the other individual rights contained in the American Bill of Rights. But the Charter represents a more contextual version of constitutionalism than the American Bill of Rights, and this shows as much in what it omits as in what it includes. Thus, two notable exceptions are a clause prohibiting the establishment of religion and any mention of property rights. The former is absent because the Charter recognizes the historic rights of denominational minorities—Catholics outside Quebec, Protestants in Quebec—to state-supported school systems. The absence of property rights was a condition for securing the support of the New Democratic Party (NDP), Canada's social democratic party, for the Charter of Rights. Although the Charter prohibits discrimination based on race, national or ethnic origin, color, religion, sex, age, or mental or physical disability, it mandates certain forms of positive discrimination: laws and programs designed to ameliorate the conditions of those who have been disadvantaged in the past because of their membership in vulnerable sectors of society are to be immune from Charter challenge.

Other sections of the Charter recognize the rights of historically privileged groups. These include the school rights of denominational minorities already mentioned and extensive coverage of English and French language rights in the realms of education and government. Section 25 of the Charter provides that none of the rights and freedoms in the Charter are to encroach upon the "aboriginal, treaty or other rights and freedoms that pertain to the aboriginal peoples of Canada." And, in a gesture at universalizing this recognition of cultural difference, yet another section states that "the Charter shall be interpreted in a manner consistent with the preservation and enhancement of the multicultural heritage of Canadians."

One reaction to the complexities, qualifications, and ambivalence in the Canadian Charter is to conclude that the document, like the political community from which it arises, is simply incoherent. Our book argues against this interpretation. The charge of incoherence against the Canadian Charter implies a unidimensional understanding of liberal democratic rights that belies, we show, even the American experience. Indeed, to frame the issue as though the problem were a lack of coherence is to miss probably the most fundamental characteristic of the politics of liberal democracies—namely, the inherent contestability of rights. Thus, the rights and freedoms set out in the Charter are packaged between two general clauses that underline the qualified commitment that Canada's constitution makers were willing to make to constitutionalizing democratic rights. The very first section of the Charter states that the rights and freedoms set out in it are subject to "such reasonable limits prescribed by law as can be demonstrably justified in a free and democratic society." Here is a clear recognition of the value pluralism inherent in liberal democratic politics: in order to enhance democracy the constitutional rights of citizens can be justifiably curtailed. At the end of the Charter, a clause extracted from a reluctant Prime Minister Trudeau by provincial premiers allows legislatures, federal and provincial, to allow a law to stand in spite of what judges may think about its inconsistency with the Charter. The special historic group rights are exempted from this "override" clause, and any laws passed under it die after five years unless they are renewed. The override clause accordingly entails a deep compromise between the traditions of parliamentary government and judicial review: on issues pertaining to the fundamental universal rights in the Charter neither judges nor elected legislators are guaranteed the last word. And just insofar as the Charter makes explicit the contestability even of second-order rights, that is, rights as to the stipulation of rights, it calls attention unmistakably to our most fundamental theme: the inescapable and essential pluralism of values in liberal democracy.

Design of the Study

Our primary research interest is the politics of rights. We therefore focus upon how both citizens and leaders in a modern democratic society respond to a wide range of issues bearing on basic rights and freedoms.

In order to hear what citizens taken as a whole have to say about rights, freedoms, and obligations, we empaneled a representative sample of them in 1987.[9] We interviewed 2,084 people in all, working through the premier center for academic survey research in Canada, the Institute for Social Research at York University. Moreover, we carried out not one but two interviews, first interviewing respondents over the telephone, then sending them a self-administered questionnaire to complete in the privacy of their homes and mail back.[10]

The idea of a representative sample of the general population is straightforward; that of leaders or "elites" is anything but. In principle, the aim is to canvass the opinions of those with their hands on the levers of power. In practice, this has meant everything from officers of fraternal organizations (for example, the Shriners) to leaders of the Parent Teachers Association to trade union officials to religious leaders (for example, officers of the Council of Churches or an influential clergyman of any denomination) to journalists to mayors and city council members.[11] For our purposes, we prefer to concentrate on decision makers, that is, on those who have their hands more immediately on the levers of governmental power.

Specifically, we devised a three-pronged approach. First, we were particularly interested in the views of those who compete directly for governmental power and, if successful, make public policy. In Canada, the incontestably appropriate focus was parliaments at both federal and provincial levels, and so a systematic sample of elected politicians from the major parties contesting federal and provincial elections at the time of our study was drawn (n = 474). Second, to represent the views of the executive branch charged with responsibility for issues of rights, a sample was specially drawn of officials from the upper echelons of those government departments most concerned in the administration of justice: the federal Department of Justice, Crown Attorneys, and ministries of the attorney general and solicitor general, at both federal and provincial levels (n = 260). Finally, because enlisting the cooperation of sitting judges is both practically and ethically problematic, we focused upon the next best thing: the pool from which judges are selected, that is, lawyers with ten to thirty years of professional experience, drawing a special sample weighted by province (n = 352). Our three-pronged conception of elite decision makers thus corresponds, roughly, with the legislative, executive, and judicial branches of government.

So much for who spoke to us; now for what they spoke to us about. Although valuing and therefore replicating a number of questions from previous studies, we wanted to focus attention on an array of issues, from wiretapping through public funding of religious schools through antihate legislation, which in our judgment are integral components of the politics of rights. Our aim, accordingly, has been to capture more of the texture and complexity of these issues by basing questions on actual cases out of which differences over democratic rights arise and are argued out. The core questions in many sections of our interviews were thus drawn from the real world of the Canadian Charter, the concrete issues to which the Charter was being applied at the time of our study. Typically in the situations encapsulated in these cases it is not the hard inner, consensual, core of a democratic right that is at issue but its outer margins, where it comes squarely into collision with another cherished right or freedom. In this way we have attempted to weave the political context through the questions and propositions about rights that we put to citizens and decision makers.

In addition, the Charter Study is distinguished by the use it makes of computer-assisted interviewing. All of the special techniques we deploy, and there are now a sizeable number of them, have been developed with an eye to understanding better the actual politics of rights. Setting aside their description until they are called into play, we nevertheless would like to say a word about the match between the larger objectives we are pursing and the new methods we are putting to use. The first objective is to study double standards through identity-substitution experiments. In arguments over rights, a pivotal premise often is parity, either in the form of a future conditional—I will agree that you have a claim to X provided you agree that I have an equivalent claim to X—or in the form of a present negative—I do not accept your being entitled to X because you do not accept my being entitled to X. Taking advantage of computer-assisted interviewing, we conducted a series of identity-substitution experiments: in each experiment a claim to exactly the same right is made but on behalf of different groups. Because the specific group a respondent is asked about is decided on an entirely random basis, we can tell with confidence whether members of one group are more likely to uphold a claim to a right if made by members of their own group.

Our second objective is to explore the force of arguments made in advance of presentation of a claim to a right. It is, for example, commonly said that rights are trump now, but there is scarcely any evidence about the force that the idea of rights actually possesses. To mention only one of our attempts to get a grip on the dynamics of claims to rights, the constitutional springboard experiment is designed specifically to test whether and for whom knowing that a claim to a public good is indeed a right increases support for the right being claimed. But political arguments do not end with a single stroke. Arguments are made; then counterarguments are made in reply.

Our third objective, accordingly, is to expand the study of the dynamics of political arguments to take account of postdecisional as well as predecisional influences. This we do through the counterargument technique, in which we ask people to take a position on a matter of rights in the standard fashion and then immediately try to talk them out of the position they have just taken by calling their attention to countervailing arguments and competing values. In short, unlike the conventional public opinion survey, our study makes arguments to our respondents. It does so because the world of actual politics is a world of argument and counterargument. And we attempt to capture this world by bringing our interviews about the politics of rights closer to the conversational form of point and counterpoint in which arguments over rights are characteristically carried out.

Major Themes

Value pluralism is the key term of our argument. The politics of rights is driven by the irreducible diversity of values in politics and the unavoidability of their coming, in one form or another and at some point or other, into conflict with one another. What is distinctive in the account of liberal democratic politics that we set out here follows from the attention we pay to value pluralism. Without attempting to be comprehensive, we want to introduce some of the main strands of arguments that are bound up in the theme of value pluralism:

- For nearly half a century, it has been settled knowledge that the stability of democratic politics rests on a bedrock of consensus on core values among the politically aware and influential: in contrast, ordinary citizens' understanding of, and commitment to, fundamental democratic values is too superficial and too fickle to hold up under pressure. This presumption that elites are the custodians of democratic values has rested on two sets of empirical findings: first, that ordinary citizens, although unanimously endorsing democratic principles in the abstract, desert in droves under pressure, and second, that the politically active and aware overwhelmingly stand by essential democratic rights even in the heat of controversy.

  We shall show that this view is wrong, not because its depiction of the general public is too pessimistic, but because its characterization of political elites is too optimistic.

- As against previous studies that have attributed a failure to stand by individual rights in specific controversies to a failure of understanding, the "error" hypothesis, we highlight the inescapable collision of values, the "contestability" hypothesis. Eliminate misunderstandings, guarantee the learning of societal values, and clashes over claims to rights will nonetheless remain at the center of democratic politics. As we show, even liberty, notwithstanding its status as a foundational value of democratic politics, can readily be challenged in the name of values of the right *and* of the left.

- If liberty is an example of a democratic value that can be challenged in the name of another, equality is an example of a democratic value that is distinctively contestable because it can also be challenged in its own name.

The politics of equality is distinctively contestable, we argue, not simply because it can be interpreted in different ways, but more fundamentally because different interpretations of it lie ideologically at opposing poles. The fact that it can be contested from within as well as from without gives to the politics of equality its distinctively doubled-edged character: Equality, obviously enough, often works to the advantage of the political left. But in part because it is contestable in its own name, it can also work to the advantage of the political right.

- Ideas matter, and among the new ideas that matter most is that of group rights. As genocidal civil wars across three continents bear witness, clashes for group supremacy have become a standard feature of twentieth-century politics; and a country like Canada, strained to the breaking point by the cleavage between French and English, seems to teach a lesson about the limits of liberal tolerance even in affluent, well-educated countries.

  As against this image of the limits of liberal democracy imposed by mass tolerance, we make a two-pronged argument. First, as we shall show, a working consensus had in fact been achieved, with a majority of English Canadians supporting the special rights of French Canadians and a still larger majority of French Canadians supporting the special rights of English Canadians. Second, as we shall suggest, the politics of group rights is inherently volatile because of selective incentives to partisan leaders to put the issue of group rights into play as part of their competitive bid for power.

- Politics, particularly the politics of rights, is dynamic, not static. Just because claims to rights are inescapably contestable, it is not enough to document the positions that either citizens or elites take when an issue is broached. It is necessary to see what happens when they are pressured to defend their position or take account of countervailing considerations. Across a number of issue contexts and as a result of our using a variety of new survey devices, our findings illustrate how support for a claim to one right can be undercut by calling attention to a competing right, not merely in the public at large but among the politically most sophisticated and aware.

• The dynamics of political ideas, including ideas about rights, cannot be understood outside the dynamics of political institutions, including the electoral system. Partly through the influence of political ideology, partly in the search for electoral advantage, political parties in pluralist democracies can and frequently do elaborate contrasting conceptions of the rights of citizens and the powers of the state. Without minimizing the risks begot by the public's ignorance, we take as a theme of equal importance the dangers begot by elites' pursuit of both power and ideology.

TWO THE THESIS OF DEMOCRATIC ELITISM

The vulnerability of democratic rights is not always the dominant theme in democratic theory—a concern for justice, for example, periodically commands more attention—but it is surely the deepest and most persistent anxiety.[1] And for all too obvious reasons. The twentieth century alone has added unprecedented chapters to the historical record of war, corruption, political persecution, and genocidal annihilation. How, then, has it been possible for citizens in certain countries to enjoy fundamental democratic rights: to vote in free and fair elections, to speak their mind on public issues without fear of governmental reprisals, to be protected against unreasonable searches or seizures? What accounts for their maintaining possession of these rights over extended stretches of time and in the face of a string of threats, both internal and external?

Part of the answer, from an American perspective, lies in the formal institutions of governance. Institutional checks and balances, after all, were the central focus of the so-called Madisonian theory of democracy.[2] But over the long run of political experience, constitutional architecture has not proven to be a sufficient or even a necessary assurance of fundamental democratic rights, and the search for an exclusively constitutional prophylaxis has come to seem a vain quest. As Robert Dahl remarked in his classic *A Preface to Democratic Theory*,

> Because we are taught to believe in the necessity of constitutional checks and balances, we place little faith in social checks and balances. [But] . . . in the absence of certain social prerequisites, no constitutional arrangements can produce a non-tyrannical republic. The history of numerous Latin-American states is, I think, sufficient evidence. . . . Whether we are concerned with tyranny by a minority or tyranny by a majority, the theory of polyarchy suggests that the first and crucial variables to which political scientists must direct their attention are social and not constitutional. (83)

Social prerequisites may take a variety of forms, economic, cultural, and political, among them;[3] but at least since Tocqueville wrote *Democracy in America,* the most notable has been consensus, that is, general agreement on what may be done politically and how it may be done.

Or so thoughtful observers of American politics, whether American or not, supposed for roughly the century between the American Civil War and the Second World War. Exactly what had been agreed on and precisely how much agreement it took to achieve societal consensus were left implicit. The heart of the matter seemed intuitively obvious. Two dangers stood out: tyranny of the majority (in the form of a numerically dominant group) exercised against a minority and tyranny of the minority (in the form of political leaders) exercised against the majority. And the primary safeguard against both was the same: the commitment of most citizens to democratic principles and practices.

Just so long as it was not possible to determine what ordinary citizens actually believed in, the sanguine assumption that they agreed on the fundamental rules of democratic politics survived. With the introduction of the modern opinion survey, the plausibility of assuming general agreement evaporated. To be sure, ordinary citizens were virtually unanimous in being willing to endorse democratic principles in the abstract. Reacting to an unpopular group or confronting an apparent threat, however, majorities of the public (often large majorities) rejected the rights of unpopular groups to express their point of view publicly and to be safeguarded by due process of law. The divergence between principle and practice, it became apparent, can be gapingly large.

In the absence of an appreciation of the gulf that can open up between democratic principle and practice even in the longest standing democracies, the problem of consensus may appear to be merely academic; and so a concrete illustration is in order. Consider the issue of whether a person should lose his job because he is, say, a communist. To make the point as plain as possible, let us suppose that his job in no way involves issues of national security or indeed any political or societal harm that can rise directly from his holding of the job. The person in our illustration, then, does not work at the State Department, is not in the army or indeed in any agency of government; he is a shoe salesman or perhaps a clerk in a grocery store working at the checkout counter. At the height of McCarthyism, as Samuel Stouffer showed in his classic study *Communism, Conformity, and Civil Liberties,* nearly two out of every three Americans believed that an admitted communist who held a job *as a clerk in a store* should be fired.[4] That so overwhelming a majority of the general public could openly and without embarrassment favor so arbitrary, punitive, and unjustified an invasion of a fellow citizen's rights surely merits attention.

One might wish to reply that this particular illustration of intolerance indicates only that ordinary citizens were swept off their feet by the exceptional circumstances of the fifties or perhaps, in a spirit of reverse chauvinism, that Americans proved to be vulnerable to hysteria over communism in a way that citizens of ideologically more varied cultures are not. But these saving maneuvers are debarred. To an alarming extent, as a lengthening series of subsequent studies has shown,[5] the general public in liberal democratic societies remains ill-informed about essential democratic practices, ready to applaud them as abstract principles but all too willing to violate them in the heat of specific controversies. The difficulty goes deeper, though. The loss of faith in the ability of ordinary citizens either to understand truly what the values of democracy require of them or to honor their commitment to them conscientiously in the heat of controversy is only one aspect of a more sweeping skepticism about the competence of ordinary citizens to attend seriously to and think coherently about the larger world of public affairs. Ordinary citizens, to judge from several generations of public opinion research, are conspicuous for the cursoriness of their attention to public issues, the shallowness of their knowledge about them, the inconsistency and capriciousness of their opinions about them, not to mention the deficiency of their understanding of the larger ideas and political principles integral to them.[6] The consequence: all too often citizens prove themselves to be either muddleheaded, failing to put their political opinions together consistently, or empty-headed, failing even to form them in the first place.

Not surprisingly, this deeper skepticism about the rationality of the public at large helped vaporize confidence in the classic claim that consensus on the part of citizens on the rules of the games is a bulwark of democratic rights. But the evaporation of confidence in the classic claim notwithstanding, faith in the fundamental intuition underlying it persisted. Surely, if democratic leaders managed to stay on the straight and narrow even in the face of political crises, it must be because restraints had been placed both on the public and themselves, and if the broader public were so fickle, then surely someone else had to be more faithful. But what form could restraint take? And how exactly could it be institutionalized?

By way of response, the concept of consensus was reworked rather than rejected. The classic studies of political tolerance had come across a striking contrast. If it was true and disheartening that the support of the general population for fundamental democratic rights was thin, it was also true and encouraging that the commitment of political elites—public officials, community leaders, legal elites, political party activists, trade union leaders, public interest group participants, in a word, people uncommonly interested in and informed about issues of public concern—was deep. And the politically informed and influential proved to be supportive not only when they spoke of democratic principles in the abstract, but also when they confronted them in controversies and proved themselves willing to defend the right of unpopular groups to express their point of view, to engage in peaceful demonstration, to enjoy the same rights of due process as other citizens, to be protected against the loss of their jobs because their point of view or life-style is at odds with the majority's.

The underpinning of fundamental democratic rights, it seemed to follow, was consensus not among ordinary citizens but rather among the politically active and aware; hence the thesis of democratic elitism.[7] Democratic societies like Canada and the United States are centered on core democratic norms, including (but not limited to) freedom of expression and assembly, due process and equal treatment under the law, and a universalistic right (following from citizenship itself) to vote in free and fair elections. The crucial societal location for support of democratic norms like these is the stratum of the politically influential and aware. As Herbert McClosky and Alida Brill (1983) remark,

> Those who function at the center (or centers) of the political culture—who serve as the political, economic, cultural, and intellectual leaders of opinion—are far more likely than those who function at the periphery to have encountered the norms and to have discovered which beliefs or values are considered "definitive" or "legitimate" and which are not. By

virtue of their social location, their greater education, their more frequent involvement in community activities, their participation in the public colloquy on questions of the day, and their affiliation with social networks whose members often discuss and hold informed views on vital public issues, they are often exposed to [and more likely to understand and be motivated to accept] the ideas and principles which constitute the society's creed. (29)

The differences observed in levels of support for central democratic values on the part of citizens at large and of the politically aware and active *are* striking; indeed, so striking as to appear self-evidently to offer a key to the problem of political stability in liberal democracies. How can countries like Canada and the United States weather political storms without jettisoning their democratic principles and practices? Because adherence to democratic values is strongest and most steadfast precisely among those with the most direct influence on and responsibility for public decisions. Political elites are not a sure bet, mind you, to stand by democratic values: to say that their understanding of and commitment to democratic values far exceed those of the average citizen is not to say that either their understanding or their commitment is perfect. But political elites are, a huge volume of research suggests, a far better bet to hold their ground under pressure than is the public at large. As McClosky has written, "The evidence suggests that it is the articulate classes who serve as the *major repositories of the public conscience and as carriers of the Creed. Responsibility for keeping the system going, hence, falls most heavily on them*" (1964, italics added).

The contention that the politically aware and influential, by virtue of taking part in politics and public affairs, acquire a distinctive commitment to democratic values and play therefore a major role in protecting democratic rights has become conventional wisdom. Though challenged from time to time (Jackman 1972; Gibson 1988), the finding that the politically aware and active are markedly more committed to democratic values than the general public has entered the stock of professional knowledge and is routinely and uncontroversially accepted as a matter of fact in textbooks (for example, Dye and Zeigler 1987). In turn, this empirical finding has led to a signal change in the normative roles assigned to the public at large and to political elites in democratic theory. Rather than citizens restraining the ambitions of leaders, the principles of leaders restrain the passions of the public. As McClosky and Brill urge, we should "take comfort from the fact, as Stouffer did, that the community leaders, who are more tolerant than the general public, are likely to exercise a disproportionate influence on public policy." (434)

The Mobilization of Bias: An Argument on Behalf of the Thesis of Democratic Elitism

Legally, rights are claims of entitlement to courses of action, and in the case of fundamental rights, claims treated as universal entitlements. It is not argued, and it would be taken as foolish on its face to argue, that some citizens but not others are entitled to freedom of expression under the Canadian Charter of Rights or virtually any other Bill of Rights. Instructively, it is not argued even that citizens are entitled to freedom of expression but other residents of Canada are not. Rather, it is stipulated that everyone or at any rate every legal adult by virtue of residence alone is entitled to exactly the same right of free expression. But if rights are legally universalistic, politically they are susceptible to particularism. They are susceptible because, politically, rights are and are understood to be two-pronged claims. A right that has become the subject of political debate represents a claim *to* particular entitlement and simultaneously a claim made *on behalf* of particular agents. This dual aspect of political rights is a key to their dynamics, for the very same claim to entitlement may be perceived as legitimate—that is, taken to be a right—if made in the name of one group but not if asserted in the name of another. To say that there is, in this sense, a politics of rights is to say that claims to rights are not merely act-sensitive—that is, contingent on what one wishes to do or how one wants to be treated—but also agent-sensitive, that is, contingent on *who* is to receive a public entitlement or benefit.

Our concern, to borrow a classic phrase, is with the mobilization of bias against the poles of political argument and thought.[8] To what extent, we want to know, is the political landscape tilted against those at the ideological extremes? Does the far right, even though located as much out of the mainstream as the far left, enjoy a comparative advantage over the far left?

It is not difficult to imagine that the left and right are differentially disadvantaged. Particularly among the public at large, the overwhelming focus of concern in the last generation was on communist subversion. But it is far from obvious that the politically aware and sophisticated now believe that the principal threat comes from the left, and indeed it is easy to imagine that they more often think it comes from the right. By way of assessing the plausibility of these speculations, the first step is to establish if there is indeed

Figure 2.1. Most-Disliked Groups (excluding racists)

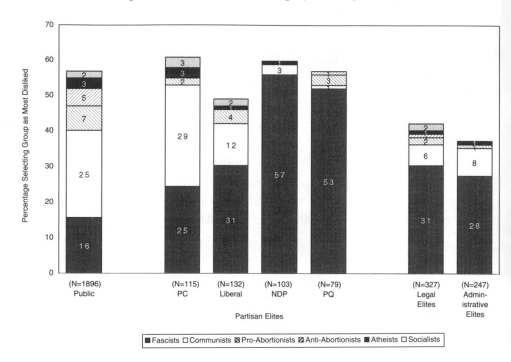

statistical significance of comparisons*:
public vs. elites as a whole: p ≤ .01; political elites by party: p ≤ .01

Note: Significance tests for the non-probability elite samples are provided as general guides only.

a consensus, whether among the public at large or among political, legal, and administrative elites, on which ideological pole is the more abhorrent. To determine whether such a consensus exists, respondents were read a list of seven groups and asked which of them they dislike the most.[9] The list was designed to include groups across the political spectrum and includes (among others)[10] communists, socialists, atheists, fascists, and pro- and antiabortionists. The percentage of the general public and of elites who dislike particular groups is set out in figure 2.1.

Which is the more unpopular, the extreme left or the extreme right? Looking at the general public, one can see at once that the extreme left, in the form of communists, is markedly more unpopular than the extreme right, in the form of fascists. Ordinary citizens are roughly half again as likely to pick communists rather than fascists as the group they dislike the most. By contrast, just the reverse is true for political elites: except for Progressive Conservatives (PC), elite groups are far more likely to select a group from the extreme right than from the extreme left as the group they dislike the most. In reviewing the reactions of elites, one cannot, of course, be surprised that New Democrats and Parti Québécois (PQ) nearly unanimously pick fascists as the group they most dislike, virtually none of them selecting communists.[11] But it cannot be suggested that the ideological outlook of senior lawyers, for example, at all resembles that of New Democrats; and they, too, are much more likely to pick fascists than communists as the group they dislike the most, as are administrative elites. In short, the horizons of concern of the public at large and of elites of diverse stripes sharply contrast. The central tendency of the general public, so far as the focus of their concern is one or the other ideological extreme, is to dislike the left; that of elites generally, to dislike the right.

But does it really matter which extreme these two groups most dislike? Consider arguably the most fundamental of political rights, freedom of expression. The trademark finding for the thesis of democratic elitism is slippage between principle and practice: both ordinary citizens and political elites endorse democratic principles stated in the abstract unanimously or nearly so; however, when they are caught up in a specific controversy, support slips noticeably more in the general public than among the politically sophisticated and active. Accordingly, the Charter Study assessed support for freedom of expression in three different ways: as a measure of support for the principle in the abstract, everyone was asked whether they agreed or disagreed with the statement, "No matter what a person's political beliefs are, he or she is entitled to the same legal rights and protections as everyone else"; as a measure of support for free expression in practice, everyone was asked, first, whether members of extreme political groups should be allowed to hold a public rally,[12] and then (after a suitable interval of time) whether the group they dislike the most should be allowed to do the same.[13]

Stated in the abstract, the principle of freedom of expression is endorsed virtually without dissent, and this is as true of the public at large as of elites (fig. 2.2). As expected, there is obvious slippage in practice, as is evident if one examines judgments about whether members of extreme political groups should be allowed to hold a public rally. Support for freedom of expression for an extreme political group tumbles among the general public, and although a majority (approximately six in every ten) still favor it, sup-

Figure 2.2. Levels of Support for Freedom of Expression in the Abstract and for Rights of "Extreme" Groups and Most-Disliked Group (excluding racists) to Hold Public Rallies

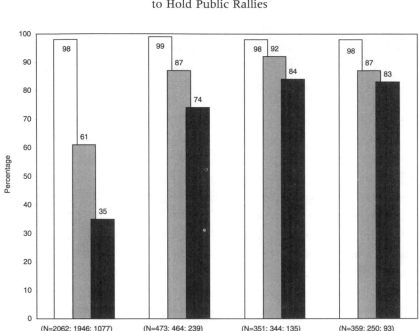

statistical significance of comparisons
extreme groups, public vs. elites as a whole: p ≤ .01; most-disliked groups, public vs. elites as a whole: p ≤ .01

port is very much lower than among elites, of whom at least eight and more nearly nine in every ten believe that even members of an extreme group should be allowed to hold a public rally (fig. 2.2). Finally, to complete the standard argument, it is necessary only to notice reactions when respondents are asked to support the rights not of a group vaguely described as extremist but rather of one he or she definitely dislikes. Support for freedom of expression plummets still further. In the public at large, instead of two in every three citizens affirming that a group should be allowed to hold a public rally, now roughly two in every three take the position that it should *not* be allowed to do so. To be sure, slippage is apparent among elites also, support for freedom of expression being significantly lower when it is the group they most dislike that they must tolerate. Yet even so, a clear majority of elites of all stripes, about two in every three, back freedom of expression.

Rights are, these results make plain, agent-sensitive: how much support there is for a fundamental right depends in a significant measure on who wishes to exercise the right, and this is true not only for the public at large but also for the politically sophisticated and aware. These results also suggest, however, that rights are agent-sensitive to a far more marked degree for ordinary citizens than for elites. The general public, so far as it focuses its concern on an ideological extreme, is more likely to fix on the far left than on the far right, while elites, so far as they focus their concern on an ideological extreme, are far more likely to do the reverse. Still more important, ordinary citizens translate their dislikes into opposition to fundamental democratic rights with far less restraint than do elites. Thus, citizens are most likely to pick a group on the ideological left as the group they most dislike, and just over one in every three believes that the group they most dislike should be allowed to hold a public rally. By contrast, although elites have the opposite ideological bias, they are far less likely to act on it: only about one in every five who pick fascists as the group they dislike the most *opposes* their right to hold a public rally. In the Charter Study, elites and the public thus seem to differ twice over: elites are, compared to ordinary citizens, more likely to focus on the extreme right rather than the extreme left as their primary source of concern; and they are also less likely to translate their concerns and dislikes into restrictive political judgments. The initial results of the Charter Study therefore match those of previous studies: fundamental democratic rights appear to be far safer when put in the hands of political and legal elites than when entrusted to the erratic judgment of the ordinary citizen.

This match between previous results and ours shows that our findings cannot be explained away by alleging peculiarities in either the political context in Canada or the sample or survey design of the Charter Study. And this matters because we show now that our study, so far from corroborating the consensus of political elites in favor of democratic rights, contradicts it.

Two Counterconsiderations: Value Pluralism and Electoral Competition

Our object is to pursue a pair of arguments. The first concerns the irreducible pluralism of values in a democratic political culture; the second, the basic architectonics of electoral competition in democratic polities.

The thesis of democratic elitism holds that the politically aware and active, by virtue of their political awareness and involvement, are more likely than ordinary citizens to master and internalize the central, constitutive values of their political culture. Where the political culture is democratic, it seems to follow, they will acquire "democratic values." It is thus tacitly assumed that whatever lessons they learn from the political culture favor democratic values. But a political culture, above all, a democratic political culture, is not all of one piece. It is pluralistic. In addition to liberty there is a host of other values, including respect for authority, the assurance of order in public life, and the importance of community and conformity. And because a society places a high value on order, for example, it does not follow that it places a low value on liberty. Political societies, most especially including democratic ones, attach and ought to attach importance to a mix of values; and part of the socialization of members of a society accordingly consists of lessons on the importance of a mix of values, if only because each of them is necessary if the politics of the country is to remain democratic.

And the consequence is critical. The thesis of democratic elitism presupposes that political elites, by offering a special measure of support for individual rights, supply a special bulwark protecting democratic politics. In fact, as we shall show, on a wide array of issues requiring political elites to balance competing considerations of individual rights and social order, their responses are indistinguishable from those of the public at large.

A second, equally fundamental consideration is electoral competition. Joseph Schumpeter famously equated the democratic method with the struggle between political parties, defining democracy itself as "that institutional arrangement for arriving at political decisions in which individuals acquire the power to decide by means of a competitive struggle for the people's vote."[14] Electoral competition, the fight among political parties for popular support in open elections, has come to define the democratic method. Political parties compete for people's votes by distinguishing themselves along a number of fronts, including from time to time issues bearing directly on conditions under which democratic rights should properly be exercised. And they do so for at least two reasons. First, issues bearing on democratic rights periodically and unavoidably become entangled with other public concerns, public safety and national security among them; and just so far as the two become entangled, one political party can gain an electoral advantage over another. Second, political parties are not simply vote maximizers. They are also, in a celebrated phrase, communities of cobelievers, at the level of activists committed to distinctive bodies of belief, to differing conceptions of the role of government in society and the economy, to alternative interpretations of the master values of democratic politics like equality, to competing resolutions of the tension between the rights of citizens and the common good. It is not necessary to exaggerate the ideological cohesiveness of parties' bodies of belief to recognize that their shared convictions will, from time to time, spill over to issues in which the rights of citizens and the needs of public order and national security collide. In short, political parties divide on issues of citizens' rights in part because of electoral competition, in part from political conviction, and over the medium run the one motive tends to reinforce the other.

Divergence in the ideological commitments of political parties, whether driven by electoral strategy or ideological conviction, is the second source of difficulty for the thesis of democratic elitism. The thesis holds that the politically active and aware adhere more closely to democratic values because they have been more thoroughly socialized into the norms of the larger political culture. People do learn as a consequence of political involvement, but what they learn depends very much on the company they keep. To take an empirically extreme, but therefore conceptually vivid example, people who immerse themselves politically in the Heritage Front or the John Birch Society may well be altered by the experience, but this transformation is unlikely to take the form of a special devotion to civil liberties and democratic rights. Political socialization, at the level of the politically active, involves exposure not simply to the values of the larger culture but also to the norms of particular political groups; and in the case of those who strive for direct political power, the primary political group is the political party. Adherents accordingly tend to be socialized into the norms of their party even when they did not initially select the party because of the attractiveness of its norms. Notwithstanding the inevitable heterogeneity of complex organizations, then, competing political parties can and frequently will diverge over claims to individual rights. Republican and Democratic activists in the United States, for example, often balance conflicts between claims to individual rights and concerns over order and security in distinctly different ways, just as do PC and NDP activists in Canada. As we shall make plain, however, the thesis of democratic elitism owes much of its plausibility to the pooling of political activists without regard to their partisan affiliations. It accordingly loses much of its persuasiveness once it is recognized that these partisan elites represent quite different policy agendas on the role of individual rights in contemporary societies and that part of the point of elections is to determine which of these alternative agendas is to shape public policy. In sum, previous research has emphasized the contrast between the average citizen and elites taken as a whole; by contrast, we shall highlight the differences in point of view between competing groups of partisan elites, demonstrating that elite-mass differences on a variety of issues of democratic rights tend to be eclipsed, both in size and in political significance, by differences in commitment to basic rights that divide competing groups of partisan elites.

Wiretapping

Arguments occur over what the public should be allowed to do as a matter of right and what government is empowered and, indeed, obliged to do to secure the public's safety. They are inevitable partly because balancing the rights of citizens and the responsibilities of government entails weighing competing values; inevitable, still more fundamentally, because balancing requires weighing competing conjectures about conceivable consequences of alternative policies. In turn, the values to be weighed and the conjectures to be evaluated play against one another as the questions of public action to be answered slide from the present to the future tense. The question is thus not merely whether citizens' freedom of action should be curtailed so that the state can deal responsibly with a crime that has been committed; it is also, and more opaquely, whether government encroachments on citizens' freedoms are in order because there is a risk that a crime threatening national security or public safety is about to be committed.

How do elites respond to threats to national security or public safety? Are they, as the thesis of democratic elitism implies, more scrupulous than the public at large in safeguarding individual freedoms? Elites are more supportive than ordinary citizens of fundamental rights such as freedom of expression and assembly, as we have seen. But does it follow that they will show a comparable solicitude for the freedom of citizens when coping with threats to national security and public safety?

Clashes over rights take place not in the abstract but in the crucible of policy choices. A classic example is the controversy over secret surveillance, or, as it is popularly (if increasingly anachronistically) called, wiretapping. Wiretapping offers a textbook example of intrusive governmental action that is clearly defensible in many circumstances but at least potentially injurious in nearly all.

For several reasons, a comparison of the judgments about the propriety of secret surveillance made by elites and by ordinary citizens offers us a good starting point. One of these reasons is perfectly obvious; the other, curiously overlooked. The obvious reason is that the need for care in authorizing secret surveillance is plain: every liberal democracy of which we are aware has been rocked by abuses of government surveillance powers. The overlooked reason is that the very studies that have become pillars of the argument for democratic elitism contain a number of instances dealing with concerns for order and safety, of which wiretapping is a striking example, in which the elite sample affords no more protection for individual rights than the general population sample.[15] These apparently anomalous results have gone unremarked, and it is surely worth determining whether the anomaly is genuine or not. Finally, the issue of secret surveillance can throw a searching light on the extent to which the politically active and aware truly learn from past abuse of governmental power and take into account the manifest risks bound up in authorizing wiretaps. If governmental abuse of secret surveillance has occurred in every liberal democracy, such abuses have received special notoriety in Canada. Indeed, a Royal Commission was specifically established not only to hold public hearings but to investigate illegal surveillance and related abuses committed by the Royal Canadian Mounted Police, including illegal break-ins, unauthorized opening of mail, and obtaining of improper access to tax data, all actions originally justified by considerations of public safety or national security.[16] Given both the notoriety and the recency of wiretapping abuses, our samples of elites must have been familiar (indeed, some on a firsthand basis) with the potential for harm in the government's police and security powers[17] and should, on any reasonable expectation, have carried away a clear understanding of the need for care and attention to circumstance in justifying an invasive practice.

Not that the issue can be reduced to either-or terms, with approval of wiretapping equated with violation of democratic rights. The question is not whether wiretapping may be legitimate—an abundance of legal decisions and police experience testify both to its legality and efficacy—but the standards of care that people must exercise in authorizing it. Much depends on circumstance: exactly who, why, and where. But how is it possible to determine if people, whether elites or ordinary citizens, exercise care in weighing the propriety of government surveillance and, in particular, whether they are attentive to the different justifications and circumstances in which an appeal to its use can be launched?

It would surely do little good to run people through a long series of repetitive questions, the standard practice in public opinion research, asking them first if they approved of wiretapping in this circumstance, then in that, then in yet another, then in still another. They could not fail to see what was at stake. Accordingly, we took advantage of computer-assisted interviewing to conduct the wiretapping justification experiment. Our aim in the experiment was to explore a variety of justifications for surveillance, but in order to avoid conditions in which a question about one might bias an answer to another, we asked each person about only one particular situation, the situation put to them being chosen at random. Thus, everyone, elites as well as ordinary citizens, was asked whether Canada's security service should be permitted to tap peoples' telephones in one of four circumstances: (1) when they are suspected of terrorism; (2) when they are suspected of being spies; (3) when they hold ideas that may lead to the overthrow of Canada's democratic system; or (4) when they are agents of a foreign government.[18]

Let us begin with the case in which justification for secret government surveillance is most compelling: when people are suspected of terrorism. In an age when terrorism has become a day-to-day risk that responsible authorities must be prepared to cope with in the regular course of their duties, it is easy to understand why many people, elites and ordinary citizens alike, will approve of the security service tapping the telephones of people suspected of plotting to put a bomb on an airplane or blow up a world trade center. The linchpin contention of the thesis of democratic elitism is that whatever happens with ordinary citizens, elites, by forming a consensus in favor of individual rights, supply a bulwark in support of democratic politics.

A solid majority of the general public, not surprisingly considering the publicity given to terrorist bombings, supports secret surveillance of terrorists. More exactly, two in every three citizens agree that "the security service should be able to wiretap the telephones of people who are suspected of terrorism" (fig. 2.3). More surprising, to borrow from the Sherlock Holmes story of the dog that did not bark, is what did not happen. The thesis of democratic elitism is organized around contrasting images: that of the public at large, susceptible to sudden gusts of political passion, and that of elites, especially political elites, anchored securely by democratic convictions. The contrasting images lead to a prediction: although the general public may be overready to approve secret surveillance, the politically aware and sophisticated should show considerably more restraint. But this is exactly what does not show up in figure 2.3. Indeed, rather than being more likely than the average citizen to resist wiretapping, elites as a whole are more likely to approve it.

Figure 2.3. Levels of Support for Wiretapping Suspected Terrorists

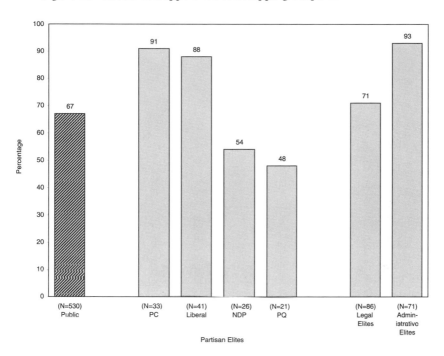

statistical significance of comparisons
public vs. elites as a whole: p ≤ .01; political elites by party: p ≤ .01; elite groups by sector: p ≤ .01

It is not true that legislative elites are equally likely to approve of the secret service wiretapping suspected terrorists—the historically dominant parties at the national level are more likely to favor it—but it is true that in no party does more than a bare majority object. Of course, a reasonable rejoinder is that terrorism is a problem of special urgency, one that puts a liberal democratic society at risk, and that there is, therefore, no inherent conflict between approving wiretapping to combat terrorists and standing by individual rights.

Just because arguments for surveillance can be made on an ad hoc basis, the proper standard for evaluating the special scrupulousness that elites are said to exercise in balancing claims of public welfare and individual rights is whether they discriminate, approving it in some instances, rejecting it in others. If they are at least as likely as the average citizen to back secret surveillance across the board, the presumption that a key safeguard for democratic politics is the special caution that elites exercise in approving

Figure 2.4. Levels of Support for Wiretapping Suspected Spies

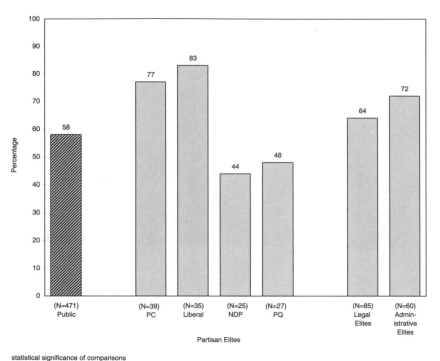

statistical significance of comparisons
public vs. elites as a whole: p ≤ .05; political elites by party: p ≤ .01; elite groups by sector: not significant

potentially intrusive governmental actions will lose much of its plausibility. Just for this reason, we show figure 2.4, which summarizes citizens' and elites' judgments about whether "the security service should be able to wiretap the telephones of people who are suspected of being spies."

Notice that the issue is defined as what is proper not in the case of individuals known to be spies, but rather in the case of those merely suspected of being spies. Notice also that no justification for the suspicion is given. Suspected by whom? And on the basis of what evidence? To the politically sophisticated, well placed to know of past abuses, the fact that neither question is addressed might in itself be a ground for reservation. But the elites, rather than being more cautious and therefore less likely to approve of secret surveillance in this circumstance, are if anything more likely to ratify it (fig. 2.4). Moreover, although again differences are apparent among legislative elites (the historically dominant parties being more likely to give their blessing to wiretapping of suspected spies), the fact deserving serious consideration is that in no party does more than a bare majority stand against the use of wiretapping on the grounds of an unstipulated suspicion.

Still, as regards either terrorism or espionage, the argument for surveillance has a natural force. Accordingly, it seemed to us essential to take account of a wider range of circumstances in which there was either no illegal conduct or an easily rebuttable presumption of illegal conduct. A paradigmatic case, for this purpose, is the "objectionable ideas" argument: secret surveillance of some group of people is necessary, it is argued from time to time, not because of any illegal acts they have committed, but because of objectionable ideas they hold. For the purposes of this test, we wanted to ensure that the ideas were indeed objectionable, and so we asked whether "the security service should be able to wiretap the telephones of people who hold ideas that may lead to the overthrow of our democratic system."

Think about what is at stake here. There is no allegation of illegal *conduct*; no suggestion that the people under suspicion have committed any illegal acts whatever, let alone made an effort to overthrow the government; there is merely the assertion that they "hold ideas" and that these ideas, for some unspecified reason, may jeopardize Canada's democratic system. The question thus serves as a classic test of what the government is or is not justified in doing to check allegedly dangerous ideas. How far may it use its intrusive power and invade the privacy of citizens to spy on their conversations and personal lives, not because of anything they have actually done but merely because of what they think? Here, surely, if elites are indeed "repositories of the public conscience and . . . carriers of the Creed," they should form a distinctive bulwark, protecting the privacy of citizens and their freedom to think as they wish, opposing government wiretapping justified by reference merely to dangerous ideas. In contrast, if the public at large is indeed the point of vulnerability, as the thesis of democratic elitism posits, then ordinary citizens should be markedly more likely to support surveillance on the same grounds. In fact, far from being more likely than the ordinary citizen to oppose wiretapping in the case of dangerous ideas, politicians taken as a whole are just as likely to support it as ordinary citizens, while legal and governmental elites are, if anything, even more likely to support it (fig. 2.5).

Equally important, as figure 2:5 also makes plain, the divisions between parties go deep on this issue. Conservatives and Liberals are markedly more likely to countenance the use of secret surveillance in the case of dangerous ideas; indeed, a majority in both parties backs the practice. On the other

Figure 2.5. Levels of Support for Wiretapping People
with Anti-Democratic Ideas

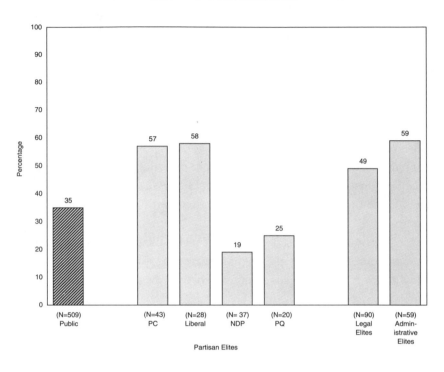

statistical significance of comparisons
public vs. elites as a whole: p ≤ .01; political elites by party: p ≤ .01; elite groups by sector: not significant

hand, New Democrats and PQ are overwhelmingly arrayed in opposition to wiretapping on this ground. One cannot suppose that party commitments translate perfectly into government decisions, but these results make plain that debates over wiretapping can start from radically different premises depending on which party forms the government.

Given the importance of the issues under consideration here, we provided for a final test, now framing the question in terms of whether "the security service should be able to wiretap the telephones of people who are agents of a foreign government." The ambiguity of this expression, "agents of a foreign government," is worth remarking. The phrase has a slightly menacing aspect, but in truth, there is nothing illegal or threatening in working as an agent of a foreign government. On the contrary, it is a perfectly legitimate line of work followed by tens of thousands in capital cities of countries around the world. And the phrase "agents of a foreign govern-

Figure 2.6. Levels of Support for Wiretapping Agents of a
Foreign Government

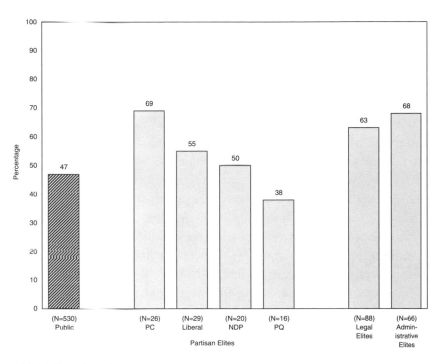

statistical significance of comparisons
public vs. elites as a whole: p≤.01; political elites by party: not significant;elite groups by sector: not significant

ment" is just the sort of empty, if menacing, verbiage that one should surely expect elites to see through if elites really do form a protective bulwark of individual rights. But, again, so far as there is any difference between the responses of ordinary citizens and of elites, it is just the opposite of what the thesis of democratic elitism predicts: elites are at least as likely as, and in the case of legal and governmental elites in particular even more likely than, the average citizen to approve of wiretapping telephones in this circumstance (fig. 2.6).

Because the results of the wiretapping justification experiment run counter to the conventional wisdom, they deserve closer examination. In presenting the results, we have followed the standard practice in public opinion research, which is to record the direction of people's positions on issues, reporting accordingly whether in a variety of circumstances people approve or disapprove of secret surveillance. But good arguments can be made that merely knowing a person votes yea or nay is insufficient. When it comes to balancing complex and conflicting considerations of public safety and individual liberty, what matters is not just which side of the fence they may wind up on, but also the conditions, reservations, and qualifications they may attach to their position.[19] It is, after all, not hard to imagine that a politically sophisticated person may approve of an operation like wiretapping but only on the explicit understanding that crucial conditions (for example, probable cause) have been met.

It is thus worth determining if people, whether in the general public or among the more politically aware and active, attach explicit reservations and conditions as part and parcel of giving approval. Just for this reason, interviewers were trained to note not only if respondents approved or disapproved of wiretapping, but also whether they spontaneously attached qualifications or reservations to their approval or disapproval. When we solicited opinions about wiretapping, we systematically flagged all responses, whether of approval or disapproval of secret surveillance, to which substantial qualifications were attached (fig. 2.7).

The intuition, of course, is that the more sophisticated and aware, by virtue of their sophistication and knowledge, will be more likely to qualify the positions they take than will the average citizen. And as one can see in figure 2.7, obviously elites, whether legislative, legal, or governmental, are indeed more likely than the ordinary citizen to qualify their positions on wiretapping. To summarize across experimental treatments, one out of every four spontaneously qualify their approval; the equivalent figure for ordinary citizens is less than one out of every ten.

Two quite different but by no means mutually exclusive interpretations can be given to this result: first, that elites, even if protesting, nonetheless approve, and in the play of politics this is what counts; and second, that their greater willingness to approve of wiretapping is an approval granted to the government on condition that the necessary and appropriate legal proprieties are complied with.

As for the first interpretation—"protesting, they nonetheless consent"—the best approach is to consider whether, as the thesis of democratic elitism requires, elites do offer a distinctive measure of support for individual rights on issues other than wiretapping. We shall shortly review a number of such issues. When the results are in hand, it will be difficult to avoid the inference that legal, political, and administrative elites are prepared to go along with wiretapping by the government in some of these circumstances in part

Figure 2.7. Qualified and Unqualified Judgments about Wiretapping
(all four experimental variations combined)

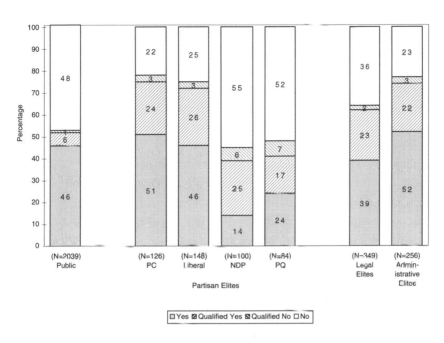

statistical significance of comparisons
public vs. elites as a whole: p ≤ .01; political elites by party: p ≤ .01; elite groups by sector: p ≤ .01

because of their association with and hence trust in government. They are being asked to have confidence in the probity and judgment not of a mysterious "they," but of people who have been their colleagues in the past and might be again in the future or, if they are not personally known to them, of people very much like others they have known long and well. Lacking direct measures, we do not claim dogmatically that this is so. The process of socialization at the heart of the thesis of democratic elitism can cut two ways, however. It can increase adherence to democratic norms. But it can also bolster confidence in the trustworthiness of public officials—indeed, just because they often *are* deserving of trust—and hence instill a readiness on the part of elites to go along with potentially dangerous intrusions of governmental power.

The second interpretation, which suggests that the greater willingness of elites to approve of wiretapping is not as disquieting as it may at first seem because they so often attach qualifications to their approval, entails two problems. First, even if, by setting aside all elites who approve of wiretapping but qualify their approval, it can be argued that they are no more likely than ordinary citizens to do so, the thesis is still sunk. For it requires that elites be far less likely than the average citizen to approve of government acts that may put individual rights at risk. Second, the role of political elites in sustaining democratic norms becomes problematic in a new and deeper way. Contrast the reactions of the different political parties to wiretapping, setting to one side all who, whatever their party, give a qualified approval.

The effect is to accentuate the differences between political parties and to increase the similarity between the historically dominant parties and the public at large (fig. 2.7). Thus, *even setting aside those who approve of it only with qualifications,* Conservatives, who previously made up the federal government, and Liberals, who make up the current one, are as likely as ordinary citizens to approve of wiretapping. Contrary to the thesis of democratic elitism, then, so far as secret surveillance is concerned, it cannot be said that the two recent governing parties offer a superior measure of security for individual rights than the general public. On the other side, if it is not true that political elites, qua political elites, strike a distinctive stance in protecting individual rights, it is true that organized groups of them do. The course of action that the NDP and PQ endorse contrasts dramatically with the one that the Liberals and Conservatives wish to chart. Whereas roughly one-half of the latter approve of wiretapping without qualification, only about one in every four or five of the former does likewise. Our point, in underlining this sharp divide within political elites, is not to suggest from the perspective of democratic theory that one camp is right and the other wrong, as though it were always right to oppose wiretapping, even if the documented record of official abuse counsels caution in its use. Our point is rather that deep disagreement exists among partisan elites over what is right, and it makes a correspondingly consequential difference which of them wins the election.

Whether one focuses on the convergence between elites and the public or on the divergence between elites as a function of party, it is difficult to interpret the findings as vindicating the claim that citizens' exercise of democratic rights is safeguarded because decisions about these rights are not in their hands but are instead vouchsafed to the politically influential and sophisticated. Before coming to any conclusion, however, we take account of a wider range of circumstances in which concerns about public order and safety collide with claims to individual rights.

Suspension of Civil Liberties: The War Measures Act

We want to put the thesis of democratic elitism to a still more severe test by exploring issues raised in the aftermath of an actual episode in modern Canadian political history, the imposition of the War Measures Act. In 1970, following the kidnapping of a British trade commissioner and a minister of the Quebec government, the prime minister of Canada, Pierre Trudeau, suspended certain civil liberties, initially across the whole of Canada, subsequently in Quebec only, taking as his authority for the suspension of civil liberties the War Measures Act. The police, pursuant to regulations passed under the act, were authorized to search and hold suspects for questioning without warrant or bail, and they did so; they were empowered to search and seize without customary legal constraints, and they exercised these powers; they were authorized to arrest people merely for being members of a legal political organization, the Front de Libération du Québec (FLQ), or indeed merely for publicly agreeing with the goals of the FLQ, and they acted on this authority.[20]

The immediate reactions to the imposition of the War Measures Act were heavily positive. The prime minister not only enjoyed popular support in the public opinion polls, but also won a near-unanimous parliamentary vote in which only NDP members dissented. In the heat of a crisis a rally-around-the-flag response is to be expected. But have political leaders, a measure of time having passed, availed themselves, as Stouffer put it, of "sober, second thought"?

Canadian political elites presumably should have given serious thought to the lessons of the October Crisis of 1970 and come away with a deeper appreciation of the enormity of the risks in suspending civil liberties so precipitously and so sweepingly. Hence we asked,

"If the cabinet says there is a national emergency, and a majority in Parliament agrees, is it all right to suspend the usual civil rights?"

Given the mechanics of parliamentary government, to say that the cabinet and a majority in Parliament must approve is, of course, to say that the government can suspend civil liberties whenever the party in control of government wishes to do so.[21] If the thesis of democratic elitism is correct in holding that political elites protect democratic rights, then we should expect them to show a far deeper appreciation than the public at large of the risks that lie in the suspension of civil rights (fig. 2.8).

If one believes that elites, political elites especially, form a high wall

Figure 2.8. Attitudes toward Suspension of Civil Rights if the Government Declares a National Emergency

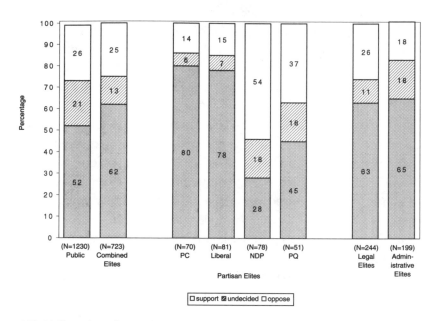

statistical significance of comparisons
public vs. elites as a whole: not significant; political elites by party: p ≤ .05; elite groups by sector: p ≤ .01

protecting civil rights against demagogic leaders and mass hysteria, where they choose to stand on emergency powers must be disconcerting. Taking elites all in all, they are just as likely, indeed, a shade more likely, than ordinary citizens to approve of the suspension of civil rights in these circumstances: 62 percent of elites, compared to 52 percent of the public agree that if "if the cabinet says there is a national emergency, and a majority in parliament agrees, it is all right to suspend the usual civil rights." No less important is the marked divergence between partisan elites. The thesis of democratic elitism emphasizes the political socialization common to all political elites, whatever their partisan commitments. Yet it is the divergence, not the convergence, of their responses that stands out (fig. 2.8). On the one side, members of the two major federal parties give overwhelming support to parliamentary suspension of civil liberties "if the cabinet says there is a national emergency." Indeed, Liberals and Conservatives are significantly more likely to approve of a suspension at the cabinet's pleasure than are ordinary citizens, which should hardly be taken as evidence that political elites as a whole have become more cautious about suspending civil rights. In contrast, only among the NDP did a majority of partisan elites oppose the parliamentary suspension of civil rights in emergency situations.[22] Ironically, a plurality of the PQ, and a clear majority of those with an opinion on the issue, favor the principle of parliamentary suspension, which suggests that even those who have been victims of this power will go along if they see themselves as being one day able to exercise it.[23]

The Politics of Order

To say that an issue of democratic rights is a live issue is to say that, in order to decide it, a choice must be made between competing values, each recognized as being valid in its own right. In so characterizing judgments about rights, we do not mean to suggest that any given individual passes his or her life occupied in an endless, exhausting tug-of-war between opposing values. On the contrary, thoughtful people work to assure that the values *they* care most about fit with one another, precisely in order to avoid dilemmas of choice.[24] The point is that however much effort people put into arranging their views consistently, from time to time they will find themselves pitched into a situation in which they must choose between them. And the reason for this is the rarity of antivalues. You may value liberty more than order— value it far more, in fact—but that is not to say that order is an antivalue for you, that you are repelled by it. It may ordinarily be outranked by liberty, but in certain situations the value of order will take on a more-than-ordinary measure of importance for you, and you will, accordingly, be forced to decide the best course of action.

Because values come into conflict not in the abstract but in specific situations, we want to compare how elites and ordinary citizens, when confronted with definite problems, manage the trade-offs between the rights of citizens to advocate their political views and the responsibilities of authorities to ensure public order and safety. We started our examination by asking,

> "Should a town or city be able to limit public demonstrations that city officials think might turn violent against persons and property?"

A genuine conflict is posed here. Public officials are surely not only permitted to forestall violence but actively obliged to do so. On the other hand, the nettle of the issue here is not whether a demonstration should be limited if there is clear evidence of a high risk of violence, but whether a demonstration should be restricted if "city officials think" it might turn violent. Which city officials? On what basis do they rest their assessment of danger? How much of an exception is being made to standing policies on this occasion, and why? Just because a public official is inclined to declare that a danger exists is not to say that one in fact exists.

These are the sorts of questions and complexities that political elites must be cognizant of if they are to play the role assigned them by the thesis of democratic elitism. It is sobering, therefore, to inspect the reactions of citizens and elites to the question of whether local officials should be able to place limits on public demonstrations because of the risk (as they perceive it) of violence. Both groups are strongly inclined to place concerns of safety and order above those of free expression in the circumstances, and that holds for legal and administrative elites as well as political elites. The only clearly contrasting reaction is offered by New Democrats. They are markedly less likely than other elites or ordinary citizens to approve of local officials exercising a regulative authority over public demonstrations, although even they more often than not will back them.

For all practical purposes, then, it would make no difference whether a public policy decision on public demonstrations were in the hands of elites or of ordinary citizens. Order can eclipse liberty among both.

Consider, therefore, a choice in which freedom of speech and established morality come into conflict and collide not implicitly but explicitly. This kind of choice captures a recurrent quandary of citizens in liberal democracy: Does "society" have a right as a matter of principle to put the expression of certain points of view out of bounds? It would be misleading to imply that we may not ourselves have a preference between the pair of alternatives on offer,[25] still more so to insinuate that one or the other alternative represented the all-round objectively correct position from the point of view of democratic theory. On the other hand, the character of a liberal democracy is not unrelated to which of the two positions achieves ascendancy. Given that it makes a difference which viewpoint holds sway, it is important whether elites resolve the conflict between the claims of liberty and morality differently from the average citizen. The thesis of democratic elitism implies that elites will be more sympathetic to the claims of freedom, more suspicious of the claim of established morality to censor expression.

To explore this conflict, we asked,

"Which of these comes closer to your own view?
(1) The government has no right to decide what should or should not be published.

Figure 2.9. Attitudes toward Limiting Public Demonstrations if Local
Officals Are Apprehensive

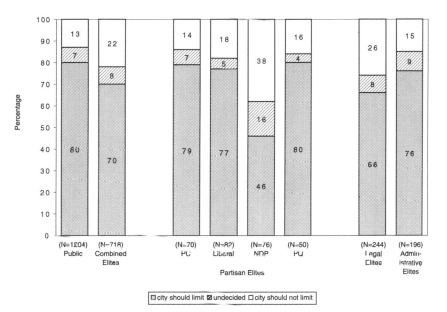

statistical significance of comparisons
public vs. elites as a whole: p ≤ .01; political elites by party: p ≤ .01; elite groups by sector: p ≤ .05

or

(2) To protect its moral values, a society sometimes has to forbid certain
things from being published."

There is relatively little difference either among the views of elites, whether
legislative, legal, or governmental, or between their views and those of the
public at large (fig. 2.10). A clear majority of the general public (approximately two in every three) believes that society has to forbid certain things
from being published in order to protect its moral values. But elites as a
whole are at least as likely as the general public to favor this censorship.

We are not unmindful of instances in which elites offer markedly more
support for fundamental rights of expression and assembly than does the
average citizen; indeed, we presented at the outset the results on slippage
between principle and practice to make this very point. But it cannot be said
that the findings we have presented on a wider range of issues, from wiretapping through suspension of civil liberties through adjudicating colliding
claims of individual rights and of public safety or morality, bolster confi-

Figure 2.10. Attitudes toward Forbidding Certain Things from
Being Published

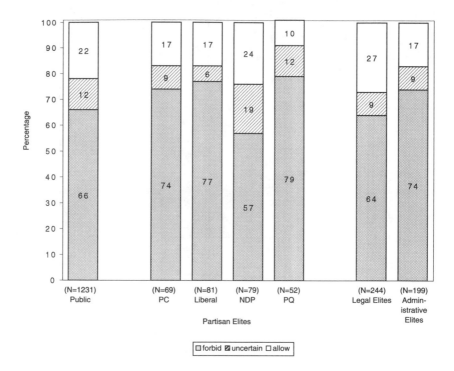

dence that elites are an across-the-board bulwark protecting democratic values. Apart from classic freedom of expression issues, what is striking is the convergence of views of the public at large and of elites as a whole, together with the divergence of views between legislative elites as a function of party.

As a final illustration, consider a clash between public concerns for safety and individual rights given a more legal construction. On any account, among the primary burdens of the concept of rights over the long stretch of history is the presumption of protection. But protection from what? As the Mill of *On Liberty* understood it, from the coercive, shaping power of society, but as Isaiah Berlin, speaking for an even longer trajectory of political experience, understood it, from the intrusive, coercive power of the state. Responding to the question, What would make a society free? Berlin said, "No power, but only rights, can be regarded as absolute. . . . there are frontiers, not artificially drawn, within which men should be inviolable" (1969, 165). There is, plainly and inherently, a balancing act between the claims of the

state to restrain, investigate, coerce, and intrude on the activities and property of citizens as part of its responsibility to assure order and safety and the
rights of citizens to enjoy "frontiers, not artificially drawn, within which
[they] should be inviolable." The question, accordingly, is whether in balancing these competing claims elites impose a different set of weights than
does the average citizen: Do elites, confronting the intrusive powers of the
state, insist on higher standards of proof before backing its right to invade the
realm of private experience?

As a paradigmatic example of where the line should be drawn, we asked
all respondents, elites as well as ordinary citizens,

> "Consider an instance in which the police see a young man they do not
> recognize walking very near a house where they know drugs are being
> sold. They search him and find he is carrying drugs. Do you think this
> search is a reasonable search, or does it violate the young man's rights?"

Just because the issue of individual rights is posed here in a legal context, the
contrast between the responses of political and legal elites is instructive.
Arguments on behalf of the thesis of democratic elitism have not been
accompanied by strict definitions of just who qualifies as an elite. Yet whoever else the concept encompasses, public officials (legislators, mayors, pres-
idents, and prime ministers) are manifestly included. Just for this reason, the
contrast between the responses of legislative and of legal elites (fig 2.11) is
the more striking. A clear majority of legal elites (and also of governmental
elites, who are, it will be remembered, primarily drawn from law-oriented
agencies) reject police action under this description as a reasonable search.
For those whose profession is the law, mere proximity to a place where
drugs are sold does not constitute a defensible ground for the police to stop a
person and search him, and such a search, so far from being reasonable,
violates the young man's rights. Not surprisingly, a majority of ordinary
citizens comes to just the opposite conclusion. What is surprising, from the
point of view of the thesis of democratic elitism, is that political elites are just
as likely as the average citizen to judge the police search to be reasonable.
Finally, the pattern of divergence *between* partisan elites presents itself again.
Thus, the vast majority of Conservatives say that the search is legitimate; the
NDP reject the search as a violation of the young man's rights; the Liberals
and the PQ split down the middle. The lesson to draw from these differences
within and between elites is this: Insofar as what counts is a readiness to
place a heavier weight on considerations of freedom—on "frontiers, not

Figure 2.11. Support for Police Search of Suspect

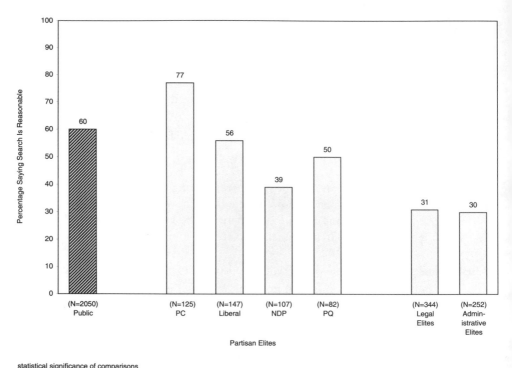

statistical significance of comparisons
public vs. elites as a whole: p ≤ .01; political elites by party: p ≤ .01; elite groups by sector: p ≤ .01

artificially drawn, within which men should be inviolable"—the cause of liberty would be better served if the average citizen made a decision on this issue as opposed to an elected member of the political party previously governing Canada.

The overall pattern of similarity between the general public and political elites *taken as a whole* and of dissimilarity *among* partisan elites holds for a variety of other issues that tap judgments about the proper power of the state to intrude on the privacy and property of citizens. These issues include whether the police should be able to search cars they have stopped for a traffic violation; whether the government ought to be allowed to read people's mail in order to catch a criminal; whether customs officials should be able to conduct body searches without a warrant if they suspect someone is smuggling drugs into the country; and whether, in dealing with muggings and other serious street crimes, priority must be given to protecting the rights of suspects or to stopping such crimes and making the streets safe.

Taking all these findings into account, one finds that the evidence consistently runs against the central claim of the thesis of democratic elitism, which is that political elites, by virtue of their greater involvement in politics, are distinctively more reliable guardians of civil liberties and democratic rights than ordinary citizens. On the contrary, political elites respond quite differently depending on which political party they adhere to. It is difficult, given this systematic divergence, to "take comfort from the fact . . . that the community leaders, who are more tolerant than the general public, are likely to exercise a disproportionate influence on public policy."[26] Too much depends on which group of political elites makes policy. What are the implications of these cross-party differences?

Schumpeter's Argument

Democratic politics, Joseph Schumpeter insisted, hinges on electoral competition between blocs of elites that are organized in the form of political parties and are battling for control of government by winning popular support. The mass public plays its role not by making public policy in conformity with its views but by choosing between competing groups of elites who are elected to act in conformity with *theirs*. The key concepts in a Schumpeterian analysis are thus *mass public* and *partisan elites, direct* and *indirect* influence. Our results have illustrated their value in elucidating the clash of rights, particularly in pointing to differences in orientation to rights between different groups of partisan elites. It is not that each and every party in a multiparty system necessarily develops its own distinctive orientation to questions of civil liberties and democratic rights. In the Canadian party system the most profound differences lie between the parties who have historically dominated the federal government—Conservatives and Liberals—and the parties who have been challenging them, certainly on a regional level—the NDP and the PQ.[27] Schumpeter's point is that the party *system* favors differentiation, not that every party differs dramatically from every other.

But how far does Schumpeter's argument apply? Is it, perhaps, peculiarly appropriate to the politics of Canada? Does the thesis of democratic elitism possibly apply to most contemporary liberal democracies even if not to Canada? Consider a strong, although indirect, test of the generalizability of our critique of democratic elitism. The leading proponent of the idea that political elites, by virtue of their involvement in politics, are "repositories of the public conscience . . . and carriers of the Creed" is Herbert McClosky, and what we shall show is that the results he has himself presented, rather than confirming his argument, support an even stronger version of ours.

A direct contrast of partisan elites' views on issues of civil liberties and democratic rights in the United States is not possible,[28] but fortunately a generation of research[29] has established the close correspondence between ideological and partisan elites in American politics. The Republican Party, at its most active and politically consequential level, is overwhelmingly conservative in its convictions, and the Democratic Party, having lost its conservative southern wing, has become comparably liberal in its sentiments.

To illustrate the politics of rights, we draw from McClosky and Brill a selection of reactions to three issues: whether the government has a right to determine what should be published; whether a person who has been arrested has a right to remain silent; and, finally, whether refusing to hire a professor because of his political beliefs is justified. The three issues are illustrative of a much larger class of issues.

Figure 2.12 A. *"Which of these comes closer to your own view? (1) The government has no right to decide what should or should not be published. (2) To protect its moral values, a society sometimes has to forbid certain things from being published."*

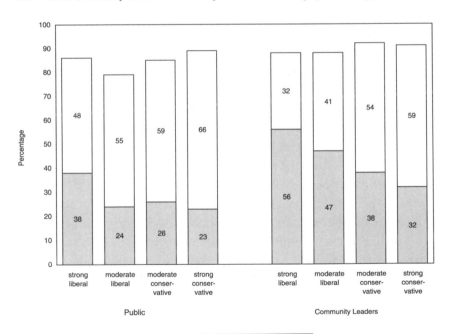

Source: McClosky and Brill 1983, table 7.9, p. 306.

Figure 2.12 B. *"Once an arrested person says he wishes to remain silent, the authorities . . . (1) should stop all further questioning at once; (2) should keep asking questions to try to get the suspect to admit his crimes."*

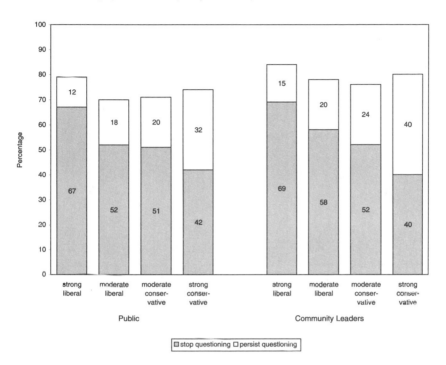

Source: McClosky and Brill, table 7.9, p. 308.

The thesis of democratic elitism holds that political elites, by virtue of their involvement in politics, outstrip ordinary citizens in commitment to civil liberties and democratic rights. But the results shown in figure 2.12 explode this claim in two ways. Conservative elites are substantially more active, aware, and sophisticated politically than ordinary citizens who describe themselves as conservative in outlook. Yet, whatever the issue (and we again underline the diversity of issues we have canvassed), conservative elites are rarely more supportive of civil liberties and democratic rights than ordinary conservative citizens. Second, whenever the responses of conservative elites and ordinary citizens who are liberal diverge, it is usually the liberal citizens who are the more likely to protect individual rights. To give one example: fewer than one in every ten conservative elites believes that refusing to hire a professor because of his unusual political beliefs is unjustifiable; by contrast, one out of every two in the general public who are strong liberals reject such a political test as unjustifiable.

Figure 2.12 C. *"Refusing to hire a professor because of his unusual political beliefs . . . (1) is never justified; (2) may be necessary if his views are really extreme."*

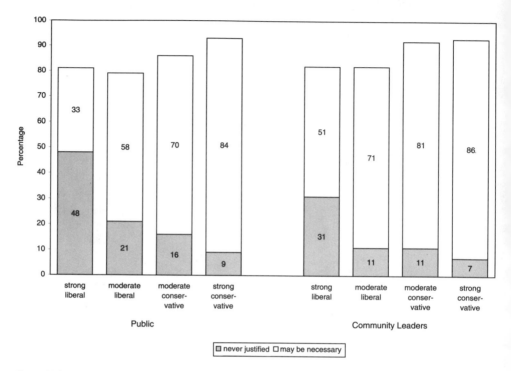

Source: McClosky and Brill, 1983, table 7.9, p. 307.

The thesis of democratic elitism counsels us that we are in better hands, so far as our civil liberties and democratic rights are concerned, by virtue of being in the hands of political elites rather than those of our fellow citizens. But in light of the consistency and strength of the findings in figure 2.12, in whose hands should we prefer to entrust our rights—political elites who are conservative or ordinary citizens who are liberal?

Concluding Themes

A tension lies at the heart of modern empirical democratic theory. The politically active, we are told, constitute a special stratum with a distinctive commitment to democratic norms by virtue of their distinctive involvement in politics: "Members of the political stratum (who live in a much more politicized culture) are more familiar with the 'democratic' norms, more consistent, more ideological, more detailed and explicit in their political attitudes, and more completely in agreement on the norms. They are in more agreement not only on what norms are implied by the abstract democratic creed but also in supporting the norms currently operating."[30] Call this the consensus thesis, for it holds that the politically active, by virtue of being politically active, come to agreement, or consensus, on democratic norms and practices while the general public does not. But a second contention threads its way through modern democratic theory. It holds that the mark of democratic politics is pluralism, pluralism at different but connected levels, among them values and actors. Thus, people plunged into the whirl of politics come up against a *mixture* of values, including conceptions of citizens' rights but also considerations of order, safety, and national security, among others. What is more, they encounter the diversity of values that makes up a national political culture from a variety of perspectives and in the company of people committed to quite different points of view. It follows from this second claim—the pluralism thesis, as we shall call it—that the objectives and political convictions of competing elites can vary from one policy domain to another and from one point in time to another. Our findings have exposed the tension between the theses of consensus and of pluralism.

In figure 2.13 we present a stylized but essentially true-to-life illustration of how the fact of elite pluralism undercuts the claim of elite consensus on civil liberties and democratic rights. For simplicity, figure 2.13 maps levels of support for civil liberties and democratic rights in a two-party system (equivalent, if more complex, representations can be graphed for multiparty systems). The solid and dotted curves describe the distribution of support for civil liberties among political elites and ordinary citizens, respectively; the solid and dotted vertical lines, the average (mean) levels of support for civil liberties among elites and ordinary citizens.

The heart of the thesis of democratic elitism is the claim that political elites reach consensus on issues of civil liberties and democratic rights; and as the vertical lines in figure 2.13 make plain, on average political elites are more committed to democratic rights than are ordinary citizens, the solid (elite) line being significantly to the right of the dotted (citizen) line. But the test of consensus entailed by the thesis presupposes that elite responses toward civil liberties are unimodal. In fact, the lesson to draw from our findings is that often they are bimodal. A large number of elites tend to pile up in support of an expansive conception of democratic rights; a large num-

Figure 2.13. Stylized Comparison of Elite and Citizen Means and Modes: Commitment to Civil Liberties

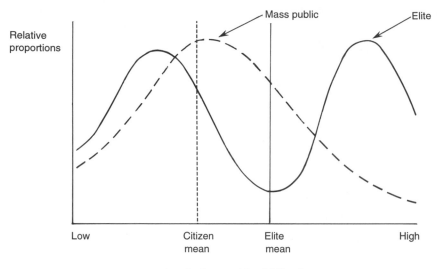

ber in support of a narrow one. The two peaks of the elite distribution drive home graphically how misleading it can be to group political elites together.

Elites with a broad conception of democratic rights do not all belong to one party and those with a narrow conception to another. The differences among partisan elites are a matter of degree and may vary from one aspect of civil liberties to another and from one political system to another. But the burden of our findings is that partisan groupings of political elites competing for popular support differ markedly both in the orientation toward civil liberties and democratic rights that they would bring to public office and consequently in the direction of the public policies they would advocate if they were to win control of government. Politics in contemporary democracies—not only Canada and the United States but also Great Britain and Israel, among a great many others—continues to supply fresh examples of how issues of civil liberties can become a central part of the electoral contest.

It is of importance, in its own right, how far citizens taken as a whole can commit themselves to democratic values and respect them not just as abstract pieties but as guiding considerations. Yet as Schumpeter insisted, the public decides only who decides public policy. The danger of mass intolerance is itself a function of the likelihood of contending groups of elites differing radically over issues of individual freedom and public order. For the decisive clash over issues of civil liberties and democratic rights is conducted between opposing groups of elites competing for control over public policy. The thesis of democratic elitism presupposes that the decisive contrast is between elite and mass public, ignoring the party system. The electoral system, however, operates to provide a choice between, not an average across, competing sets of elites. And the fallacy of democratic elitism consists exactly in its indifference to which partisan elites prevail.

THREE THE CONTESTABILITY OF RIGHTS

Democratic rights come in all sizes and many shapes. Some represent long-standing and deeply grounded claims; others have surfaced only recently. Most are political, explicitly dealing with public affairs; others are only obliquely so, defining what is private and personal against the claims of what is public and political. It would be an exaggeration to say that the variety of democratic rights forms a definite, agreed-on hierarchy, but substantial agreement obtains on a set of core rights. We want to deepen our examination of democratic rights by exploring this core set, concentrating on the rights of freedom of expression and freedom of assembly.

Exploration is in order because there is a paradox integral to the politics of rights. On the one side, it is uncontroversially agreed that freedom of speech and of assembly are and have long been at the center of democratic rights; on the other side, it is just as clear that these same rights are often at the center of some of the deepest disagreements in both contemporary democratic thought and practice. Why do we find ourselves arguing, so vehemently and so often, about the very core of what we have, as participants in a democratic polity, long since presumably agreed on? What are the forms that these arguments about core democratic rights take now? What do they tell us about the strains and dynamics of contemporary liberal democracies?

Tolerance of Intolerance

What makes for a politics of rights is that claims to rights, even core democratic rights, can be legitimately contested. But it is just the contestability of
rights that has been emphasized least. Consider a standard way of framing
the issue: "There are always some people whose ideas are considered bad or
dangerous by other people. For instance, somebody who is against all
churches and religion. If such a person wanted to make a speech in your
community against churches and religion, should he be allowed to speak or
not?"[1] From the point of view of citizens sympathetic to freedom of expression, the question verges on being open and shut. Of course, he should be
allowed to speak, and if someone cannot see the principle behind this, then
he or she really has not grasped what free speech is. Or consider a second
example: "Should an unpopular group be allowed to hold public rallies in
our cities?" Again, from the point of view of citizens friendly to the value of
liberty, the answer is obvious and immediate: yes, of course, a group should
not be denied the right to express its views merely because it happens to be
unpopular. In turn, the concentration—not exclusive, to be sure, but heavy
nonetheless—on open-and-shut cases has subtly encouraged an overin-
tellectualized conception of the politics of rights. Nearly everyone supports
fundamental democratic rights stated in the abstract: their failure to take the
position they manifestly should in support of free speech or due process, it
has therefore seemed to follow, must reflect a failure of comprehension on
their part, a failure to understand how an abstract right of which they
approve applies to a specific issue. Given that questions posed about fundamental rights in most studies tend to be obvious from the perspective of a
person committed to democratic rights, the problem thus seems primarily a
failure of learning—and by implication, it is a problem that can be cleared up
if people will only understand better the requirements of democratic values.

We call this the error thesis. It would be foolish to deny the importance of
ignorance in human affairs, not least in public affairs. Substantial numbers
of ordinary citizens decline to support fundamental democratic rights when
confronted by others they find threatening, and they do so not because they
wish to do so or even recognizing that they are doing so, but because they do
not understand what is required of them to adhere in the grip of controversy
to the democratic values they profess in the abstract. But error is only part of
the problem. Disagreements over fundamental rights often are genuine disagreements: reasonable people knowledgeable about individual rights fre-

quently disagree as to what ought to be done. The crux of the politics of democratic rights—indeed, what makes for a politics of rights—is that rights, even fundamental rights, are intrinsically contestable.

To say that rights are contestable is to say that they present themselves as live issues in current political life, open to argument and debate. Claims to rights, moreover, are open to debate from two quite different sides: from values most often associated with the political right, as we saw in the previous chapter, but also from values most closely associated with the left, as we shall see in this chapter. Specifically, we focus on the paradoxical challenge to the norm of political tolerance that arises from the idea of social tolerance.

The call for social tolerance has become a hallmark of the politics of the last quarter-century. If the recognition of the need for justice on behalf of minorities, very much including women, is still imperfect, as by any standard it surely is, the increased attention paid it represents a profound change. We shall map concern over assuring tolerance in two companion contexts: on behalf of racial and religious minorities and on behalf of women. In both, we explore how the very strengthening of a commitment to social tolerance has now made the value of political tolerance contestable in a way it was not before.

The paradox of whether a democratic polity is under an obligation to tolerate the intolerant was debated, a generation ago, in terms of the dangers of internal subversion by communists (for example, Hook 1962). But the quandary of whether intolerance is to be tolerated is more demanding when applied to prejudice than to extreme political belief. It has breached, as we shall show, the once consensual commitment of the politically engaged and aware to freedom of speech and assembly.

This new paradox of tolerance of intolerance has given rise to unfamiliar dilemmas over fundamental rights of thought and expression, and to understand these new dilemmas, a new approach has been necessary. For a generation, students of public opinion have surveyed levels of support for fundamental democratic rights both among the larger public and among strategic political and social elites. Many of these studies—those by Stouffer, by McClosky and his colleagues, and by John L. Sullivan and his colleagues—have become classics, establishing an array of empirical findings, analytical concepts, and techniques of measurement of continuing value. But on whatever other points these studies have disagreed, in all of them the supporting of a democratic right has meant the expression of a preference in favor of a right under special, indeed, atypical, conditions. The customary objective in the study of public opinion is to put the people being interviewed at their ease. Great care is taken to neutralize any pressure on them, whether by the wording of the question or through the manner of the interviewer, to favor or oppose a specific democratic right. It matters, of course, whether citizens in a democratic society will support freedom of expression even in this social vacuum. But politics is about *argument*. It is about getting people who start off on one side of an issue to join your side or at least to leave theirs. And part of what it means to say that there is a politics of rights is to say that the positions people take on questions of rights are subject to challenge. People attempt to persuade others. They attempt to induce them to qualify, give up, even reverse the positions they have taken. Where people start off politically matters, but what counts is where they wind up after the pushing and shoving of political argument.

It is necessary to take seriously the idea of political argument. However valuable it is to know whether citizens will support a fundamental democratic right in the absence of pressure, it is still more important to go on and to ask whether they will hold on to their positions in the face of pressure to change them. Will citizens who support freedom of speech stand firm if they are presented with a plausible reason for changing their minds? Can those who initially oppose freedom of expression be induced to support it?

To throw light on the role of political argument, we shall introduce the counterargument technique. Once people have taken a position on an issue of rights, we attempt to talk them out of it by calling their attention to a countervailing consideration. By mapping persistence and pliability in the face of political counterarguments, we can get a new grip on the contestability of rights.

Racism and the Politics of Tolerance

Liberal democracies have moved over the last quarter century to grapple with the historic problem of racial injustice. The campaign against racism has become a prominent item on the public agenda, perhaps most conspicuously in the United States, but to a degree that surely would have astonished even the most politically sophisticated observer in the 1930s and 1940s in liberal democracies generally. Which makes it the more important to ask: To what extent is the problem of racial intolerance approached in terms of the individual history of each liberal democracy? To what extent is it defined by the distinctive experience of the liberal democracy over which it has thrown the deepest shadow, the United States?

By way of exploring alternative terms in which the problem of racial intolerance can be posed, a special experiment was performed. The Ku Klux Klan is a preeminently American institution, and, capitalizing on this, we sought to determine if Canadians are more likely to find racism objectionable under an American label. Accordingly, when we asked respondents to pick the group they most dislike, randomly one-half of the time the list of groups presented to them included the "Ku Klux Klan," the other half of the time "racists."[2]

Manifestly, the issue of racial intolerance stands out as more objectionable when presented under the specific, albeit foreign, label of the KKK, and this is as true for elites as for the public at large (fig. 3.1). But even when the generic label is used, ordinary citizens are at least as likely to pick racists as

Figure 3.1. Percentages of Citizens and Elites Selecting the Ku Klux Klan or Racists as Most-Disliked Group

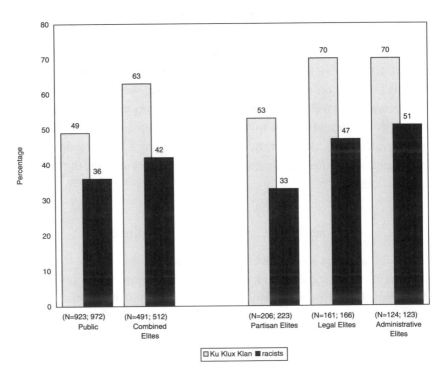

statistical significance of comparisons for both experimental variations
public vs. elites as a whole: p ≤ .01; elite groups by sector: p ≤ .01

communists as the group they most dislike (cf. fig. 2.1), and elites are at least as likely to pick racists as fascists. Given how peripheral the issue of racism has been in Canadian history (compared, for example, to the American experience), it is striking how many Canadians pick racists as the group they most dislike; the phenomenon suggests just how powerful the distinctive historical experience of the United States has been in shaping the emerging transnational culture of liberal democracy.

Intolerance of Intolerance

It speaks well for the standing of tolerance as a value in Canadian political culture that so many should attach so much importance to the dangers of racism. But it is necessary, just for this reason, to call attention to the quandaries of the politics of rights. For the very desire to achieve the value of racial tolerance now poses one of the principal threats to political tolerance.

Suppose that you detest racism. It does not follow that you *ought* to deny racists freedom of expression. The key question is not whether racism is a noxious idea: it is rather whether a person or group may be prevented, because their ideas are noxious, from engaging their fellow citizens in a debate on matters of public interest. David Duke, to take advantage of a recent and salient American example, represents a point of view that many people find objectionable and wish to speak against. However, it is a long and potentially frightening step to move from speaking out against his views to asserting that he may not speak out. To deny his right to speak is to exercise a veto on who has a right to run for public office; in a liberal democracy this is an extraordinary step to take. And, as we shall see in considering the legal actions regarding individuals like Ernst Zundel (discussed in the next section), on the Canadian scene it is an open question whether racists should be able to express their views publicly in rallies and elsewhere.

Both the power and the peril of the term *racist* speak to the nature of symbolic politics. *Symbolic politics*, as we use the term, refers to a disposition to respond to a political issue in light of broader, vaguer, more emotional concerns that the issue has come to symbolize. By taking advantage of the experimental variation of "racists" and "Ku Klux Klan" in the list of groups we presented to people in asking about their least-liked group, we can throw some light on the symbolic character of racial intolerance as a contemporary issue.

People should not be faulted for answering in good faith questions asked them in the course of an interview. If they are told that a group is racist, they are not being unreasonable in supposing that it genuinely is. But objectively there is a decided difference in the grounds for denying the Ku Klux Klan a permit to hold a rally and denying a group labeled as racists a permit. We do not want to suggest that it is normatively correct to deny a permit to the Ku Klux Klan, yet there are grounds for contesting its claim to one. The Klan is a group marked not only by its commitment to ideas that one can rightly describe as noxious, but also by its history of overt acts in furtherance of these ideas. The Klan has engaged in murder, intimidation, assault, and general thuggery. It has earned the scorn in which it is widely held, not simply by virtue of the noxious ideas it advocates, but also as a consequence of the violent and illegal acts it has committed and continues to commit in the service of these noxious ideas. There are, accordingly, substantial and concrete grounds for objecting to the Ku Klux Klan's efforts to stage a public rally, grounds that, in truth, are not immediately available if one were confronted merely with a group labeled as racists. Or, to think of another salient American example, this time from the sorry era of McCarthyism, it is now generally agreed that it was reprehensible and a serious violation of civil liberties to curtail the legitimate activities of communists, even in the face of the argument then made on the other side that the Communist Party was dedicated to the violent overthrow of the American Constitution, was closely linked to a hostile, nuclear-armed power, and hence was properly subject to suppression. No one, however, contends that contemporary racists in Canada present a parallel threat. No actual racist group of any substantial size with a history of illegality or link to a foreign power is attempting to overthrow the Canadian government; and in contemporary Canadian politics, no group dedicated to racism is politically active and in a position to win even one seat in Parliament, let alone to form a government at a local, provincial, or federal level. The political threat of racism is, in a word, negligible. But such obvious differences between the Ku Klux Klan on the one hand and racists on the other are not likely to count for very much for a person whose political thinking is pitched at the level of symbolic politics. Characterization of a group as racist becomes an encompassing description. No distinctions need be drawn between racists and the Klan, between noxious ideas and illegal conduct. The designation *racist* supplies all that one needs to know.

That ordinary citizens think about politics in symbolic terms is not remarkable. Given their uneven attention to public affairs, it is to be expected that they should often respond in terms of the symbolic politics of the issue. But surely political, legal, and administrative elites can be expected to adhere to a different, more demanding, standard. Their judgments, one might suppose, will reflect the distinctions to be made between claims made on behalf of the Ku Klux Klan and those on behalf of (otherwise unspecified) racists—unless, of course, the term *racists* has become so politically loaded as to obscure the difference between noxious ideas and illegal conduct.

Whatever the hazards when individual rights clash explicitly with concerns for public safety, elites do, as we noted earlier, exhibit consensus in support of rights to free expression for unpopular groups (see fig. 2.2). Notice that it is not merely that elites are more likely to stand by freedom of expression than are ordinary citizens. The decisive consideration is instead the degree of agreement among elites. Only so far as elites overwhelmingly support freedom of expression in the heat of controversy can it be said that consensus prevails among them; indeed, by convention at least two-thirds must be willing to stand by a democratic right for a consensus to prevail in its favor.[3] Because this is what obtains, as we have seen, when elites and the public make judgments about the free speech rights of groups other than racists that they dislike, it seems a safe bet that the same should be true when elites make judgments about whether racists ought to be allowed to hold a public rally.

In fact, it is a bad bet. In figure 3.2 we summarize the willingness of elites and of the public at large to agree that members of the group they most dislike should be allowed to hold a public rally, breaking down each depending on whether the group they dislike is racists or some other group (for example, fascists or communists). Let us look first at the responses of the public at large. It makes very little difference whether the group they disliked most is racist or not: in either case only about one in every three supports the right of the group they most dislike to hold a public rally (see fig. 3.2). By contrast, it makes a striking difference to elites whether the group they find most objectionable is racist. If the group is not—if it is instead run-of-the-mill politically objectionable—then elites indeed form a consensus to protect its rights, with nearly four in every five of them in agreement that the group, whether fascists or communists or whatever, is entitled to hold a public rally to express its point of view. However, if the group that elites most dislike is racists, the situation is quite different: just as many oppose the right of the group to hold a public rally as support it. It is true that elites are more

Figure 3.2. Support of Citizens and Elites for Freedom of Expression of Most-Disliked Group (nonracist or racist groups)

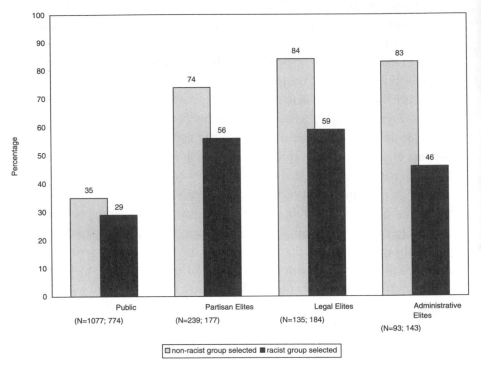

statistical significance of comparisons
non-racist vs. racist groups, for partisan elites: p ≤ .01; for legal elites: p ≤ .01; for administrative elites: p ≤ .01

likely to support the rights of racists than is the public at large. But there is little comfort in this. Taking the elite sample as a whole, as many are opposed as are in support. Elites cannot by any standard be said to have formed a consensus in defense of the fundamental right of racists to freedom of expression.

This result matters for two related reasons. On the one hand, racists are *the* group most often picked out by elites as the group they most dislike; on the other, it is racists—or, perhaps more accurately, people charged with being racist, a potentially enormous group because it is ill-defined—whose basic rights are now subject to public challenge. Hence the new dilemma of contemporary liberal democratic politics: precisely when it comes to one of the hottest issues of current politics, elites are unwilling to give unqualified support to the fundamental right of free expression, not out of an inherent intolerance on their part, but rather out of an intolerance of racial intolerance.

Value Conflict: Basic Distinctions

Liberty, we have seen, is a contested value in part because politically it raises a double-barreled question: who should be allowed to do what? Even if one sets this aside, however, liberty is an inherently contestable value. There is a fundamental tension in the notion of rights, whether detailed in a written constitution or not, with which every liberal democracy must wrestle. No right, not even freedom of expression, can be exercised without limits. It is consensually agreed that citizens do not have a right to utter directly dangerous speech, the paradigmatic example, of course, being the prohibition on falsely crying, "Fire!" in a crowded theater.[4] How to determine such limiting circumstances has been immensely challenging. In confirming limits on insulting or obscene speech, for example, American judges have at times been forced to resort to denying that something someone said was speech at all.[5] In Canada, the Charter of Rights has distinctively institutionalized the contestability of rights through a constitutional invention, namely, section 1 in the Charter of Rights and Freedoms, the Limitations Clause. This clause stipulates that the charter "guarantees the rights and freedoms set out in it subject only to such reasonable limits prescribed by law as can be demonstrably justified in a free and democratic society." Considered by itself, the guarantee of free expression appearing in section 2(b) of the Charter of Rights is set out in language every bit as unqualified as its American counterpart. And Canadian courts have given very broad interpretation to these guarantees in recognizing no restrictions on the content of the expressions guaranteed by the charter. The inevitable limitations on the right to free expression are arrived at not through reading limitations into the rights themselves, but through separate consideration of limitations under the auspices of section 1. In doing so, limits on free expression have been justified on a number of grounds, notably the promotion of other values, for example, tolerance, equality, and respect for individuals and communities.

The principle of freedom of expression, so far as it derives, for example, from the liberalism of John Stuart Mill's *On Liberty,* is based on its value as an instrument of truth. On this account, it is only through the "collision of adverse opinions" that the truth can be grasped. A broader argument can be mounted, however. For one thing, the core idea of a liberal democratic society is that of a government accountable to a public that can freely express its views and withdraw its consent. For another, free expression is an essential aspect of the dignity and the full development of the person. These fundamental values clearly underlie the guarantee of freedom of expression in section 2(b) of the Charter and jurisprudence arising in this area. But just because liberty is so deeply conjoined with other values, and most especially because of the link between liberty and self-realization, the right of free expression has become contestable in new ways. We want to explore the new contestability of liberty, focusing on arguably the leading edge issue in the new politics of tolerance: antihate legislation.

Affirmative Tolerance: The Case of Antihate Legislation

The principle of tolerance, as applied in contemporary liberal democracies, harbors a number of antinomies. Perhaps the most central, certainly the most salient of these concerns the requirements of tolerance in the face of prejudice. The idea of tolerance, whatever its philosophical dimensions, is a historical idea, impossible to understand apart from its history, including its recent history. Arguments over rights are arguments embedded in a context, and the context of these arguments changed decisively with World War II and the Jewish Holocaust. Six million people gassed, shot, starved, buried alive. It was—it is—difficult to accept the horrors wrought by anti-Semitism. Never again: that seemed surely the lesson, a lesson to be applied on more than one front, most especially including the eruptions of anti-Semitism and denial of the reality of the Holocaust.

Tolerance, it seemed to liberals of the nineteenth century, required one to accept not only a diversity of beliefs and values within a liberal society but also, and as important, the freedom to express these beliefs and values, whether held by majority or minority. Two issues thus need to be distinguished. First, whether citizens in a liberal democracy are obligated to allow others to organize their lives around the beliefs and values central to them, consistent with ordinary law, even if these beliefs and values are at odds with those of the majority. Second, whether adherents of beliefs and values that are at odds with those of the majority in a quite specific way, by virtue of being intolerant, should be allowed to proselytize on behalf of them. Tolerance demands the first, but it has seemed less obvious to many liberals in the twentieth century that it requires the second. Indeed, so far from requiring the second, a positive commitment in behalf of tolerance is now said to require a positive effort against intolerance.

We want to explore the notion of "affirmative tolerance" in the context of the legal cases surrounding the activities of James Keegstra and Ernst Zundel. The disposition of the two cases by the Supreme Court of Canada reveals something of the difficulties that liberal societies have in balancing support for free expression against a desire to discourage racial intolerance. Keegstra was charged with the Criminal Code offence of "willfully promoting hatred against an identifiable group" as a result of his making anti-Semitic statements to his Alberta high school class. In ruling on the case the justices of the Supreme Court unanimously agreed that the hate propaganda provisions of the Criminal Code infringe upon the guarantees under the Charter of Rights regarding freedom of expression. The Court, however, split 4–3 in deciding under section 1 of the Charter that this infringement was a reasonable limit upon freedom of expression.[6] The majority recognized that the Charter protected free expression irrespective of content but decided that other legislative purposes can "warrant overriding a constitutional freedom" (698). In upholding hate propaganda sections of the Criminal Code, the Court decided that, in a society committed to equality and racial tolerance, as Canada is, the value of preventing the potential harm of hate propaganda can outweigh the value of freedom of expression.[7]

In the second case, Zundel, the publisher of several pamphlets denying the Holocaust, was charged with spreading false news by publishing statements harmful to the public interest that he knew or ought reasonably to have known to be false.[8] Once again, the Court noted that "section 2(b) of the Charter protects the right of a minority to express its view, however unpopular it may be" (732). The decision in the Zundel case thus hinged, as it did in Keegstra's, not on whether the Charter's guarantee of free expression protected his activities, but rather on whether there were reasons for limiting the right to free expression in light of section 1. Once again, the Court split 4–3, only this time the majority ruled that the legislative purposes of the false news section of the Criminal Code under which Zundel had been charged were neither sufficiently precise nor important enough to warrant overriding the Charter's guarantee of freedom of expression. The dissenting minority argued that the public's interest in "furthering racial, religious and social tolerance" warrants restricting freedom of expression by preventing the "wilful publication of injurious lies" (736).

The Zundel and Keegstra cases expose the new collision between the values of free expression and of tolerance in contemporary liberal societies. And the differing outcomes in the two cases as well as the split decisions and the narrow margins of decision speak eloquently to the difficulty of resolving these conflicts decisively. The values of free expression and racial or religious tolerance remain in tension in Canadian society even though they both draw on the same underlying liberal principles. To illuminate this tension, we focused on antihate legislation, asking all respondents,

> "Do you think it should be against the law to write or speak in a way that promotes hatred toward a particular racial or religious group?"

From the perspective of the classic civil libertarian, the potential of legislation along these lines is chilling. One can detest hatred of racial or religious groups, yet see in the vagueness of the provision—"to write or speak in a way that promotes hatred"—a menace to liberty. Who is to decide? On the basis of what kind of evidence? What, exactly, does it mean "to promote" hatred? Can one in fact compellingly draw a line between the thoughts and feelings that a person has toward a racial group and the actual behavior that he or she exhibits toward them? Is one obliged to do so? None of these questions is unreasonable or unimportant, but none of them, it seems fair to say, is given much in the way of consideration when ordinary people, asked their opinion, weigh the desirability of antihate legislation. The response of the general public is one-sided (fig. 3.3). Seventy-four percent of ordinary Canadians believe in laws prohibiting speech or writing "that promotes hatred toward a particular racial or religious group."

It is tempting to write this reaction off as evidence of good intentions, even perhaps as proof of the vagueness of good intentions of ordinary citizens, politically naive and inexperienced as they tend to be. A very different response, one that is more measured and balanced and aware of the pitfalls of criminalizing speech however noble the objective, might be expected to characterize the responses of elites. But the reaction of elites is just as lopsided in support of antihate legislation as that of ordinary citizens (fig. 3.3).

What does it mean to support antihate legislation? What is the nature of the commitment? The issue of antihate legislation hinges on competing claims of tolerance expressed in two different and, from the perspective of the project of legislation, opposing values: the need to promote freedom of expression and the need to combat prejudice. What needs to be determined, therefore, is how people react when these opposing values clash before their very eyes.

Figure 3.3. Support for Anti-Hate Laws

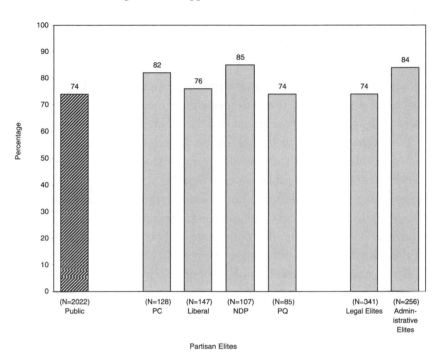

And to bring about a clash of values is the function of political argument. One person takes a position on an issue, then another, if she disagrees, tries to talk him out of it. How does the second person try to accomplish this? Most generally, by calling the first person's attention to a competing consideration, a consideration she has reason to believe both of them think important, a consideration, moreover, that should induce the first person to qualify, abandon, or even reverse his initial position.

To introduce the role of argument into the study of public opinion, we have devised the counterargument technique. We want to see what happens to people's ideas about political rights when others talk back to them. Counterarguments are therefore prepared in advance. Then, as soon as a person has taken a position on an issue, taking advantage of computer-assisted interviewing, the appropriate counterargument automatically appears on the interviewer's screen, and the interviewer tries to talk the respondent out of the position he or she has just taken.

Consider people who, when asked their views on antihate legislation, reply that there should be a law against inciting hatred of a group. Immediately on taking this position, they were asked,

> "If this results in less freedom of speech about important public issues, would you feel differently about it being against the law?"

In figure 3.4A we lay out the proportions of respondents initially favoring antihate legislation who feel differently after their attention is explicitly called to the competing consideration of freedom.

The incidence of change is high indeed. Among the general public, very nearly half declare that they would change their position if freedom of speech about important public issues suffers. By any standard, the willingness of one in two to reconsider their position is formidable, and it suggests how deceptive the politics of antihate legislation can be. If partisan political elites, examining public opinion polls, were to choose a position on the issue on the basis of political advantage, their initial choice would be to back antihate legislation. The level of public support for it is overwhelming: about three in every four citizens favor it, as we saw. However, that support does not represent an unconditional commitment for many, and if the attention of citizens favoring antihate legislation is drawn to the value of freedom of speech about important public issues—as inevitably it would be in the course of serious public argument—the majority in favor of antihate legislation vanishes.

But is this pliability of support for antihate legislation only one more variation on the now-familiar sermon of the superficiality of ordinary citizens' political ideas? After all, it has become a commonplace of modern political commentary that ordinary citizens know and care little about many political issues and hence invest little of themselves in any of the positions they take. Surely, it follows that they can readily be induced to abandon the positions they take on many issues.

It does not pay to underestimate the superficial engagement of many citizens with political issues, but it is very likely a mistake, in light of the results for elites, to attribute the pliability of the public's support for antihate legislation simply to their political naivete and lack of political awareness. Consider the reaction of elites who support antihate legislation and then are challenged with a counterargument (fig. 3.4A). Approximately four in every ten say they would feel differently about the desirability of antihate legislation if a threat to freedom of speech on other important public issues were to result. This is not quite as many as among the general public, but it is

Figure 3.4 A. Pliability of Support of Antihate Laws

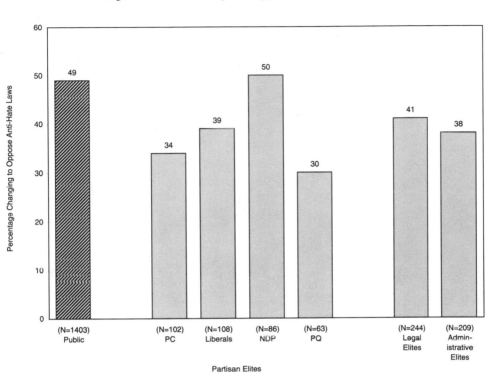

for all practical (and political) purposes very nearly the same. Moreover, the pattern of variation *among* elites suggests that the reason for their willingness to reconsider a position on the issue is less that they do not care about the issue of antihate legislation one way or the other, but precisely that they do care and care about both sides of the issue. Thus, the willingness to withdraw support for antihate legislation in the face of a counterargument calling attention to the importance of freedom of expression is highest among the NDP, the very group that attaches the highest importance to freedom of expression.

The clash of values bound up in the issue of antihate legislation is logically symmetrical: just as a person who has given priority initially to fighting prejudice may be vulnerable to an appeal to freedom of speech, so a person who has supported freedom of speech and thus opposed antihate legislation may be vulnerable to an argument about the dangers of prejudice. Accord-

Figure 3.4 B. Pliability of Opposition to Antihate Laws

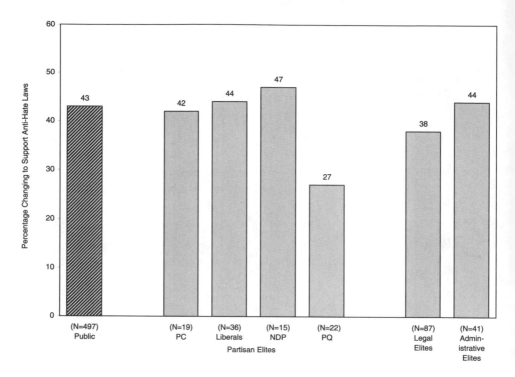

ingly, by way of assessing empirically the pliability of opposition to antihate legislation, we immediately asked every respondent who opposed an anti-hate law,

> "If this results in more racial and religious prejudice, would you feel differently about it NOT being against the law?"

It could be argued that people who, having resisted the temptation to take the easy course and adopt the socially popular position of combating racial and religious hatred out of a concern for freedom of speech, will be more likely to stick to their guns than people who went with the tide of social opinion. But the results of the counterargument against the freedom of expression position belie this expectation, illustrating instead how a clash of values, and hence a pliability of positions, is built in to both sides of the issue of antihate legislation (fig. 3.4B). Thus, contrary to the "hard core minority" hypothesis, the rate of pliability in the face of a counterargument is nearly as high among opponents of antihate legislation as among proponents. For example, 43 percent of opponents change their mind when their attention is called to the risk of increasing prejudice, as compared to 49 percent of proponents. Among governmental elites, 44 percent of opponents change their mind, compared to 38 percent of proponents, while the comparable figures for legal elites are 38 percent and 41 percent, respectively.

The key feature of the findings is the similarity of elites and ordinary citizens. If the crucial consideration had been the remoteness, the lack of reality of the issue, then ordinary citizens, for whom politics is by orders of magnitude more remote and abstruse than it is for elites, should be markedly more pliable in their preferences about antihate legislation than elites. But opposition to antihate legislation is nearly as pliable among elites as among ordinary citizens (fig. 3.4B). And the sheer frequency with which elites do in fact change their minds, reconsidering their opposition to antihate legislation if their attention is called to the competing risk of prejudice, further buttresses the view that there is a conflict of values, an intense and immediately evident conflict, built in to the project of criminalizing certain forms of previously protected speech in the name of tolerance.

This conflict of values between combating prejudice and protecting freedom of expression imparts a volatile character to the politics of affirmative tolerance. The affirmative effort to assure tolerance has come to center on the deployment of institutional authority—most often public, though increasingly private, too (in the form, for example, of universities)—to promote tolerance by criminalizing as intolerant the expression of racist views. The politics of affirmative tolerance, the results on antihate legislation suggest, are inherently volatile because of the immediacy and intensity of the conflict underlying them. From the perspective of agents of authority, public and private, who wish actively to punish expressions of intolerance there is a preponderance of support to combat intolerance. The effort to combat intolerance thus seems to hold out to elites the opportunity to combat religious and racial prejudice, surely worthwhile in itself, and, also important, the opportunity to take credit for a popular policy. But once an effort is actually made to apply affirmative tolerance, as our results make plain, a popular reaction in exactly the opposite direction is more than possible. When and if the potential risk to freedom of expression is underlined, a substantial fraction of those initially favoring criminalizing intolerance, perhaps as many as one-half of them, could change sides; and together with those initially opposing affirmative tolerance they would constitute a new majority, a majority now in opposition. Hence the volatility of the politics of affirmative tolerance. Tempted by large majorities, elites may take policy initiatives to compel tolerance, but in implementing these initiatives they risk evoking, like an elastic band snapping back, an intense reaction in the opposite direction. And the effect of this volatility of popular reactions is to assure that issues of tolerance have a built in potential for sudden dramatic shifts in public preferences, and so are contestable not merely philosophically but politically.

Censorship, Pornography, and Feminism

Claims to rights are contestable because, as a matter of principle, they cannot be immunized against counterclaims, and just for this reason, in developing a political theory of rights, one must examine when the claim to freedom of expression collides with competing values. There is, however, more than one kind of collision. The most obvious kind occurs in explicitly political contexts: for example, when a group with controversial or noxious views wants to hold a public assembly to air its point of view. A less obvious kind occurs in contexts not necessarily construed as political, and perhaps the most urgent contemporary example of such a collision is that between classical liberal claims of freedom of expression and the claims of some modern feminists that liberty for pornographers is oppression for women.

On many fronts, an effort is now being made to suppress the publication or public showing of sexually explicit materials on the grounds that it not only injures the women shown in the materials but, still more fundamentally, endangers women throughout the society (for example, MacKinnon 1993). It may be objected that the issue of whether sexually explicit materials should be banned has nothing essential to do with fundamental democratic rights. On this view, political rights are explicitly and centrally tied up with politics. To be sure, a notable feature of contemporary life is precisely that claims to "rights" are frequently made in the context of "private" as against "public" institutions and obligation: children, for example, now invoke notions of due process or inalienable rights in disputes with their parents.[9] But these claims, it is argued, are merely analogies, and their very profusion shows that the idea of the political has become confused and incoherent in contemporary cultures by being made synonymous with any claim, in any context whether political or not, for guaranteed treatment.

We reject the suggestion that the idea of political rights has a fixity, established *sub specie aeternitatis* independent of historical or cultural context.

On the contrary, as political theorists like Michael Walzer (1983) argue, claims to rights are contestable because they are ultimately and inescapably context-dependent. But, having said this, we must also say that the notion of context is shadowy. It is tempting, and indeed common, to take the national political culture, which marks a distinctive way of life, as the context in which political rights are to be understood. But it is far more difficult than is usually imagined to identify empirically the distinctive boundaries of national political cultures; and there is much to recommend recognizing that arguments over rights in Canadian politics, by virtue of being framed as questions of rights, tend to be embedded not exclusively in the context of Canadian or even English political culture but rather in the larger background of the culture of contemporary liberal democracy.

To say that censorship of sexually explicit materials becomes an issue of political rights is to say that competing considerations can be evoked on either side of the issue, and it is necessary, therefore, to understand how competing rights or claims are evaluated, not when viewed in the abstract or in isolation, but when pitted against one another. When an issue becomes controversial, it becomes the center of political argument, a process that exposes people to a swirl of competing considerations, together with an invitation to reconsider their position. Political arguments over rights are live arguments. People care about more than one thing, have more than one value, not because they lack a definite political point of view (although many do) but because they have one. A political point of view, like liberalism, can be coherent, but it is not monistic just insofar as it is liberal. It does not aim at just one goal, to the exclusion of all others; rather, it represents a pluralistic assemblage of related concerns that at some levels are mutually reinforcing and at others capable of coming into conflict. How does this pluralism bear on the politics of rights? As we shall show, although elites *initially* are more likely to oppose censorship of sexually explicit films than ordinary citizens, because they also are more likely to have a definite point of view politically, they are more likely to surrender their support of freedom of expression in the face of a countervailing argument.

The clash over antihate legislation, we remarked, has hinged at the level of the Supreme Court on the section 1 limitations clause of the Charter of Rights. The Court has also brought section 1 to bear sharply on freedom of expression issues involving sexually explicit materials. Yet the limiting of free expression in this area, at least at the level of the Court, has been based not upon concern over violating or offending social or religious norms, but rather, as with hate propaganda, on the argument that such materials can be seen to cause harm to an identifiable group, in this case, women.

In Canada as elsewhere, sexually explicit material has become the site for sharply contested claims over the reach of public speech. A coalition of proponents, led by feminists, has attempted to take the issue of pornography outside the context of free speech, arguing that it involves discrimination.[10] On their view, the public dissemination of much sexually explicit material victimizes women, either firsthand, if they are themselves forced to see it, or secondhand, insofar as they suffer at the hands of others who have been brutalized by exposure to pornography. So viewed, criminalization of the public dissemination of sexually explicit materials represents a redress of a civil tort, not an instance of censorship. Indeed, far from being an invasion of free speech, the feminist argument maintains, the criminalizing of pornography represents an attempt to assure freedom and equality on behalf of women who have been demeaned and silenced by a climate of opinion that brutalizes women generally. On the other side, it has been argued that the attempt to repress, whether through criminal law or administrative regulation, the treatment of sexually explicit themes in literature, sculpture, photography, novels, and films is censorship pure and simple.

This issue recently came before the Supreme Court of Canada in the Donald Butler case.[11] As the owner of a sex shop, Butler was charged with possessing, displaying, and selling obscene material in violation of a Criminal Code provision that "any publication a dominant characteristic of which is the undue exploitation of sex, or of sex and . . . crime, horror, cruelty and violence shall be deemed to be obscene."[12] In a unanimous (8–0) decision, the Court ruled that the Criminal Code infringed upon the Charter of Rights guarantee of freedom of expression in section 2(b). Nevertheless, as in the Keegstra antihate case, the Court, in referring to the Charter's limitation clause (section 1), decided that the overriding objective of "the avoidance of harm to society . . . is a sufficiently pressing and substantial concern to warrant a restriction on freedom of expression"(455). Moreover, the Court held that "material which may be said to exploit sex in a 'degrading or dehumanizing' manner will necessarily fail the community standards test, not because it offends against morals but because it is perceived by public opinion to be harmful to society, particularly women" (454). Once again, the Court decision hinged on a trade-off between the value of freedom of expression and another liberal value, this time the dignity of (female) persons.

It is of course not a new venture for public opinion studies to explore attitudes toward censorship.[13] But we believe that to make out the actual politics of rights, it is not enough to follow standard practice and examine citizens' opinions in the neutral setting of the conventional public opinion interview. It is necessary to track people's preferences in the course of political argumentation. People have more than one attitude, more than one concern; and just because their first thought is to take one side of an issue does not mean that they cannot be persuaded to take the opposite. The politics of rights is more complex, more fluid than has been customarily supposed.

The basic pattern of the politics of rights is defined by the disparity in support for fundamental rights between the general public on one side and political elites on the other. If fundamental rights are caught up in specific conflicts rather than confronted in the abstract, previous studies show that elites offer strikingly more support than do ordinary citizens. But at just this point these studies stop. They measure initial positions, people's first reaction to a clash of rights, and leave it at that. But that is like measuring what people think at the beginning of a political argument, then omitting to measure what they think at the end of it. And political argument makes a difference. Indeed, as we shall show in the case of censorship and pornography, although elites are more likely than ordinary citizens to oppose censorship of sexually explicit movies, they are even more likely than ordinary citizens to be talked out of their opposition by a counterargument.

As a starting point, everyone was asked,

"Do you think that films that show sexually explicit acts should be allowed or should they be banned?"

The responses show that ordinary citizens are split more or less down the middle: half favor allowing sexually explicit films, half favor banning them; in contrast, elites are markedly more likely to oppose banning of such films (fig. 3.5). In fact, with the single exception of Conservatives, a solid, in most cases an overwhelming majority of elites believe that sexually explicit films should be allowed.

This finding is consistent with previous studies of democratic rights.[14] But what happens when people's views are challenged? Will those whose first impulse is to oppose censorship stick with their support for freedom of expression? Will those whose initial wish is to ban sexually explicit films swing around in support of the principle of freedom of expression once they

Figure 3.5. Opposition to Censorship of Sexually Explicit Films

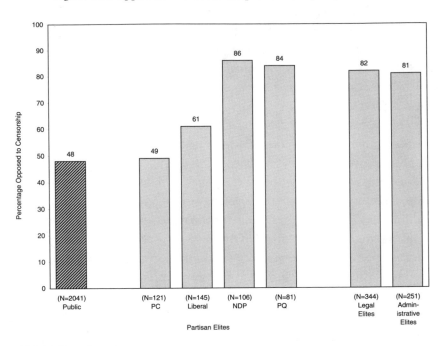

statistical significance of comparisons
public vs. elites as a whole: p ≤ .01; political elites by party: p ≤ .01

see the price of censorship in terms of democratic values? Will elites, under pressure, maintain their commitment to freedom of expression more often than ordinary citizens? To answer these questions, after people had pronounced themselves in favor of or opposed to banning sexually explicit films, they were presented with counterarguments designed to call their attention to a countervailing consideration. Specifically, if they had supported banning sexually explicit films, they were asked,

> "Would you feel differently about banning such films if that means less freedom of choice for adult Canadians in the films they watch?
> Yes, feel differently.
> No, feel the same."

Alternatively, if they had opposed banning sexually explicit films, they were asked,

> "Would you feel differently about allowing such films if that means that films degrading women might be seen by larger parts of the public?

Yes, feel differently.
No, feel the same."

The crucial question is the extent to which the climate of opinion on issues of civil liberties changes when the larger public and elites have their attention called to competing considerations on both sides of an issue. Supporters of censorship among the general public, having declared themselves in favor of banning sexually explicit films, were confronted immediately with a counterargument invoking the competing value of freedom of choice. Yet overwhelmingly they maintain their original position. Approximately four in every five declare that even if censorship infringes on freedom of choice, they remain in favor of banning sexually explicit films (fig. 3.6). Moreover, the reactions of elites who support banning sexually explicit films are virtually *identical* to those of the average citizen. Again, approximately three in every four who initially favored censorship maintain their position, even after having had their attention called to the damage that censorship can do to the principle of freedom of choice, and this holds for elites of every description, legislative, legal, and governmental (fig. 3.6). In short, the side of the issue that favors censorship holds its ground even when the risk of infringing on the principle of freedom is explicitly called to their attention.

But a key part of politics, including the politics of rights, is that conflicts can be asymmetrical. Just because one side holds up under pressure does not mean the other will. Indeed, much of the political dynamics of issues of civil liberties hinges not simply on whether more people favor than oppose specific civil liberties, but whether, when their positions clash, opponents of censorship are as firmly committed to their position as proponents are to theirs. Accordingly, we also report the comparable proportions of stability and defection to a counterargument (fig. 3.6), prefiguring the reasoning in the Butler case, which asks opponents of censorship if they would still be in favor of allowing such films to be seen if "that means that films degrading women might be seen by larger parts of the public?" This is, of course, not the same counterargument that proponents of censorship received, and it may be objected that any difference between the pliability of the two may be a function of the difference in the strength of the two counterarguments. But because issues of civil liberties hinge on choices between competing values, people taking one side of the issue open themselves to a different objection from people taking the opposite side. To assess the strength of

Figure 3.6. Pliability of Support for and Opposition to Censorship of
Sexually Explicit Films

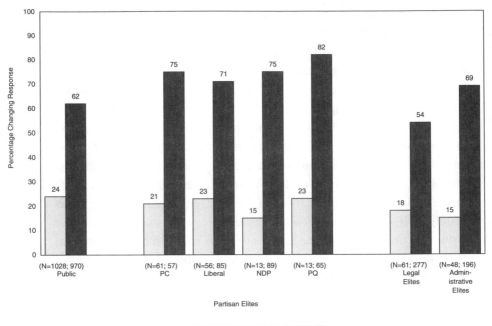

commitment to a position, it is necessary to assess their reactions to the
counterarguments that will be directed against them in real life; and as
people who favor censorship tend to be met with the objection that freedom
suffers in consequence, so people who oppose censorship of sexually explicit
films are now met with the objection that women suffer in consequence.

Consider first the reactions of ordinary citizens whose first response is to
oppose censorship of sexually explicit movies. Their response to counterar-
gumentation is quite different from that of proponents of censorship.
Whereas proponents are very likely to maintain their commitment to censorship after being exposed to a counterargument, opponents of censorship
are disproportionately likely to give ground after their attention is called to
the risk of degrading women. Thus, six in every ten citizens who support
freedom of expression give ground in the face of a counterargument compared to only one in every four who favors censorship (fig. 3.6).

This asymmetry in pliability—opponents of sexually explicit films holding their ground, proponents yielding it—is telling. Imagine, by way of a

thought experiment, that public argument were to erupt over censorship of films. At the beginning of the controversy, the two sides would be almost evenly matched: as we saw, one-half of the general public opposes this form of censorship, one-half favors it. But the impact of argumentation on the two sides is likely to be anything but identical. Indeed, attending to the probabilities of defection in the face of a counterargument consistent with figure 3.6, the best guess is that approximately two in every three citizens would favor censorship of sexually explicit films, only one in every three would oppose it. These figures are only estimates, and a variety of other factors would need to be taken into account, among them, the likelihood of exposure to countervailing considerations, which is in turn a function of, among other things, the relative sizes of the war chests of the opposing activists. Nevertheless, over a wide range of plausible assumptions, the most likely outcome is plain: an issue of rights on which the opposing sides in the general public are at the start evenly matched will become, through political argument, politically one-sided, with the balance of public opinion in the end being unsympathetic to freedom of expression.

This may be taken as yet one more chorus in the familiar refrain that democratic rights are not in safe hands so far as they are in the hands of ordinary citizens. But to appreciate the true potential of political argument to shape the politics of rights, it is essential to take account of the reactions of elites, above all, political elites, to counterarguments. The accepted position is, of course, that fundamental rights receive an extra measure of support from elites, and indeed, just by virtue of a consensus among elites, fundamental democratic rights receive the support that they require to withstand storms of intolerance on the part of ordinary citizens. So far as elites do indeed play the role of custodians of democratic values, protecting them against popular onslaught, two things ought to be true. First, supposing they initially supported censorship, they should overwhelmingly swing around, in defense of liberty, once their attention is called directly to the threat posed to the value of freedom of expression. Second, and still more crucially, supposing they initially favored allowing the showing of sexually explicit films, they should hold their ground in defense of freedom of expression in the face of a challenge to their position. But as figure 3.6 makes plain, on this highly charged issue the suggestion that elites are, so to speak, more likely to correct a misstep on the principle of freedom of expression is dead wrong. In fact, those among the elites who favor censorship tend to stay in place, even when the countervailing value of freedom of choice is invoked explicitly:

indeed, approximately three in every four elites persist in favoring censorship even "if that means less freedom of choice for adult Canadians." The second expectation—that elites initially opposed to censorship will hold their ground in the face of a counterargument—fares even worse. Consider the responses of elites, and above all political elites, who initially take a position in favor of freedom of expression in the form of sexually explicit films and are then asked if they will reconsider their position on the grounds that such films are "degrading to women." So far from being markedly *less* likely than the general public to qualify or surrender their position under pressure, taken as a whole they are *just as* likely to withdraw their support for freedom of expression if challenged with the argument that such films are degrading to women, and indeed, political elites are *more* likely than the average citizen to yield under pressure.

It should not be concluded that elites will withdraw their commitment to freedom of expression in the face of any and every counterargument. But as our findings suggest and, in fact, as the full train of events in the Butler case revealed, where the counterconsideration is itself rooted in the values of liberalism, elites can be swung around from a civil libertarian position just like citizens at large. To speak of competing values is not to speak of competing philosophies. Just because a political philosophy like liberalism is pluralistic, it can come under challenge from *within*. For liberals are most likely to abandon the liberal value of freedom of expression when the challenge to freedom is rooted in the plurality of values that they, as liberals, cherish.

Reprise

The politics of rights is not static. Rights are claims, and claims are contested, bolstered, qualified, expanded, withdrawn, and redrawn. Claims are inherently and unavoidably contestable because they inevitably and conspicuously evoke counterclaims. And just for this reason, it is deeply deceptive to give an account of the contemporary understanding of fundamental rights in the abstract. Claims to rights come alive only contextually, and we must therefore try and catch sight of claims and counterclaims to rights in play to see how they collide with one another in the course of actual argumentation. We have accordingly gone beyond the conventions of the standard public opinion interview and explored the fate of claims to fundamental rights when the claims are subject to challenge. Our aim has been to drive home how familiar ideas about freedom of expression, which may appear settled and uncontroversial, remain live issues. Arguments over fundamental rights are live issues, moreover, not simply in the sense of sometimes lacking a consensually agreed-on solution, but in the deeper sense of often representing genuine predicaments in which citizens sympathetic to liberty and tolerance and comity, as well as those more closed-minded and illiberal, can find it difficult to assent to even fundamental democratic rights. In this spirit we have traced some quandaries of contemporary liberal democracy, including the dilemma of the tolerance of racial intolerance and the reconception of political and aesthetic freedom of expression under the spur of the new feminism.

FOUR EQUALITY: A CHAMELEON VALUE

Equality has been a foundational value of liberal democratic politics. Less obvious is the nature of the foundations it has helped to establish. What gives a special stamp to equality as a political value? Why does it so distinctively engender, as J. R. Pole (1993) has remarked, a fissiparous politics? The answer, we suggest, is that equality is a complex rather than a unitary idea. It embraces a variety of domains of life and social goods capable, as Michael Walzer (1983) has argued, of taking on different but coherent meanings in different cultures or even in the same culture at different times. And the pluralism of equality as a value, we argue, is the key to its distinctively discordant role in contemporary politics. The politics of equality does not consist simply in a clash between those who favor and oppose it. Rather, it is centered in the clash between images of equality differently conceived. Douglas Rae has captured exactly this spirit of pluralism, asking, "Is equality a plan for a great cathedral, whose walls and buttresses fit together in a progressively more complete and stable structure, each occupying its proper space, the whole consisting in interlocking parts? Or is equality the blue print for a contradictory structure—a jester's church—some of whose walls and buttresses can be raised to the sky only as others are leveled to the ground?" (1981, 2) Equality resembles a jester's church very much more than a great cathedral. It encompasses a plurality of concerns and acquires its special political dynamic because its various conceptions can both complement and conflict with one another. Our objective, accordingly, is not to ascertain whether citizens and elites do or do not value equality, but rather to canvass the variety of meanings they ascribe to it.

In working through what equality means, we shall focus in this chapter on several usages. Briefly, these are (1) equality as a symbolic value; (2) economic equality; (3) equality and individualism; and (4) equality of status and esteem. These do not exhaust the ways in which equality is used as a foundational value, but they do illuminate some of the principal implications of equality as a value in contemporary liberal democratic politics.

Our objective is to map patterns of consensus and cleavage regarding the value of equality, and this requires comparison. The comparisons at the center of our analysis of the value of equality in Canadian culture are three-fold. There is, first, the natural comparison between Canadian political culture and American—natural because the two countries are similar and yet distinct. Second, there is the pivotal comparison between the Canadian public and their elites, particularly political decision makers who are charged with determining public policy. Finally, there are comparisons among elites. In liberal democracies, public influence takes more than one form and is embodied in more than one strategic institution; hence our tripartite examination of political, administrative, and legal elites. All three are of interest, not least lawyers. As Tocqueville and many others since have observed, the legal elite plays a crucial role in interpreting and institutionalizing equality in liberal democratic societies.[1]

By and large, the politics of equality has been assumed to be transparent: equality is a value of the political left. The greater equality's appeal in public debate, the greater the electoral opportunity of the left, other things being equal; conversely, the more equality recedes into the background, the deeper the shadow over the left's electoral chances. It would be perverse to deny that the left has a comparative advantage (in some sense) when the politics of equality becomes paramount. But equality has many facets, and some of them offer a potent weapon not to the political left but to the political right.

Finally, we distinguish between the symbolic politics of equality and its substantive politics, concentrating in this chapter on the symbolism and in the next on the substance. By the symbolic politics of equality we have in mind public contests centered on the importance of equality as a value—on the amount, as it were, of public esteem that it deserves. We choose the term *symbolic politics* not to denigrate the political weight of such contests, but rather to highlight the reflexive character of equality as a political value. Political appeals on behalf of equality take on very different meanings depending on the perspective of the audience. Perspective has much to say, as we shall also demonstrate, about whether appeals to equality as a value work to the advantage of the political left or political right.

That equality is, politically, a double-edged sword is our theme. Sometimes it is a weapon of the left, sometimes a weakness of the left, sometimes a weapon of the right. To drive this home, we shall explore two dimensions of political equality on which the right enjoys an unequivocal advantage in popular support over the left. The first involves a set of themes having to do with individual responsibility, opportunity, achievement, and merit. The second turns on a set of attitudes toward moral equality, that is, an array of beliefs as to whether people deserve equal respect notwithstanding differences in morally irrelevant criteria like national origin or sexual orientation.

Equality as a Symbolic Value

What place does equality hold in the Canadian political culture? Does the role of equality as a symbolic value distinguish the deeper dynamics of liberal democratic politics in Canada as against those of its nearest neighbor, the United States? How does equality interact with other values to define the incentives and constraints of everyday politics?

In a classic article on conservatism, liberalism, and socialism in Canada, Horowitz argued that Canada and the United States are new societies, both founded as fragments thrown off from Europe.[2] But the Canadian fragment was distinctively streaked, as we noted in chapter 1, with a tory touch—an accent of conservative, hierarchical, organic values. This difference between the two countries, Horowitz insists, makes all the difference to the ideological dialectic played out in the history and politics of both countries. The very impurity of the fragment in the case of Canada—the fact that it incorporated, in addition to liberal, rationalist values, the organic, corporate, hierarchical values of community—allows the full development of the idea of equality to be dialectically realized. As Horowitz argues,

> In a liberal bourgeois society which has never known toryism, the demand
> for equality will express itself as left-wing or democratic liberalism. . . .
> The government will be required to assure greater equality of oppor-
> tunity. . . . In a society which thinks of itself as a community of classes, the

demand for equality will take a socialist form: for equality of condition rather than mere equality of opportunity; for cooperation rather than competition; for a community that does more than provide a context within which individuals can pursue happiness in a purely self-regarding way. (49)

Hence the paradoxical representation of Canadian culture as *both* more elitist, hierarchical, and deferential *and* more egalitarian and collectivist than the American.[3]

How closely does this picture capture the Canadian political culture, not as it was at the time of its founding, but as it now is, a few years after the adoption of the Charter of Rights? Our starting point is the place formally accorded to equality as a value, the amount of public esteem paid to it in both popular and elite cultures. As a first approximation in seeing how important equality is as an abstract principle of politics for Canadians, we asked people if they basically agreed or disagreed with the statement,

"If people were treated more equally in this country, we would have many fewer problems."[4]

The comparison between Canada and the United States has long been taken by those on both sides of the border to define what is distinctive about each. Consider, therefore, the reactions of ordinary Canadians and Americans (fig. 4.1A). What is striking is their similarity. North of the border, 71 percent of ordinary citizens believe that there would be fewer problems if more people were treated equally; south of the border, 61 percent believe this.

It is by no means necessary to conclude that Canadians and Americans are identical in their responses to equality as a value, only that they are (at least in this initial test) exceedingly similar. But if the convergence of citizens north and south of the border stand outs, so too does the divergence of different elites. Equality has a markedly higher standing in the political realm than in the realms of either law or administration (fig. 4.1A). With the exception of Progressive Conservatives, to be sure, the bulk of political elites believe in the societal utility of equality. By contrast, legal and administrative elites divide into nearly equal proportions over the proposition that the larger society would have fewer problems if its members were treated more equally. There is, then, a suggestion of a disjunction: equality has an honorific standing in the political realm that it does not enjoy in the same measure in other elite realms.

Figure 4.1 A. *"If people were treated more equally in this country, we would have many fewer problems."*

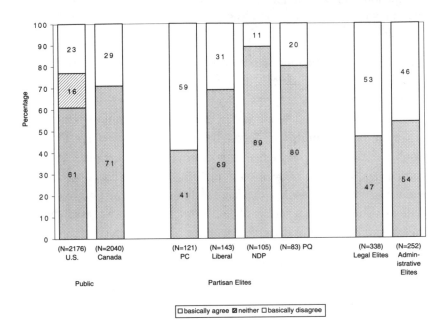

statistical significance of comparisons
political elites by party: p ≤ .01; elite groups by sector: p ≤ .01

Both of these findings—the similarity across borders and the dissimilarity across elite realms—are evident in responses to another question, which gauges the extent to which contemporary practices fall short of the degree of equality judged to be necessary and desirable. Specifically, we asked if people agreed with the following statement:

"One of the big problems in this country is that we don't give everyone an equal chance."

The responses of Canadians and Americans are virtually interchangeable (fig. 4.1B). Canadians are just as likely as Americans (but no more so) to place equality on an honorific pedestal. The evidence so far may not be decisive, but it raises a cautionary flag. National stereotypes to the contrary notwithstanding, equality enjoys much the same standing in the minds of ordinary citizens on both sides of the border, and the cautionary lesson this finding suggests is that a surprising measure of transnational homogeneity

Figure 4.1 B. *"One of the big problems in this country is that we don't give everyone an equal chance."*

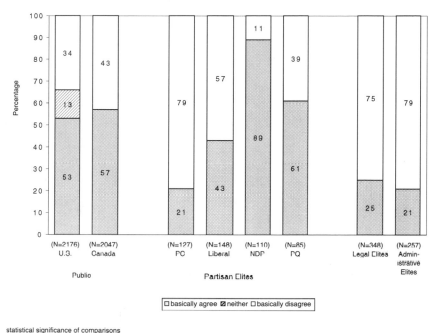

statistical significance of comparisons
political elites by party: p ≤ .01; elite groups by sector: p ≤ .01

in major departments of political life has been achieved *so far as the popular culture is concerned.* But the characterizations of popular and of elite culture need to be kept sharply distinct; and a disjunction in the standing of equality as a value in different realms of elite culture is again discernible.

This disjunction within the elite culture calls out for attention. Put broadly, our finding is that equality as a value commands markedly more deference among explicitly political elites than among elites generally. But this broad description requires refinement. Political elites themselves vary considerably in their response to equality as a symbolic value; what is more, the lines of cleavage among them and consensus between them and the larger public form a striking pattern (fig. 4.1A and B). Relative to other partisan elites, Conservatives belong to the political right, and they are out of step with the larger Canadian public in terms of the aspects of equality represented in figure 4.1A and B. They are nearly twice as likely as Canadians as a whole *to disagree* that "there would be fewer problems if more people were treated equally"; and they are similarly discordant in their

Figure 4.1 C. *"We have gone too far in pushing equal rights in this country."*

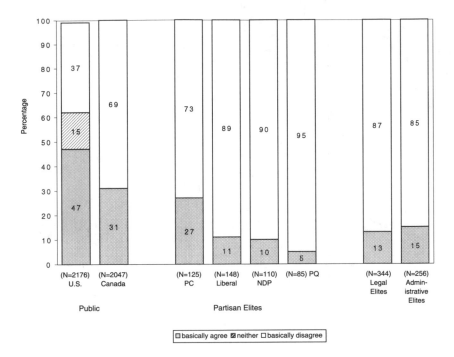

rejection of the suggestion that "one of the big problems in this country is that we don't give everyone an equal chance."

Equality, however, is a "chameleon value." Its meaning, its appeal, depends on the political context. Consider, for example, reactions to the following statement:

"We have gone too far in pushing equal rights in this country."

This construction of equality, which identifies it with equal rights, underlines the importance of political context. Contrast the reactions of ordinary Canadians and Americans (fig. 4.1C). For the first time, the two markedly differ. On the one side, a clear majority of Canadians (nearly seven in every ten) *disagreed* that we have gone too far "in pushing" equal rights; on the other side, Americans are evidently ambivalent, nearly half of them *agreeing* that they have gone too far in pushing equal rights. By this standard, Canadians and Americans differ: Canadians affirm egalitarianism; Americans equivocate over it. But the ambivalence of Americans to pushing for equal rights is not evidence of a weaker commitment to equality considered by itself, but testimony to the fact that people react to equality as a value not in isolation but in a political context. In the United States, that context is race, and the resentment and frustration surrounding the politics of race patently color the reactions of Americans. In contrast, equality construed as equal rights is free-floating in Canada; hence the remarkably uniform level of support it receives not only across different kinds of elites—legislative, legal, and administrative—but also among partisan elites. To be sure, PC legislators are more likely than the members of other parties to agree that we have gone too far in pushing for equal rights, but the truth is that the difference is slight, and what is more impressive by far is the rejection of the idea that we have gone too far on the part of every group of elites, including PCs.

The politics of equality arise, as the contrast between Canada and the United States suggests, partly from the association of the larger value of equality with specific causes and controversies. But the politics of equality is more fundamentally grounded in the variety of ways in which the value of equality itself can be construed.

Equality as an Economic Value

What does it mean to speak of the politics of equality? What distinguishes the politics of equality from those of any other central value? Broadly, our argument is this: Political parties in a liberal democracy like Canada tend to represent, at their upper reaches, communities of cobelievers, and in the characterizing of their distinctive bodies of belief, equality is a key element. Political parties tend to be distributed along a left-right dimension—in the Canadian party system the NDP falls to the left and the PC to the right of the Liberal Party. The standard presumption is that a party of the left enjoys a comparative advantage in the politics of equality: the more salient the considerations of equality, the larger the advantage of the left. We suggest instead that part of the point in recognizing that equality has multiple meanings is that equality can work to the advantage of parties of the right and to the disadvantage of parties of the left.

It is commonly supposed that clashes over economic inequality expose the built-in conflict between democracy and capitalism. A different and perhaps more useful interpretation is that the historical conjunction of the two favors a particular construction of both equality and liberty, precisely to moderate the clash between the two. Liberty is thus read to include the freedom of all to hold and to accumulate property, in consequence of which some will amass more than others; and equality is construed not as equality of condition (as Tocqueville, for example, understood it) but as equality of opportunity. Our concern, therefore, is to explore whether and how far the principles of capitalism and the economic inequality that follows from them are taken to be legitimate in the minds of contemporary members of liberal democracies. Among these principal tenets are the legitimacy of the market system; the grounds and hence the acceptability of poverty; the explanation for and hence the acceptability of success; and of course, the standing of equality itself as a governing consideration in the distribution of income.

A place to begin is with beliefs about "the profit system" and its beneficent or malign consequences. Accordingly we asked people to finish the following sentence:

"The profit system
(1) often brings out the worst in human nature
or
(2) usually teaches people the value of hard work and personal achievement."

Respondents had an additional pair of options: they could avoid taking any position either by rejecting both of the substantive alternatives or by declaring they could not decide between them.[5]

How legitimate is the profit system in contemporary liberal democracy? How closely contested a principle is it? The reaction of Canadians is one-sided (fig. 4.2A). Of ordinary Canadians expressing an opinion about the value of the profit system, approximately three in every four declare that it improves rather than coarsens the character of people who adhere to it. They reject the idea that the profit motive engenders greed and selfishness. They instead take the view that it builds character, that it helps people appreciate the importance of effort, persistence, and personal achievement. To be sure, roughly one-fifth of Canadians do not express an opinion one way or the other, choosing instead to say that neither alternative expresses their point of view or, alternatively, that they cannot decide between them. Do these results suggest that *only* 60 percent of Canadians support the profit system, while the remainder, a sizeable minority, are either outrightly negative toward it or choose to avoid making a positive commitment to it?

A comparison of Canada and the United States is enlightening. The United States, after all, is the epitome of a capitalist society, and although the operations of the market are in fact concretely constrained in many ways, the ideology of the free market is symbolically in the ascendancy there if

Figure 4.2 A. *"The profit system . . . (1) often brings out the worst in human nature; (2) usually teaches people the value of hard work and personal achievement."*

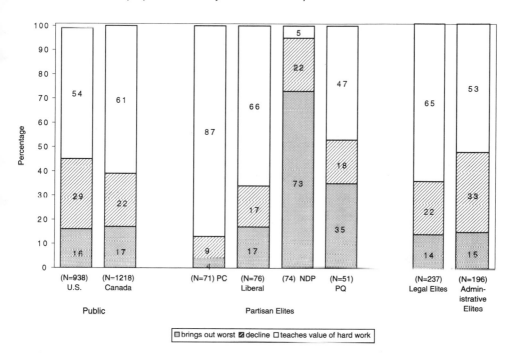

statistical significance of comparisons
political elites by party: p ≤ .01

anywhere. Yet one is struck by the similarity of views in the two countries (fig. 4.2A).[6] Indeed, support for the profit system is, if anything, higher in Canada than in the United States: 61 percent as against 54 percent declare that it "teaches people the value of hard work and personal achievement." But it is not wise to make much of small differences; we should instead emphasize the similarity.[7]

Perhaps the distinctiveness of the Canadian political culture is lodged elsewhere. Perhaps the way to gauge the central, distinctive tenets of a political culture is to attend to those at its center, not those nearer its periphery. The ordinary Canadian, like the ordinary American, may subscribe to the profit system, but how about Canadian elites? Are they not more likely to hold to a different, more distinctive orientation?

It is tempting to believe that the distinctive temper of a culture is better represented by those at its center, and just for that reason, the consensus on

Figure 4.2 B. *"The poor are poor because . . . (1) they don't try hard enough to get ahead; (2) the wealthy and powerful keep them poor."*

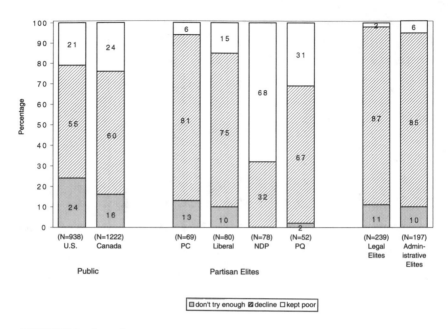

statistical significance of comparisons
political elites by party: p ≤ .01

the profit system is notable (fig. 4.2A). Asked to endorse or reject the profit system, nearly all elites come down on the same side of the fence as most Canadians. The views of Liberals and of legal elites, for example, are indistinguishable from those of ordinary citizens, while those of Conservatives are in the same direction but substantially more positive. This larger pattern of consensus on the legitimacy of the profit system is paradoxically underlined by the one sharp deviation from it. The PQ stance is marked by a discernible measure of hostility to the profit motive, but the response of the NDP stands out. Among everyone else, whether elite or member of the general public, the modal position favors the profit system not merely as conducive to economic growth and prosperity, but as instrumental in shaping individual character, teaching people "the value of hard work and personal achievement." In contrast, the NDP, and they alone, take as their majority position the view that the profit system "brings out the worst in human nature."

Ideas about the moral value of the profit system are only one thread of a

Figure 4.2 C. *"People who have made a lot of money . . . (1) have usually done so at the expense of other people; (2) are proof of what you get if you are willing to work and take advantage of the opportunities all of us have."*

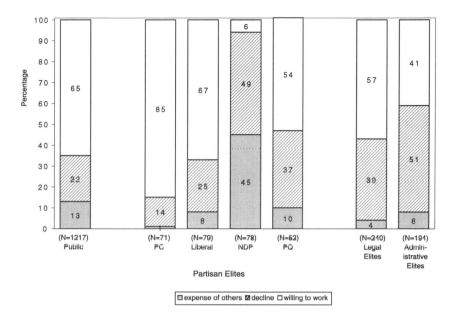

statistical significance of comparisons
political elites by party: p ≤ .01

larger pattern of beliefs about success, failure, and individual accountability, and it is important first to characterize the broader emotional and moralistic tone in which Canadians approach the issue of poverty and wealth. By way of capturing the affective tone they find appropriate to judgments of poverty and wealth (and, not less important, the tone they find inappropriate) we asked our respondents to choose between two endings for the following sentence:

"The poor are poor because
(1) they don't try hard enough to get ahead
or
(2) the wealthy and powerful keep them poor."

Both alternatives are floridly judgmental. Poverty is attributed on the one side to character failings of the poor; on the other, to deliberate class exploitation. On both accounts, poverty is to be understood in terms not of cause and effect but rather of moralistic blame. And, ironically, just for this reason

Figure 4.2 D. *"In a fair economic system . . . (1) all people should earn about the
same; (2) people with more ability should earn higher salaries."*

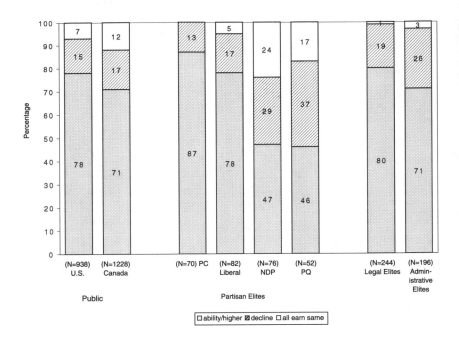

statistical significance of comparisons
political elites by party: p ≤ .01

the responses of Canadians are especially revealing. The ordinary Canadian
(and the ordinary American as well) finds both alternatives unacceptable.
Six in every ten Canadians decline to choose either alternative. And the rate
of refusal is still higher among elites, including the PC, with only a solitary,
hence revealing, exception: the NDP (fig. 4.2B). Whereas most elites refuse to
take either alternative, at least two in every three NDPers express an actual
preference—and without exception, of those expressing a preference, poverty is attributed to deliberate class exploitation. The NDP thus is an outlier
again on the value of equality, not just in the position it takes on the causes
of poverty, but also in its view that this way of thinking about poverty's
causes makes sense; an outlier, moreover, measured not only against the
popular culture but against elite beliefs, too.

Let us, though, reverse the question and ask how Canadians account not
for poverty but for wealth. Images of success offer at least as revealing a
mirror to reflect a culture as do images of failure. More specifically, to understand the compass of equality as a value, it is important to consider whether

inequality, particularly in the form of wealth, is in itself displeasing, if not illegitimate then at least tainted. Thus we asked respondents to complete this sentence:

"People who have made a lot of money
(1) have usually done so at the expense of other people.
or
(2) are proof of what you get if you are willing to work and take advantage of the opportunities all of us have."

The alternatives capture the quite different normative judgments that can be attached to wealth. At one pole wealth can be seen as proof of the merit of the people who amassed it, evidence of their willingness to work, to be clever, and to exploit the opportunities that came their way. At the other pole, consistent with the adage that "every great fortune began with a great crime," the normative premise is reversed: to have accumulated a lot of money is itself an implicit proof of chicanery. Focusing first on the responses of ordinary Canadians, we see an asymmetry between the willingness to advance accounts of success as against failure (fig. 4.2C). Whereas the largest number of ordinary citizens declined to endorse either explanation of poverty, nearly eight in every ten are willing to make a judgment about wealth. Offering a clear sign of the center of gravity of the popular culture, moreover, an overwhelming number of these take the position that making a lot of money is "proof of what you get if you are willing to work and take advantage of the opportunities all of us have." Economic inequality is thus not only not an offense against the norms of a liberal democratic society, but may be a badge of an individual's merit. And this holds for the elite culture, too. To be sure, this note of inegalitarianism is more muted, given the larger numbers of elites who decline to take a position. But the modal view among them unmistakably links individual enrichment and achievement. Indeed, across the variety of elites, only a handful are willing to interpret making a lot of money as a sign of exploitation. Only a handful, that is, with one exception: the NDP; and New Democrats again differ not in degree but in kind. In their case, and only in their case, is a majority of those expressing an opinion in favor of the view that making a lot of money is done as a rule "at the expense of other people." Compare their reactions with those of the PQ, whose orientation to a number of aspects of equality is most similar to theirs. Nearly one in every two in the NDP legislative elite believes that individual economic success comes at the price of exploitation of others, as compared to only one in every ten in the PQ; conversely, 54 percent of the PQ take economic success as proof of individual effort and initiative, as compared to only 6 percent of the NDP. And the gulf between the views of the NDP and those of the average citizen yawns still wider, with the public at large being ten times as likely as the NDP to see economic success as proof of individual merit.

Contemporary liberal democratic polities are committed to equality as a value in a way that their predecessors were not. The existence of this commitment is undeniable; we want to understand its terms better. And an indispensable step in this process is to understand that a quite sincere commitment to equality does not preclude an acceptance of inequalities. Even in a polity that regards equality as a foundational value there are acceptable inequalities.

Consider equality of income. How far is it legitimate for people to earn quite different amounts of money? How far is it desirable as a matter of moral principle that everyone should earn about the same? We asked respondents to complete the following sentence:

"In a fair economic system
(1) all people should earn about the same
or
(2) people with more ability should earn higher salaries."

It would be unreasonable, surely, to expect that any significant segment of Canadian society would be in favor of root-and-branch equality, unconditionally opposed to differences in individual effort or aptitude receiving economic recognition. But in the characterization of a climate of opinion what is telling is not absolute levels of support for a policy position or point of view, but rather relative differences in levels of support. With this in mind, notice first the similarity of views between the ordinary Canadian and the ordinary American (fig. 4.2D). Only a handful, roughly one in every ten, believe that everyone should earn the same. The thrust of the popular culture is in exactly the opposite direction. The average citizen, if he or she has an opinion, is overwhelmingly of the view that the more able should earn more, and this is to all intents and purposes as true of the average Canadian as of the average American.

The principle that there are acceptable inequalities is thus a part of the popular culture. It is, however, a contested or, perhaps more accurately, a contestable principle in the elite culture. On the one side, through large areas of elite culture—among legal and administrative elites most clearly but among political ones, too—there is manifestly support for the acceptability of economic inequality. On the other side, the legitimacy of income inequality is by no means so firmly grounded along one portion of the political spectrum; or more exactly, it is not so much that inequality as a principle is rejected but rather that it is not accepted. Consider the responses of both the NDP and the PQ. Although they are perhaps slightly more likely than the ordinary citizen to assert that everyone should earn the same, their center of gravity lies in a rejection of the view that the more able should earn more. They differ, in short, not by their overt support for strict egalitarianism but in their reluctance to endorse inequality.

It is a distinguished tradition to represent the Canadian political culture as distinctive and to identify its distinctiveness with the special standing of equality as a political value. The Canadian political ethos, as Horowitz and others have urged, incorporated at its origin not only liberal but also feudal elements; and, as Horowitz argued, precisely because it had in the nineteenth century a tory touch, the Canadian political culture in the twentieth century developed a socialist streak. Canadian public policy does have a distinctive socialist streak, but not, our findings suggest, because there is a distinctive streak of specifically economic egalitarianism in Canadian popular culture. On the contrary, if equality is construed as economic equality, the spirit of the Canadian ethos is as inegalitarian as that of the American. Indeed, the politics of equality in Canada is constrained precisely by the legitimacy of economic inequality in nearly all parts of the popular and elite culture, the chief exception being the parliamentary left. Equality, construed as economic equality, operates to the disadvantage of the legislative left, although not—given the more centrist position of the Liberals—maximally to the advantage of the legislative right.

Yet to equate equality as a value simply and solely with strict economic parity is a narrow reading; indeed, a forced and even artificial reading. Discussions of equality in contemporary liberal democracies like Canada are not confined to and arguably are not even concentrated on the assurance of nearly equal shares of material goods. Rather, the argument over equality has become a more complex, more encompassing debate about the responsibilities that individuals should shoulder and the obligations that others, in the form of the state, owe them not simply to enforce their rights under the law but to assure their broader well-being. It is to an exploration of contemporary assumptions about individuals as citizens and of individualism as an outlook that we now turn.

Individualism

Ideas about individualism change across domains of life. They take one form with respect to questions of religion, another for issues of economics. Individualism set in a political context is our focus.

It no doubt sounds odd to speak of individualism as a central thread in Canadian political culture: odd because individualism is a favored characterization of the American political culture. The so-called American style of individualism is taken to consist of a characteristic attitude of toughmindedness toward the claims of others for assistance—not an out-an-out refusal to countenance help under all circumstances but a rooted presumption that people must first help themselves. In contrast, the Canadian ethos is reputedly tender- rather than toughminded, more immediately open to the suggestion that claims for public assistance should be honored. But the conventional stylization of the Canadian ethos is based not on a chronicling of the actual opinions and sentiments of Canadians but on an inference from the political history and national literature of Canada. By way of suggesting the need for fresh consideration, therefore, consider reactions to the following assertion:

> "Too many people want someone else to help them solve their problems instead of solving them themselves."

The response of Canadians is one-sided: four in every five agreed that too many people want others to solve their problems rather than solve them on their own; only one in every five disagreed (fig. 4.3A). Elites see the problem in very much the same terms as ordinary citizens: across the board they echo the complaint that too many of their fellow Canadians want someone else to take care of their problems rather than to take care of them themselves. The only dramatic contrast is supplied by the NDP; they alone reject the view that too many nowadays want others to solve their problems.

This finding argues for the need to look with a fresh eye at the Canadian popular culture, judging not in terms of the formal works of the official or literary culture but on the basis of what ordinary Canadians think and say. Given that our concern here is with individualism in the context of politics and public policy, from what vantage point should the idea of individualism be approached? According to the Mill of *On Liberty*, first, from the state's; and then, from society's. To begin with the state: What are Canadians entitled to expect, in the eyes of their fellow Canadians, from government? In asking this question, we are not suggesting that the ordinary Canadian has pondered at length political philosophy and attempted to fix precisely the boundaries between public and private. But if there is not a public philosophy there

Figure 4.3 A. *"Too many people want someone else to help them solve their problems instead of solving them themselves."*

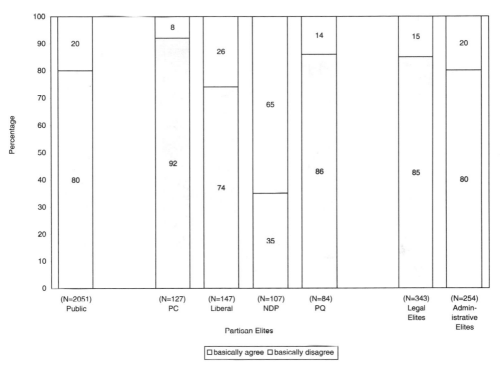

statistical significance of comparison
political elites by party: p ≤ .01

is a public mood, a clear and evident sense of what government and citizens, all in all, should seek to accomplish. Two questions especially are useful in capturing popular beliefs about the responsibilities of citizens and the obligations of the state; both are designed to elicit not the exact boundaries of autonomy but the prevailing affect, or feeling tone, surrounding discussion of independence and assistance. The first is this:

"Even if I fail, I would rather be free and stand on my own feet than have to depend on the government."

Respondents were asked if they mainly agreed or mainly disagreed with this sentiment of self-reliance.

The overall tenor of public opinion is plain. The ordinary Canadian is four times as likely to agree as to disagree with the statement (fig. 4.3B). Again, no fissure between the popular and the elite culture taken as a whole is visible. On the contrary, the thrust of responses across administrative, legal,

Figure 4.3 B. *"Even if I fail, I would rather be free and stand on my own feet than have to depend on the government."*

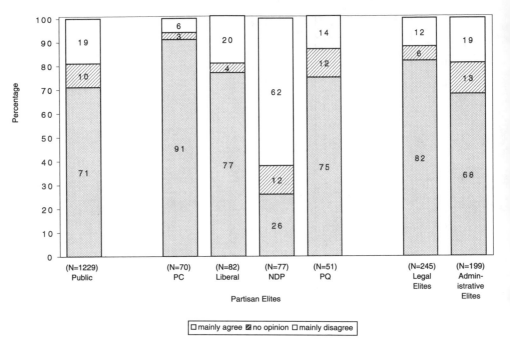

statistical significance of comparisons
political elites by party: p ≤ .01

and legislative elites, with one exception only, parallels the public mood, the one exception to the endorsement of self-reliance being again the NDP. The larger point, however, is that popular ideas about autonomy are Janus-like. It is not that a position is taken in favor of self-reliance *simpliciter*, to be repeated in any and all circumstances. Rather, the overall weight of the popular culture favors some expressions of autonomy but rejects others. And just because of this, one's impression about the public mood and of the position of any group relative to it can shift dramatically from one aspect of equality to another. Consider reactions to the following proposition:

"I am glad that I have a government that looks after me in so many ways."

One can see immediately a difference in the overall balance of public opinion (fig. 4.3C). Nearly six in every ten Canadians favor government assistance, and the reactions of elites, including those of the NDP, are essentially alike, with the possible exception only of lawyers, who by a slight margin are more likely to disagree than agree.

Figure 4.3 C. *"I am glad that I have a government that looks after me in so many ways."*

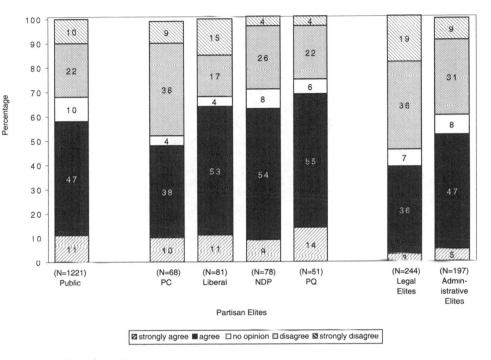

statistical significance of comparison
elites by sector: p ≤ .01

What should be made of this? Is this evidence that public opinion is made up of knots of self-contradictory beliefs? Or evidence that most people will simply agree with whatever statement is put in front of them?

There is a loose-jointedness to public preferences. But it is a mistake to take evidence that people can appreciate more than one definition of a situation as proof that they are muddled or inconsistent. Normatively, one can believe that one ought to stand on one's own without relying on assistance from the government and, at the same time, appreciate having a form of government that would give assistance if and when it is necessary and appropriate. And, empirically, the ordinary Canadian sees scarcely any connection whatever between believing that people should stand on their own two feet without depending on the government and being grateful for a government that looks after them in many ways, the correlation between views on the two being a minuscule .10. Neither can the failure of ordinary Canadians to draw a stronger connection between the two idea-elements be

Figure 4.3 D. *"Competition, whether in school, work, or business . . . (1) leads to better performance and a desire for excellence; (2) is often wasteful and destructive."*

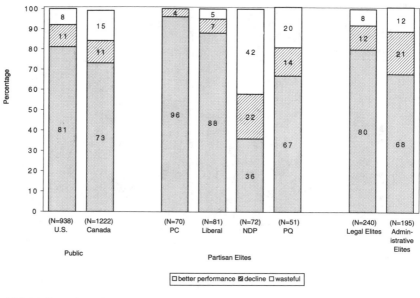

statistical significance of comparisons
political elites by party: p ≤ .01

attributed to the characteristically frowsy reasoning of mass publics. For our samples of legal, administrative, and legislative elites are not significantly more likely to connect the two, the correlation for the elite sample being only .13. Ideas about individual autonomy and responsibility are Janus-like because no one strikes just one stance toward the world. What is appropriate varies with the problem one is confronting, and what appear to be muddled inconsistencies among the ideas that citizens hold to a degree reflect a decent respect for the complexities of their relations to government and the need to strike different balances between individual autonomy and social solidarity at different times and in different political contexts.

What about individualism viewed from the perspective of society? Ideas about competition raise the issue of individualism in an intriguing way because the value attached to competition can speak simultaneously to two quite separate levels: individuals and the society as a whole. Just this division between levels helps clarify the sense in which both Canada and the United States are and are not cultures of individualism. Consider responses to the following proposition:

"Competition, whether in school, work, or business
(1) leads to better performance and a desire for excellence
or
(2) is often wasteful and destructive."

Patently, the ideal of competition pitched at the aggregate level enjoys broad support in the public as a whole. Far and away most Canadians (nearly three in every four) believe that competition stimulates achievement; in contrast, fewer than one in every five believe that its effects are "wasteful and destructive" (fig. 4.3D). Americans, to be sure, are slightly more likely than Canadians to take a positive view of competition, but notwithstanding the fact that the difference between the two countries is statistically significant, it is substantively trivial. The plain fact is that competition is valued in both countries and, as the responses of parliamentarians, lawyers, and public officials indicate, valued not only in the popular but also in the elite culture, again with the exception of the New Democrats.

Competition is thus a consensual value in both popular and elite cultures. But it is too facile to say only this. For individualism can take on a different hue, a noticeably diminished tone, precisely at the level of individuals. To capture this we asked, "How important is it to compete against others to see how good you are?" The issue now is not whether, taken as a whole, we are all better off thanks to competition but whether each of us personally benefits from competition. And the benefits from competition are not productivity and achievement: they are self-knowledge and realization of one's self-worth. The responses reflect these differences. The reaction of the Canadian public is notable (fig. 4.3E). Ordinary Canadians give competition as a means of self-assessment a remarkably low rating: less than a fifth judge it to be very important; indeed, the modal view is that it is *not* important. Does this mean that the veil has fallen, that the "true" attitude of Canadians toward individualism has been revealed? Stereotypes—of countries as well as of people—die hard. It has been an ingrained belief for more than a century that Americans are individualistic and Canadians are not. It is, accordingly, all the more instructive to compare the importance that Canadians and Americans attach to individualism as a form of self-realization. There is no difference of consequence: Americans are no more likely than Canadians to rate "compet[ing] against others to see how good you are" as very important; indeed, just like Canadians, their modal view is that it is not important.[8]

Individualism is the form that egalitarianism took in the nineteenth century, and in some of its expressions, above all, in the idea of equal oppor-

Figure 4.3 E. *"How important is it to compete against others to see how good you are?"*

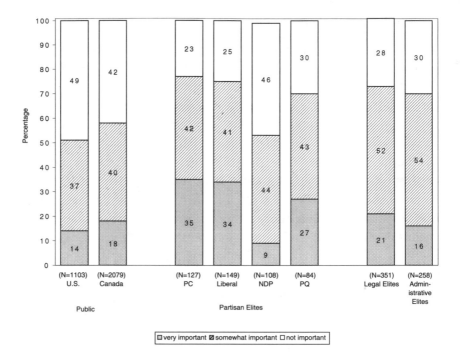

tunity and individual opportunity, it remains the form in which egalitarianism has the power to be a dominant theme in the popular culture. Taken as a whole, it underwrites the contention that individual merit cannot be inferred from the accidental and contingent features of people's social circumstance. The child of an immigrant may outdo the offspring of an established family, given the opportunity to do so. Individualism understood as a body of ideas that tie together the dignity of individuals apart from considerations of social status, the importance of achievement, initiative, and effort, and the need to assure opportunity for individuals to realize and demonstrate their merit has as strong a hold in the Canadian as in the American culture. Equality in the late twentieth century, however, has taken on a new dimension. It has come increasingly to involve a specifically focused commitment on behalf of the moral and civic equality of groups historically stigmatized and victimized because of differences in their appearance, background, or ostensible beliefs. How fully are Canadians committed to this aspect of egalitarianism?

Equality as Equal Status

A root meaning of equality in contemporary liberal democratic society, as John Rawls and others have argued, is equality of status. Of course the notion that each member of a liberal democratic community counts for as much morally as every other is notoriously an abstract proposition. But the issue of the moral equality of members of a political community cannot be confronted in the abstract. The presumption that some in the community are inferior or tainted or by their nature undependable or even dangerous always takes concrete forms, even if the forms vary from one historical moment to another. At this moment in Canadian society, the presumption of equality of esteem is most tested in its application to those who stand out by virtue of their race and ethnicity, their sexual orientation, or their country of origin. Without suggesting that the premise of equal respect should be explored only in these contexts, we are persuaded that a barometer of the commitment of Canadians to moral equality is their stance toward racial minorities, homosexuals, and immigrants.

Equality construed as equal respect hinges on a willingness of people to accept others as being, if not as good as they, at any rate not inherently inferior to them. And it finds its paradigmatic expression in an insistence that others, even if different in appearance or orientation, are entitled to equal treatment. A group historically tainted and stigmatized because of its members' alleged moral aberration is homosexuals. The perception of moral deficiency encouraged a belief that homosexuals are both untrustworthy and unworthy of enjoying the same rights as other citizens. Public policy has been changing rapidly in this area. Since 1990, lower courts in Canada have held that sexual orientation is a constitutionally prohibited ground of discrimination under the Charter of Rights and have added sexual orientation to the prohibited grounds of employment discrimination under the Canadian Human Rights Act.[9] The courts have led the way on many of these changes, the politicians often playing a role in simply deciding not to appeal a court decision recognizing the rights of homosexuals. Yet the representation of the values of a political culture in the form of judicial decisions by no means corresponds to the values of the members of a political community. And it is the willingness of Canadians to grant equality of esteem to homosexuals that we want to explore.

Our principal concern is the willingness of citizens to judge that fellow citizens who happen to be homosexual are nonetheless entitled to be treated the same as any other citizens. We are not suggesting that the farrago of contemptuous images of homosexuals is not deserving of study, only that such images are secondary to our purpose. For what we most want to determine is the willingness of Canadians to grant homosexuals equal status, to judge them entitled to have the same rights and be allowed the same opportunities as others. We asked respondents to complete the following sentence:

> "For the most part, local ordinances that guarantee equal rights to homosexuals in such matters as jobs and housing
> (1) damage Canadian moral standards
> or
> (2) uphold the Canadian idea of human rights for all."

The issue is framed in terms of equal rights: homosexuals should have legal assurance of equal access to such necessities as jobs and housing. There is no mention of special treatment for homosexuals and no suggestion that by virtue of being homosexual they should enjoy special privileges or be allowed to do or say what others would not be allowed to do or say.

How willing are Canadians to believe that homosexuals should have equal rights, so defined? The first thing to note is that homosexuality is not a taboo subject. No more than the customary number decline to take a position, about 17 percent declaring either that neither of the two alternatives put before them is acceptable or that they cannot decide between them (fig. 4.4A). The central tendency in the reactions of the Canadian public is to reject, by a margin of approximately three to one, the suggestion that local ordinances guaranteeing equal rights for homosexuals in jobs and housing will damage Canadian moral standards, seeing them instead as consistent with "the Canadian idea of human rights for all."

What interpretation should be placed on these figures? Do they indicate a decisive majority in favor of equal rights for homosexuals? Or is the right conclusion to draw less rosy? More Canadians (or fewer) could be shown to support equal rights for homosexuals by changing the wording of the question put to them. But that does not mean that the interpretation of these results is completely arbitrary. What is crucial is comparison—comparison across different groups and across different probes.

The first of these is between Canadians and Americans. It would surely make a considerable difference to our sense of these results if Americans turned out to be far more likely to approve of equal rights in the same circumstances for homosexuals. The reactions of a sample of Americans to an essentially identically worded question (deleting only the reference to

Figure 4.4 A. Support for and Opposition to Guaranteed Equal Rights in Jobs and Housing for Homosexuals

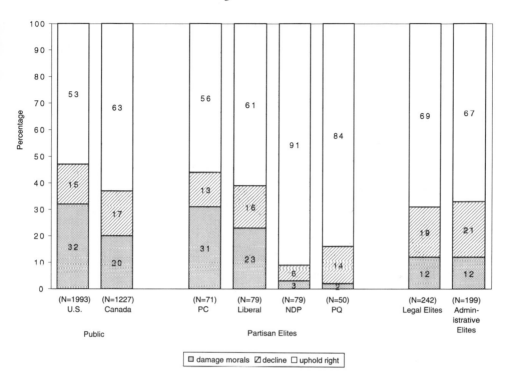

statistical significance of comparisons
public vs. elites as a whole: p ≤.01; political elites by party: p ≤ .01

Canada) are shown also in figure 4.4A, though the American study was conducted in California,[10] and a variety of studies have shown levels of tolerance to be characteristically higher in the West than in the United States as a whole. Canadians appear to be slightly more committed to equality of status for homosexuals than Americans. On the one side, Americans are more likely to respond that laws guaranteeing equal rights for homosexuals will damage moral standards; on the other side, Canadians are more likely to respond that such laws are consistent with larger standards of human rights. The differences are not vast, but plainly the ordinary Canadian is at least as supportive of equal rights for homosexuals in jobs and housing as Americans from an affluent and tolerant part of the United States.

A conspicuous number of citizens in both countries either decline to

Figure 4.4 B. Support for Equal Child Custody Rights for Lesbian Mothers

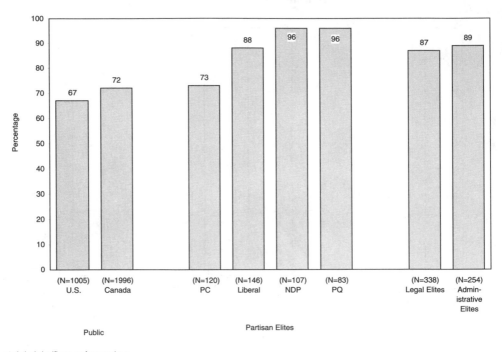

statistical significance of comparisons
public vs. elites as a whole: p ≤ .01; political elites by party: p ≤ .01

support equal rights for homosexuals or explicitly oppose them, and this deserves emphasis given *the variability of responses on the part of partisan elites.* Legal and administrative elites resemble the ordinary Canadian, although they are both slightly less likely to oppose and slightly more likely to support equal rights ordinances for homosexuals. On the other side, NDP and PQ overwhelmingly support laws assuring homosexuals equal status; indeed, there is scarcely a breath of opposition in either party. By contrast, approximately one in every three Conservatives believes such laws harm moral standards. These results reinforce our critique of the thesis of democratic elitism: the absence of consensus among partisan elites gives a political opening to popular intolerance that it might otherwise not be able to earn on its own.

We want to explore further attitudes about homosexual rights, both because they are important in their own right and because they throw light

Figure 4.4 C. Support for Equal Rights for Homosexual Teachers

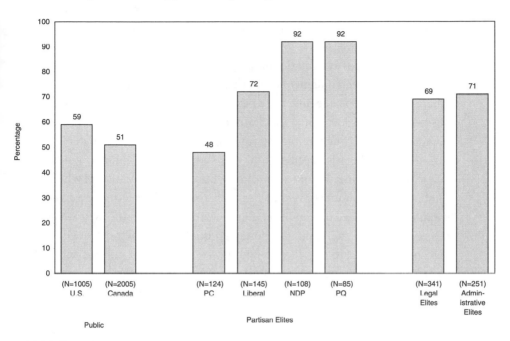

statistical significance of comparisons
public vs. elites as a whole: p ≤ .01; political elites by party: p ≤ .01

on the contemporary tendency in political thought to conceive of equality in large part as consisting in equality of status or respect. Such a tendency is not without merit, but some of its awkward aspects are usefully illuminated by attending to reactions to a group like homosexuals. Perhaps chief among these is the ease with which a term like *status* can obscure the extent to which judgments about equality are context-dependent. People do not as a rule have a judgment about the status of homosexuals, if the idea of judgment is meant to convey that they cleave to one and only one position. Judgments of equal status vary in part because the consequences of equality of status vary. To illustrate, let us turn from judgments about status in the context of jobs to views about child custody. Specifically, we asked,

> "Would you approve or disapprove of a law allowing lesbian mothers the right to be granted custody of the children in a divorce, if the court finds her otherwise capable of taking care of the children?"

The implications of acknowledging equal standing to homosexuals in this context differ from those in the case of jobs or housing. In the latter, people claim a good (in the form of either a job or housing) that they do not possess and wish to acquire; in the former, people claim a good (in the form of a child) that they possess and do not wish to lose. Quite beyond the familiar asymmetry between judgments about gains and losses in general, there is a difference between believing that a person should be debarred from obtaining something he does not at the moment have on the grounds that he is a homosexual and believing that something that a person legitimately possesses and is otherwise entitled to enjoy should on the same grounds be taken away from her. To underline this asymmetry, the question of whether a lesbian mother should have the right to custody of her children in a divorce is explicitly premised on condition that the court find her otherwise capable of taking care of the child. Support for equal status for homosexuals is perceptibly higher in this second context in the popular culture and still more so in the elite culture (fig. 4.4B).

Controversial claims, though sometimes advanced in the abstract, tend to be affirmed or rejected in specific contexts. We cannot give anything like a comprehensive gloss on the ways contexts vary, but we can point to an especially important feature: the risks or threats that granting particular claims to equal status may carry for third parties. By way of illustrating this, we asked,

"Do you approve or disapprove of allowing homosexuals to teach school in [the respondent's province]?"

Overt opposition to homosexuals jumps sharply (fig. 4.4C). Instead of roughly one in three ordinary Canadians expressing opposition, as in the child custody case, the number now is essentially one in every two.

Does the variation in support for equality for homosexuals apparent in figure 4.4 point to a telling feature of political reality or is it merely a familiar reminder that responses in public opinion surveys can oscillate from one question to another? In the American results, representing a completely independent study conducted in an altogether different country, the identical pattern of variation is unmistakable: there is manifestly more support for lesbians obtaining child custody than for homosexuals being teachers.

How should this *pattern* of cross-claim variation be interpreted? It is customary to speak of claims to rights being contestable insofar as they create conflicts of competing values, and although this manner of addressing the issue can always be tailored to fit a problem, it sometimes obscures what is at issue. The right of a lesbian mother to custody of her children was deliberately put before respondents in such a way as to neutralize concern for the well-being and safety of the children; hence the explicit assurance that the court finds the lesbian mother otherwise fit to care for her children. In contrast, the question concerning the right of a homosexual to be a teacher carries with it an implicit threat—in the eyes of those who dislike and fear homosexuals—to the well-being and safety of students in his charge. Talk of competing values does not capture what is at issue here. Claims for equal status on behalf of groups like homosexuals, apart from narrowly defined and highly focused constituencies like the religiously orthodox, are contestable less because competing values come into conflict than because risks to third parties are highlighted.

It is appropriate to speak of a value or norm being engaged in behalf of the claim to equality of status—certainly it would be labored to talk of support for such claims being the product of prudential or consequentialist calculations. People support a claim for equal status on behalf of a group like homosexuals, insofar as they do support it, primarily because they perceive it to be the right, that is, the morally appropriate, thing to do, not because they reckon such support to be in their self-interest or to the material advantage of the larger economy or society. But if it does make sense to speak of equality of status as representing a norm or value, it is a norm of a particular kind. Most obviously, there is a remarkable variability among legislative elites, running from about one in two of PCs to eight in ten among both PQ and NDP (fig. 4.4A). It makes little sense to speak of a societal or cultural norm, given this range of variation. Beyond this, in reflecting on what it means to speak of a norm of equal status, we are struck by the level of support for homosexuals' rights among the legal and executive elite groups. Though lower than among either the NDP or PQ, it is all the same substantial, about two in every three for both legal and administrative elites; and it is representatives of these groups who have spearheaded in the courts and elsewhere some of the more important recent changes in gay rights. In this light, the NDP and PQ do not so much deviate from as lead the way in an emerging norm on issues of homosexuals' rights. The subject of emerging norms calls attention to one of the politically consequential features of some claims to equality. Talking of a norm of equality conveys a misleading impression of fixity. Ideas of what is right and wrong and of what is fair and acceptable in a domain like equal status are moving targets. They shift with time, and their movement over time corresponds to their pattern of diffusion, beginning characteristically with the specific sponsorship of a partisan or ideological vanguard, then spreading—unevenly across the political elite, if only because of their ideological and partisan provenance—and taking root in the broader reaches of elite culture, not least among legal and administrative elites.

Our concern here is, of course, with support for a presumption of equality of status and respect across a range of historically stigmatized groups. So we want to turn from attitudes toward homosexuals to those toward immigrants. The reaction of Canadians to immigrants is interesting in its own right. Canada has become a political community whose past is ever more tenuously related to its present: since the end of World War II, people born not only outside Canada but, more relevantly, outside the "founding nations," have come to make up what is often referred to as a "third force"[11] in Canadian culture and society. Accordingly, we put before respondents a vaguely expressed, deliberately loaded proposition, asking them whether they agreed or disagreed with the statement,

> "People who come to live in Canada should try harder to be more like other Canadians."

Our aim was to get a sense of whether people's reactions to new Canadians tend to be negative and judgmental or positive and accommodating. Responses revealed a divergence between popular and elite culture, but truncated in a way that emphasizes the special status of representative political elites (fig. 4.5A). The popular culture is less welcoming, less inclined to grant equality of status to new Canadians. Thus, very nearly two in every three Canadians agreed that people who have come from elsewhere to live in Canada should make more effort to be like other Canadians. In contrast, the same proposition is *rejected* by legal and administrative elites and, indeed, rejected by exactly the same margin. Yet in light of this disavowal the response of political elites is the more telling. It is true that New Democrats resoundingly reject the suggestion that new Canadians are failing to assimilate as they should; but they are the only partisan elite who responds this way. Conservatives, Liberals, and PQers are evenly divided. The scent of xenophobia that leaks through the contention that those new to Canada are failing to fit in properly does not deter significant numbers of political elites from openly endorsing the proposition. Conspicuous is the consensus of

Figure 4.5 A. *"People who come to live in Canada should try harder to be more like other Canadians."*

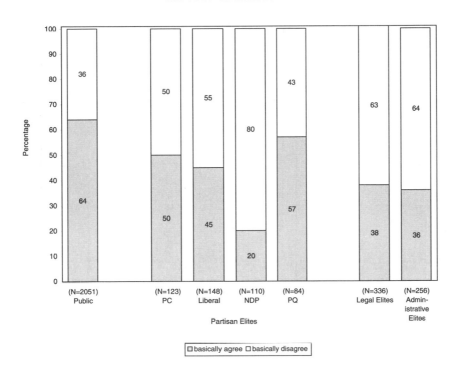

statistical significance of comparison
public vs. elites as a whole: p ≤ .01; political elites by party: p ≤ .01

political elites, with the exception only of the New Democrats, and perhaps specifically worth noting are the reactions of the PQ.

By and large, the PQ's views on issues of equality are most similar to those of the NDP and most dissimilar to those of Conservatives. Yet here the pattern is the other way around: their response is most similar to that of Conservatives and most dissimilar to that of the NDP. Why do PQers, who embraced with virtual unanimity the principle of equal respect applied to homosexuals, depart from it when applied to immigrants? Because, as the everyday record of Canadian politics has demonstrated and our findings illustrate, the PQ is distinctively committed to preserving and enhancing the autonomy of French Canadian culture; and that commitment undercuts their willingness to embrace the universalistic outlook that underwrites equality of respect. To say this is not to argue that the PQ is prejudiced against immigrants.

Figure 4.5 B. *"Immigrants often bring discrimination upon themselves by their own personal attitudes and habits."*

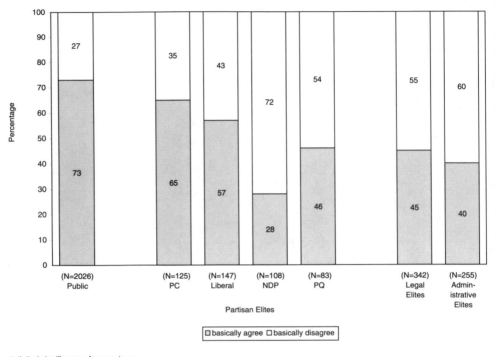

statistical significance of comparisons
public vs. elites as a whole: p ≤ .01; political elites by party: p ≤ .01

Indeed, partly to show that this is not the case, we asked everyone if they agreed or disagreed with the statement,

"Immigrants often bring discrimination upon themselves by their own personal attitudes and habits."

Notice the reaction of the PQ: they are markedly less likely to agree with this dismissive sentiment than the public as a whole and significantly more likely to disagree with it than Conservatives or Liberals. This is revelatory because it suggests not that it is immigrants per se to which the PQ takes exception, but rather that the reservations PQ'ers have about according equal respect to immigrants hinge on the special importance they attach to the preservation of French Canadian culture. Similarly, French Canadians as a whole are more likely than English Canadians to believe that immigrants should try harder to be more like other Canadians, yet no more likely to believe that

Figure 4.5 C. *"While it is all well and good to celebrate one's heritage, it is more important for new immigrants to learn what it is to be Canadian than to cling to their old ways."*

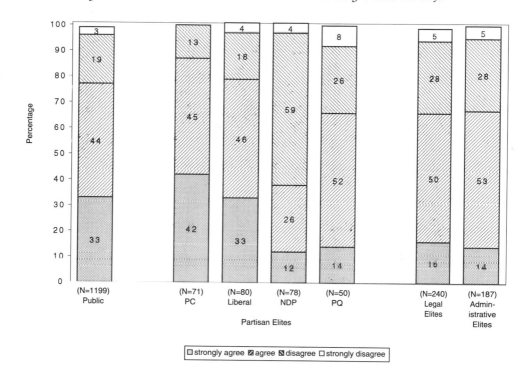

statistical significance of comparisons
public vs. elites as a whole: p ≤ .01; political elites by party: p ≤ .01

immigrants who are victims of discrimination are to be blamed for the very discrimination that victimizes them (data not shown).

Finally, the full range of results suggests that the PQ are under strain, not from a greater commitment to conformity per se, but from the threat they see immigrants as posing to French Canadian culture distinctively. It is not that PQ elites depart from a norm of elite culture in insisting that immigrants conform to "Canadian" customs and values, but rather that, in refusing to accord equality with respect to the customs and values of immigrants, PQ elites deviate from the central tendency of their own point of view. Consider responses to the following proposition:

> "While it is all well and good to celebrate one's heritage, it is more important for new immigrants to learn what it is to be Canadian than to cling to their old ways."

Among the public at large approximately three in every four support this insistence on conformity, and, strikingly, support is as high or higher still in the major party elites: nearly 80 percent of Liberals and close to 90 percent of Conservatives want new Canadians not to "cling to their old ways" (fig. 4.5C). In contrast, the PQ is less, not more, insistent on assimilation to Canadian, not Québécois, norms: indeed, around a third of them reject the idea that new immigrants should learn to be Canadian, although the NDP, it should be noted, is still more likely to do so. The point we want to underline is that the PQ's views on equality of status tend to parallel those of the NDP with the exception of the greater difficulty the PQ have in giving equal respect to those whose culture and customs differ because of the greater importance they assign to protecting and strengthening theirs.

The issues we are considering are intrinsically difficult. There are no absolutely certain answers; all that can be done is to try to identify the principal thrust or tendency of a person's or group's line of thought. A heritage culture that sees its identity under threat tends to attach a compensatory importance to conformity to its institutions and attitudes. In turn, it can itself pose a threat to groups who, because of their own sense of distinctiveness, wish not to conform.[12] But without minimizing the special importance attached in French Canada to conformity with the culture of French Canada, we can see further evidence of the parallelism between PQ and NDP in their beliefs about moral equality if we examine attitudes toward ethnic and racial minorities.

Consider reactions when Canadians are asked,

"How important is it to make a special effort to protect ethnic and racial minorities?"

Viewed in the abstract, it might appear that virtually everyone would declare that protecting ethnic and racial minorities is "very important." After all, there is no cost attached to *saying* this, and perhaps no idea has become more commonplace in the social analysis of prejudice than that people are nowadays under pressure to say the socially desirable thing. In fact, only about four in every ten ordinary Canadians believe protection of ethnic and racial minorities to be very important. Still more arrestingly, legal and executive elites pretty much echo the stance of the general public.[13] Thus, only 50 percent of the legal sample and of the executive rate a special effort to protect ethnic and racial minorities to be very important, as compared to 43 percent of the general public. Against this backdrop, the reactions of political elites are more telling. Again, an impressive *range* of reactions is evident between the parties least and most committed to special efforts to protect minorities; and, again, the *pattern* is the same, with the PC anchoring one pole and the NDP the other. Still, two points stand out. With the exception of Progressive Conservatives, political elites taken as a whole are more likely to attach special importance to protecting ethnic and racial minorities than either the public as a whole or the other varieties of elites we have canvassed. Second, the reactions of the PQ and of the NDP are virtually indistinguishable: *both* attach high importance to protecting minorities.

Still, it must be admitted that phrasing the issue of equal status in terms of protecting the rights of minorities has something of a stilted quality. Putting the issue in overly formal terms may invite overly polite answers. So we probed attitudes toward minorities at a more "gut level," to investigate the emotional flavor of people's willingness to denigrate them. We accordingly asked everyone if they mainly agreed or mainly disagreed with the following statement:

> "The trouble with letting certain minority groups into a nice neighborhood is that they gradually give it their own atmosphere."

The level of agreement with this insinuation is, relative to any reasonable standard, high among the general public. Roughly a third of ordinary Canadians agreed with the suggestion that "certain minority groups" tend to take over—and, by implication, to degrade—the neighborhoods in which they live (fig. 4.6B). We say this proportion is high by any reasonable standard to counter the reflex presumption that only when fifty percent plus one agree with a sentiment in a public opinion survey does it count politically. The proportion agreeing with this sentiment tends to be lower—between one fifth and one quarter—among elites but, considering the crudity of the sentiment being expressed, this should by no means be considered a small number. This result should be taken as a warning, we would suggest, of when the reluctance to accord equal status to new Canadians is most likely to erupt. The problem is most difficult to contend with when others, who differ in background or some aspects of behavior, are represented as violating the value of conformity; and even if it is only a minority who are exercised in these circumstances, it is nonetheless a quite substantial minority both in the popular and in the elite culture.

The claim of minorities to equal status, many now believe, can be strengthened if it can be translated into the language of rights. In liberal

Figure 4.6 A. *"How important is it to make a special effort to protect ethnic and racial minorities?"*

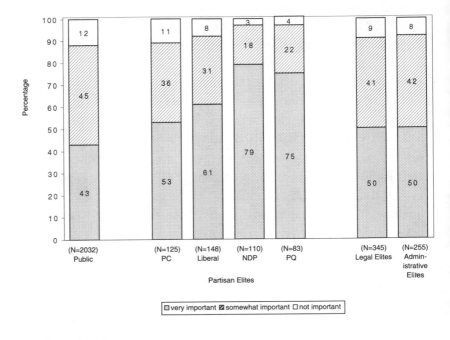

statistical significance of comparisons
public vs. elites as a whole: p ≤ .01; political elites by party: p ≤ .01; elite groups by sector: p ≤ .01

democratic polities, it is said, rights have become trump. But however popular it has become to say this, and however true it may be in certain segments of modern society, it is by no means obvious that talk of rights trumps very much in the popular culture. To make a claim as a matter of right and, still more, to invoke the language of equal rights to validate a claim is to put a specifically political cast on a demand. But it is insensitive to the darker aspects of the politics of the last two decades, to suppose that invoking the language of equal rights will necessarily be trump in the popular culture. And as for the elite culture, given the greater importance of ideology there, we suspect that the effect of invoking the language of equal rights is less to evoke support across-the-board than to impose a "political logic" on a claim.

To explore these possibilities, respondents were asked to choose between the following two alternatives:

"The laws guaranteeing equal job opportunities for blacks and other minorities
(1) should be made even stronger

Figure 4.6 B. *"The trouble with letting certain minority groups into a nice neighborhood is that they gradually give it their own atmosphere."*

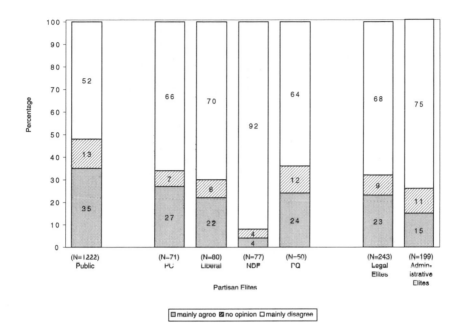

statistical significance of comparisons
public vs. elites as a whole: p ≤ .01

or
(2) sometimes go too far."

One way to make plain that rights are *not* trump, certainly among the ordinary public, is to consider the reactions of both Canadians and Americans. The politics of rights is easily more salient and has proceeded for longer in the United States than in Canada. The ordinary American is far more likely to believe that laws guaranteeing equal rights for blacks and other minorities go too far than they are to believe that they should be made stronger (fig. 4.6C). Indeed, 59 percent believe they go too far while only 19 percent believe they should be stronger. In contrast, the situation is more balanced in Canada, approximately equal numbers falling on both sides of the issue.

How should we interpret the *comparatively* greater support for equal rights legislation in Canada? Is it evidence that rights are trump, if not in the United States, then in Canada? Or is the greater support in Canada a reflection of the lesser salience of the politics of equal rights in Canada? Most obviously,

Figure 4.6 C. *"The laws guaranteeing equal job opportunities for blacks and other minorities*
. . . (1) should be made even stronger; (2) sometimes go too far."

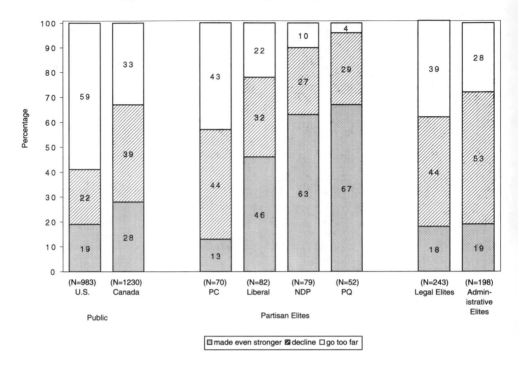

statistical significance of comparisons
political elites by party: p ≤ .01; elite groups by sector: p ≤ .01

to say that Canadians are less likely than Americans to believe that equal
rights go too far is not at all the same thing as saying that they support
strengthening them (see fig. 4.6C). Moreover, the full array of responses
reveals that the symbol of laws assuring equal rights has by no means
achieved a hegemonic position even within the elite culture. Consider legal
and administrative elites. Because they are at one remove from the world of
politics, they are a bellwether. Their endorsement of a new idea can be taken
as evidence that it has made headway and is in the process of becoming a
socially dominant view. But notice the actual reactions of legal and administrative elites to equal rights laws. Quite apart from the striking proportion of
them who decline to take a position at all (itself a striking commentary), the
most common position voiced is that laws guaranteeing equal rights for
blacks and other minorities go too far. To be sure, the PQ and the NDP, and to a
lesser extent the Liberals, most often voice support for equal rights laws

being made even stronger, but their response stands out chiefly for being at variance with the predominant tendencies among Conservatives as well as among legal and administrative elites in both the elite and popular cultures.

Equality as a value, all of the results of this chapter suggest, occupies a more equivocal, more problematic place in contemporary liberal democratic culture than is usually recognized. Equality is a primary value of liberal democracy, but it is also an issue in the politics of contemporary democracies, which is to say that it is politically contested insofar as the success (or failure) of claims to particular forms of equality spell the success or failure of other values and groups in society. To say that a value like equality is politically contested is to recognize that people take positions relative to it out of a desire to do what they regard to be morally right. Of course, part of the dynamics of the argument over equality as a value, like the argument over any public good, is grounded in the desire of political elites to win or to hold onto political office. But because the issues at stake are matters of value, of right and wrong, the main motor powering arguments over equality is convictions of right and wrong, not electoral self-interest.

Our findings have shown that elites, particularly political elites, defend positions on one or another aspect of equality that they would surrender if gaining popular support were their only or even their primary objective. It is difficult to think of any other reading of the left's commitment to equality as a value. Their support for equality across a range of contexts is striking. No less impressive is their isolation. So far from equality being a value that the left can capitalize on, we have seen that the position of the political right more nearly matches that of the public at large in terms of economic equality and correlative ideas of individual responsibility and achievement and in terms of moral equality—that is, the willingness to treat others as deserving of equal respect notwithstanding their being different in, say, national origin or sexual orientation. We have seen, moreover, that just insofar as an appeal to equality is read not as an appeal to a value they share but as a critique of their conduct, the political right rather than the left will reap the advantage. The very reflexiveness of equality as a value makes it politically double-edged.

Our purpose in this chapter has been to consider the complexity of values as symbolic political resources, exploring how equality as a value can favor the political left or right according to how it is formulated. But now we want to change focus and examine beliefs about equality as they find expression not in normative presuppositions but in political issues themselves.

FIVE THE POLITICS OF EQUALITY

Equality occupies a commanding place in contemporary polities for two apparently contradictory reasons: first, it fuels a historic argument over what the government should do on behalf of citizens who have less than others; second, it has thrown up a whole new class of claims to group versus individual rights. Thus equality has paradoxically come to define central themes both of continuity and change in democratic politics.

Equality as a value enters politics at a variety of levels but most conspicuously and vitally in the form of disputed proposals for public action. Historically, the clash over equality has centered on redistributive politics, and this clash, above every other, has served as a gauge of the overall temper of a political culture. Judged in terms of redistributive politics, the center of gravity in Canada is to the left; in the United States, to the right. Yet complex patterns of beliefs about redistributive politics exist. Why does the party in favor of redistribution not always win given that more of the voters would perceive themselves to benefit than lose from redistribution? Partly because of the strains, the competing tendencies of thought, to be found within any political culture. In the Canadian political culture there is an element of resistance to (some forms of) redistributive politics centered on the concept of welfare, a resistance every bit as pronounced north of the Canada–U.S. border as south of it.

It would, however, be a mistake to equate the politics of equality with the politics of redistribution. The reach of the politics of equality has been transformed and, in turn, has transformed the politics of public policy not because the idea of equality represents a Hegelian historical force inexorably working through its dialectic logic, but because of a pair of related developments, one extrinsic and the other intrinsic to Canadian politics. The first of these is the emergence of a transnational political culture. Premises of political thought initially emerging from the clash of forces specific to one particular country are being more widely diffused; and, although the United States is by no means the only source of new premises of political thought for liberal democratic cultures, it has proven to be the principal model for new directions in the understanding of equality. The second development, national rather than transnational, is the adoption of the Charter of Rights in Canada. The Charter represents a profound reorientation of Canadian politics, one that has taken institutional forms, most visibly in the reallocation of influence to courts (Russell 1983). But basic categories of political thought, equality among them, have also been redefined. What counts as equal standing? Who is entitled to it? What may and ought to be done to assure it? All these questions, which only a generation earlier had seemed settled, were reopened with adoption of the Charter.

The reconception of equality has developed along two principal axes. The first of these is captured in section 25 of the Charter of Rights, which spells out the special status of Aboriginal rights; the second in section 15 and in particular 15.2, which embeds affirmative action in constitutional politics. Until recently the issue of Aboriginal rights received relatively little attention in the mainstream of democratic theory. But now it is prompting a reconsideration of equality in liberal democratic thought.[1] Historically, the idea of equal rights has worn two faces. One is to assist those who have less to secure more. So viewed, equal rights drives an argument that those who have been deprived of their rights or hampered in the exercise of their rights should have the same rights, exercised under the same conditions, as anyone else. Concern about Aboriginal rights fits comfortably with this view of equal rights, but it clashes with a second face: no citizen or group of citizens should have rights above and beyond the rights of every other citizen or group of citizens. But it is just the idea of unique rights that now seems to many to be required to meet the unique status of Aboriginals as both bearers of rights under the Charter and holders of rights outside it.

Questions like this belong by convention to the province of political philosophers and are supposed irrelevant to the study of public opinion and political culture. This is a mistake. Citizens may not work out systematic answers to complex questions about conflicting conceptions of rights. But they nonetheless wrestle with some of the questions. In looking at the answers they are prepared to offer, our aim is not to discover the lineaments of a formal political philosophy but to take serious account of citizens' conceptions of fairness, informal and incomplete as they may be. It is, after all, not necessary for ideas of justice to be polished to spark political conflict. Clashing intuitions of fairness more than suffice, and these drive debate over the final dimension of equality we shall examine, namely, affirmative action. Precisely because clashing intuitions of fairness lie behind responses to affirmative action, beliefs about what ought to be done have an intrinsically contingent character.

Redistributive Politics

In the exploration of patterns of consensus and cleavage over publicly contested policies centering on equality the place to start is the role assigned the state. What is government allowed or, still more crucially, what is it obliged to do in the name of equality? We approach this question by locating it in the larger context of historical and analytical comparisons of Canadian and American cultures. It has long been part of the received wisdom that a fundamental dimension defining the distinctiveness of the two is equality, but the implied contrast has always had an unacknowledged volatility, Canada at some times and the United States at others being the more egalitarian. The reason for this volatility is a crucial duality in the idea of equality. On one interpretation, equality in the sense of equal standing is opposed to elitism; on the other, equality in the sense of collectivism is opposed to individualism. The historical construction of the place of equality in the American and Canadian political cultures has oscillated depending on which interpretation is implied.

Our concern here is with the realm of public action, with differing conceptions of the latitude of state action and individual responsibility, and so we begin with equality construed in terms of collectivism–individualism. Respondents were asked to complete the following sentence with one of two preformulated endings:

"In the matter of jobs and standards of living, the government should
(1) see to it that everyone has a job and a decent standard of living

or

(2) let each person get ahead on his own."

The contrasting responses of the two national political cultures strikingly correspond to the intuitive historical judgment of the Canadian political culture as the more collectivist and the American political culture as the more individualist (fig. 5.1A). In Canada the modal view is that the "government should see to it that everyone has a job and a decent standard of living," one out of every two respondents (and two out of every three expressing an opinion) accepting the collectivist alternative. In the United States, the situation is exactly the reverse, nearly one out of every two respondents (and two out of every three expressing an opinion) saying instead that "the government should let each person get ahead on his own."

So much corresponds to the familiar picture. But let us examine more closely the contrasting reactions of elites. The fairly high rates of refusal to

Figure 5.1 A. *"In the matter of jobs and standards of living, the government should . . . (1) see to it that everyone has a job and a standard of living; (2) let each person get ahead on his own."*

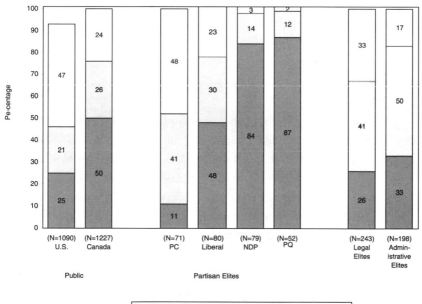

Figure 5.1 B. *"While equal opportunity to succeed is important for all Canadians, it's not really the government's job to guarantee it."*

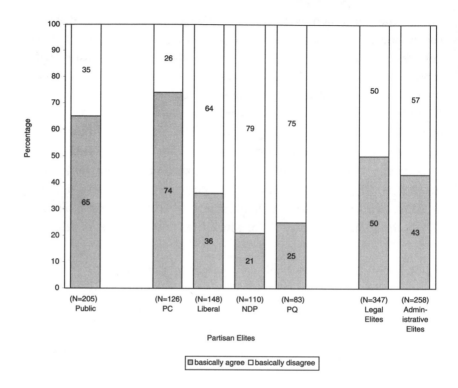

statistical signficance of comparisons
political elites by party: p ≤ .01

take a position in some elite sectors warrant caution, yet a line of cleavage divides the explicitly political segments of the elite sample (whether representative or administrative) from the legal segment. The modal position of lawyers with a view on the matter is that the government should let everyone get ahead on his or her own. Conversely, with the exception only of Conservatives, the modal position of elites who have explicit governmental responsibilities (whether in Parliament or in ministries of justice or in the office of solicitor generals) manifestly favors the view that the government should see to it that everyone has a job and a decent standard of living. This fissure is politically of interest, of course, because the lawyers we interviewed were selected precisely because they are representative of the pool of candidates from which federal and provincial judges are selected, and there is therefore reason to believe that the views they express are representative

Figure 5.1 C. *"Social insurance programs (like old age pensions and family allowances) should be based on family income, so people who don't need this type of assistance don't get it."*

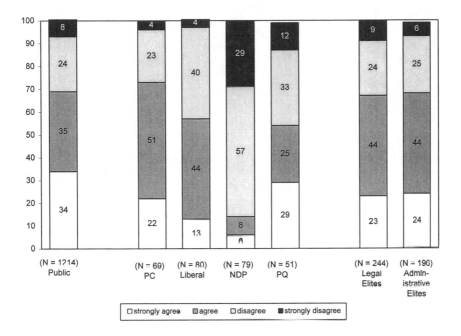

□ strongly agree   ▨ agree   □ disagree   ■ strongly disagree

of the broad outlook judges characteristically take to the bench. It does not follow that the legal decisions they make in their role as judges correspond mechanically to the social and political views they hold as individuals. But, equally, it would be naive to suppose that their convictions about the proper role of government and the responsibilities of individuals are irrelevant to their judicial behavior.

The suggestion that governmental and legal elites differ markedly in their judgment about the responsibility of government in assuring jobs and a standard of living is broadly right (fig. 5.1A). But political (that is, partisan) elites manifest a more pronounced degree of variation. Judged against the center of gravity for the public as a whole, it is now Conservatives who are very much out of step: only a relative handful of them (one in every ten) explicitly say that government has the responsibility to assure everyone a job and a decent standard of living. In contrast, the ideological thrust of the

Figure 5.1 D. *"Doctors and hospitals should not be allowed to extra bill or charge patients more than what the government health plans pay them."*

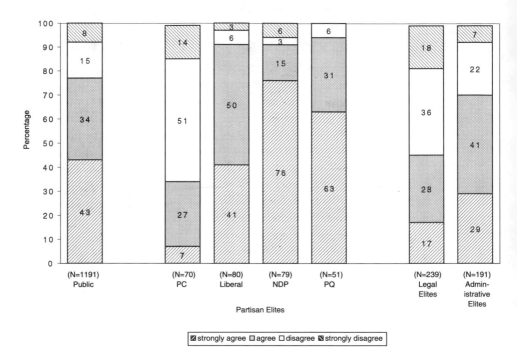

statistical significance of comparisons
public vs. elites as a whole: p ≤ .01; political elites by party: p ≤ .01; elite groups by sector: p ≤ .01

NDP now corresponds to the central tendency of the general public, reversing—or nearly so—the pattern we have so often seen before. We say nearly reversing because strategically the position the NDP enjoys (relative to the public as a whole) on this aspect of equality is not in all respects equivalent to the one the Conservatives often enjoy. It is true that the modal tendencies of both New Democrats and ordinary citizens correspond on the issue of governmental responsibility for standards of living. But notice that the advantage the NDP enjoys is by no means confined to it. The central tendency of every party but the Conservatives matches that of the public as a whole on this issue; and, indeed, if what counts is the degree of correspondence between a party and the public, the party most resembling the public mood is not the NDP but the Liberal Party.

It would be a mistake to attach too much importance to the exact degree of correspondence between a party's position and that of the larger public's inclinations, except insofar as a one-sided commitment to a position on the part of politically sophisticated and organized people bespeaks an adamancy that a party will find hard to compromise or obscure. Beyond this, in capturing the play of redistributive politics—in recognizing the readiness and speed with which large numbers of citizens will line up first on one side of the issue of redistribution, then on the other—we think it useful to introduce the concept of a belief repertoire. For many aspects of politics, including redistributive politics especially, people tend to have a number of beliefs they can call upon, beliefs that point them in politically different directions but that are themselves not necessarily in conflict with one another. It is perfectly reasonable to have more than one thought or attitude that bears upon a large, complex issue like redistributive politics—indeed, just because it is reasonable, most of us do.

As an illustration of the idea of a repertoire of belief, consider the issue of individual responsibility and government assistance posed, for the sake of argument, in these terms: "While equal opportunity to succeed is important for all Canadians, it's not really the government's job to guarantee it" (fig. 5.1B). The pattern of responses, particularly on the part of the Canadian public, contrasts sharply with that in figure 5.1A. Instead of two in every three who express an opinion favoring government responsibility, now two in every three favor individual responsibility; and, it follows, instead of the Conservatives distinctively deviating from the public mood, they now, uniquely, embrace it.

Is this evidence of mere incoherence on the part of the ordinary citizen? How can one believe both that the government should guarantee jobs and that it is not the government's job to guarantee people an equal opportunity to succeed? There is, increasingly, an awareness that ordinary citizens often have multiple and (from some points of view) conflicting attitudes they can draw on in responding to a subject like equality, but this is most often taken as evidence that their thinking about it is inconsistent and muddled, as proof that they lack a genuine attitude and have only a miscellany of conflicting considerations to call upon. In a word, their thinking about politics is ambivalent through and through.[2] The notion of ambivalence, however, carries overtones of conflict, of a person caught between opposing beliefs, seesawing between them, uncertain which to commit to. No doubt there are such people, but more often the notion of a belief repertoire seems appropriate:

citizens can legitimately take more than one position regarding a subject like equality—they can appropriately have, so to speak, more than one arrow in their quiver politically—without being inconsistent or muddled or conflicted in their thinking or feelings. Indeed, the key to comprehending the built-in tendency of redistributive politics to oscillate, first favoring one pole and then the other, is to recognize that—apart from one particular ideological point of view—the alternative emphases on government and on individual responsibility do *not* conflict. People are not under any pressure to resolve their position in favor of one or the other because from more than one perspective it is perfectly appropriate and sensible to believe that individuals should do everything they can to take care of their problems *and* that government should assure everyone an equal opportunity to succeed.

Three pieces of evidence square with the suggestion that citizens have multiple beliefs in the same domain, differing in their political implications but cohabiting without strain. First, the correlation between support for government guarantees of standards of living and a belief that it is not the government's job to guarantee equal opportunity to succeed is trivial among the public as a whole (r = −.09); more or less so among the major parties (Liberal r = −.09, PC = −.17); and marked only among the New Democrats (r = −.36). The "mere inconsistency" hypothesis could fit the first and fourth correlation but not the second and third. It may be reasonable to suggest that ordinary citizens, politically inattentive and unsophisticated as they tend to be, fail to see the relation between the two, but it is hardly defensible to suggest that Liberal and Conservative parliamentarians do so for the same reason. Instead, taken together the correlations suggest, first, that these two elements of belief are not taken to be interdependent (such that an acceptance of one entails a rejection of the other) in the abstract, and second, that this pair of elements collide only when viewed from a particular ideological perspective, namely, the left, which singly defines them as inconsistent.

The politics of redistributive equality has an oscillatory dynamic in part because large numbers of the public as a whole simultaneously hold multiple attitudes, and they have a persistent tendency to do so because these attitudes are not felt to be inconsistent. Opposing points of view at the elite level can each attract electoral support that is difficult to extinguish and that can, given the appropriate circumstances, be enlarged. In short, popular ideological "tides" tend to be short-lived partly because a movement toward one pole of equality does not require a movement away from the other.

A failure to appreciate that equality is multifaceted leads to oversimplified portraits of the beliefs of individuals and to still more oversimplified portraits of the temper of political cultures. People often have available more than one belief or attitude to guide a response; and they have more than one attitude available because they have to deal with more than one type of problem even within a common field of concerns like equality. From this point of view, the variety of responses to equality reflects not merely the inevitable inconsistency of individuals, but also the genuine diversity of issues bundled up under the heading of equality. Consider a pair of principles central to redistributive politics. The first is universality of benefits. Since the Great Depression, the unacceptability of means-testing benefits has been an axiom of redistributive politics. It is taken for granted by policy-makers and analysts of the left that requiring people to show need on their part to qualify for public benefits is demeaning and, if made a requirement of public policy, will evoke politically ruinous protest. But what policy experts believe citizens believe and what citizens actually believe are not necessarily identical. To provide a demanding test on the issue of means-testing, we included social insurance programs, like old age pensions, to which ordinary Canadians might well think they had made or would make a full contribution on their own through their working career and were therefore entitled to a full return of benefits on retirement. Specifically, we asked everyone the extent to which they agreed or disagreed with the statement, "Social insurance programs (like old age pensions and family allowances) should be based on family income, so people who don't need this type of assistance don't get it." The results show how equality is not only a double-edged sword politically, serving as a weapon for the political right as well as left, but also a rather sharp sword (fig. 5.1C). Consider first the position of the public: 68 percent of them are in favor of means-tested benefits. Notice now how closely the position of Conservatives matches that of the public: 70 percent of PC's are similarly in favor of means-tested benefits, with a substantial majority of Liberals (56 percent) in agreement. For that matter, a majority of the PQ (54 percent) also favor means-tested benefits, as do still larger majorities among legal (67 percent) and executive elites (68 percent), who, as so often on equality issues, are very much like the Progressive Conservatives. Only the NDP differ, staking out a position at odds with the views of all the other groups. The NDP political elite overwhelmingly reject means-tested benefits. Given that the NDP is the only group that rejects the principle of means-testing it is easy to appreciate why the Conservatives encountered so little opposition in first introducing "clawback" provisions in taxing family allowance payments, then revamping the program to eliminate payments to those above certain income levels.[3]

But the primary characteristic of public opinion that imparts an oscillatory character to redistributive politics is the simultaneous availability of alternative beliefs that can be mobilized by political elites on behalf of explicitly redistributive policies. Consider by way of a final example, reactions to the issue of "extra-billing."

Everyone was asked if they agreed or disagreed with the statement, "Doctors and hospitals should not be allowed to extra bill or charge patients more than what the government health plans pay them." Here the political high cards lie with proponents of redistributive politics. A large majority of the public (three in every four) is opposed to extra-billing, as is an (even larger) majority in the NDP (more than nine in every ten). In contrast, nearly two in every three Conservatives favor extra-billing, with lawyers again being more similar to the PC than to anyone else. It is, however, worth remarking again on the special topography of electoral politics when the NDP represents the central thrust of the general public. Extra-billing is indeed an issue that the NDP can make political hay with, but—and politically this needs to be underlined—so can most of the other parties: specifically, 91 percent of the Liberals and 92 percent of the PQ are opposed to extra-billing. In short, even when the NDP clearly has good cards to play in the politics of redistribution, it has no monopoly on good hands.

The politics of redistribution is only one dimension of the new politics of equality; new insofar as claims made in the name of social justice have been cast into a distinctive form by the adoption of the Charter of Rights. Two of the principal spurs to the new politics of equality are Aboriginal rights and affirmative action.

Aboriginal Rights

The concept of Aboriginal rights, for all its apparent constitutional recency, can be traced back to the early contacts of European colonizers with North America's Aboriginal inhabitants. An early manifestation was the Proclamation of 1763 following England's conquest of New France. The proclamation stipulated that settlers could not take land directly from Indians. Land could be settled only after the Indians had ceded title to the Crown. In effect, this recognized that there was an Aboriginal right to inhabit and use the land until it was formally ceded to the sovereign and that Aboriginal peoples could govern their own affairs.[4] Notwithstanding the implied rights in the proclamation, however, lying behind it and driving it forward was a policy of European colonization that treated Indians as savages. Government policy aimed at removing Indians from the advancing path of European settle- ment. The long-run aim was to "civilize" the Indians by getting them to adopt European ways. In the meantime, the Indians were to be protected from corruption by being placed on and confined to reserves and converted into Christian farmers. Following Confederation, under the terms of the Indian Act, they were treated as wards of the state. These policies continued through the 1960s.

In 1969, the Liberal government of Pierre Trudeau issued a Statement on Indian Policy that set assimilation and the dismantling of special programs for Indians as the fundamental goals of government policy. Consistent with Trudeau's vision of liberal citizenship, Canada's Aboriginal peoples were to enjoy no less (and no more) than equal access to the ordinary rights and opportunities of other Canadians. Native peoples' bitter opposition to this policy led ultimately to its reassessment and to new approaches in negoti- ating land claim agreements. These agreements are essentially modern treaties with Indian and Inuit peoples who had never entered into land cession treaties. A major stimulus for this approach of negotiation was the decision of the Supreme Court of Canada in the *Calder* case in 1973 stipulat- ing that an Aboriginal right to occupy and use traditional land existed until it was extinguished. The Court split 3–3 on the ways those rights might be extinguished. The significance of this case is that vast areas of Canada are occupied by Indians and Inuit peoples who have never ceded title to their land or had their title ended by parliamentary legislation. Moreover, these lands harbor reserves of oil, gas, water, and other resources. The land claim agreements arrived at to date have entailed the extinguishing of Aboriginal title in exchange for substantial cash payments to native peoples, outright collective ownership of land in and around their communities, hunting and fishing rights in the larger surrounding areas, and the establishment of insti- tutions of local self-government. Other negotiations have been charac- terized by calls for recognition of Aboriginal peoples' right to self-govern- ment as well as for a share in the proceeds from resource development on native lands.

What gives a distinctive stamp to the claims of Aboriginals (and not only in Canada) is a special conjunction of principle and political circumstance. On the one hand, the constitutional legitimacy of the principle of unique rights—that is, the principle that Indians have, by virtue of their status as Indians, rights other Canadians cannot claim—has clearly been established. On the other hand, the legal content of these unique rights—the description of the concrete public benefits that Indians can distinctively claim and the conditions under which they can claim them—has not been authoritatively defined or even broadly circumscribed. The only reference to Aboriginal rights in the Charter of Rights (sections 1–33 of the Constitution Act, 1982) is in section 25. It reads, "The guarantee in this Charter of certain rights and freedoms shall not be construed so as to abrogate or derogate from any aboriginal, treaty or other rights or freedoms that pertain to the aboriginal peoples of Canada." This is a "saving" clause, protecting or shielding Aboriginal rights from being overridden by other rights set out in the Charter, for example, by the equality rights set out in section 15. Aboriginal rights are dealt with somewhat more directly in another section of the constitution, adopted at the same time as the Charter. Under section 35, "The existing Aboriginal and treaty rights of the Aboriginal people of Canada are hereby recognized and affirmed." This formulation, in referring to "existing Aboriginal" rights as well as "treaty rights," recognizes rights based on the native peoples' original occupancy of the land as well as on the promises made to natives through treaties but leaves considerable uncertainty as to what exactly these rights are. Consequently there has been more or less continuous effort to negotiate and clarify the meaning of these rights.

One substantial product of this effort has been a constitutional amendment in 1983 clarifying that any rights obtained under current and future land claims agreements are included among the treaty rights recognized by the Constitution. The amendment also established that Aboriginal and treaty rights "are guaranteed equally to male and female persons" in order to obviate, on the basis of constitutionally protected Aboriginal rights, traditional forms of discrimination against women in communities. A constitutional definition of existing Aboriginal rights, however, remains elusive.

Up to and including the failed attempt to amend the Constitution through the Charlottetown Accord of 1992, the most difficult issue in the ongoing negotiations between representatives of the federal and provincial governments and native peoples has been explicit constitutional recognition of their inherent right to self-government. For more than a decade native groups have lobbied and negotiated for this recognition. With the Charlottetown Accord an agreement on this question was achieved, at least at the level of political leadership. Following the defeat of the accord, however, explicit constitutional recognition of the Aboriginal self-government right remains to be achieved.

The rights of Aboriginals, though grounded in section 25 of the Charter and section 35 of the Constitution Act, are far from settled. The full scope and meaning of these rights have yet to be translated into specific guarantees constitutionally. The rights of Aboriginals thus provide a dramatic stage on which the politics of rights can be played out. Not only is there a clash of competing rights, each constitutionally privileged, none unequivocally and unconditionally dominant; additionally, there is bound to be a test of political strength because the Charter of Rights assigns a special status to Aboriginals but does not specify their special rights.

Several court cases have begun to define Aboriginal rights more precisely, but the process is far from over, giving an open-ended character to the "unique rights" of Aboriginals. This makes analysis of the acceptance by Canadians of the unique rights of native peoples a special case. But it is special only in degree, not in kind, and it is not peculiar to Canadian politics: a number of liberal democratic polities, not the least being the United States, have it on their agenda. Constitutionally secured rights all in all, and not just the rights of Aboriginals, are inherently contestable if only because they necessarily take the form of abstract rules: citizens, section 2b of the Charter holds, have a right to "freedom of thought," not a right to think *this* or *that* thought. The right must be put abstractly because it is impossible to compile a list of all its permissible applications at any moment in time or to foresee how abstract rights will be construed in the future. A politics of rights, that is, a contest over the authoritative determination of the meaning of a right at specific moments and places, thus exists if only because the announcement of rights is abstract. And even apart from the inevitable indeterminacy of rights, because of their inherent abstractness there would be a politics of rights. For the crucial point is precisely that rights come in the plural. There is not just one right or even one set of rights: the Charter sets out a plurality of them—rights for more than one group and more than one set of rights for any given group. Inevitably these rights come into conflict, for the act of validating one often quashes another.

It is misconceived to expect the average citizen to be able to adjudicate the conflicts among Charter rights or to rule, with precision, on the application of rights in specific controversies. That is not our project. Our aim is, to borrow Montesquieu's phrase, to understand "the spirit of the laws" and in particular to take advantage of the terms in which citizens construe the issue of Aboriginal rights to throw light on two questions of increasing importance in contemporary democratic thought. First, how do citizens and decision makers react to the principle that Aboriginals, by virtue of being Aboriginal, hold rights that other Canadians do not? in other words, how does the idea of unique rights fare against a background defined by the principle of equal rights? And second, in a politics of multiplying rights, to what extent can the Charter of Rights legitimate a claim to a right?

Let us take the second question first. We want our analysis of attitudes toward Aboriginal rights to contribute to a political theory of rights, and an element in a specifically political theory of rights is a consideration not simply of whether citizens and decision makers recognize and support the rights set out in the Canadian Charter of Rights and Freedoms, but also whether the Charter itself can serve to legitimate these rights in their minds. After all, one argument made in favor of establishing the Charter in the first place is that a written constitution serves as an instrument of civic education. A constitution enshrines, not merely encodes, both the identity and basic principles of a political community. Insofar as it becomes a symbol of political identity and legitimacy, a constitution can legitimize in the minds of citizens the basic rights of citizens.

But does a written constitution in fact do this? To get leverage on this question, we designed a special experiment called the charter springboard experiment. Its purpose is to determine if the Charter can serve as a springboard, that is, whether citizens and decision makers are more likely to accept a right as legitimate because the Charter of Rights declares it to be a right. In the springboard experiment, one-half of the respondents were asked, "Should native peoples be treated just like any other Canadian, with no special rights or should their unique rights be preserved?" and the other half were asked the same question prefaced by the assertion, "Canada's constitution recognizes the unique rights of Canada's native peoples." Given the randomization of question versions, more support for the unique rights of native peoples among respondents who heard the introduction is compelling evidence that the Constitution serves not merely a passive role of supplying a record of agreed-on rights but also a dynamic role of creating legitimacy for the very rights it records.

Two features of our presentation of the data should be remarked. First, the results are presented for elites taken as a whole because (1) support for Aboriginal rights is in any event higher among decision makers, and hence a ceiling constrains the range of observable effects, and (2) the manipulation

Figure 5.2 A. Charter "Springboard" Experiment: Unique Rights
of Aboriginals

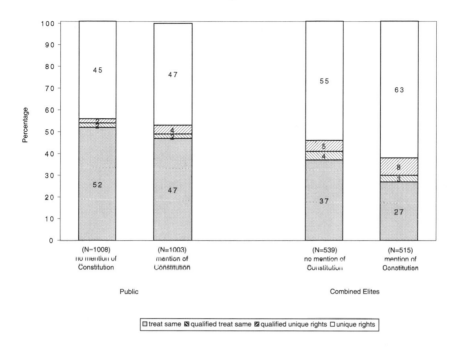

statistical significance of comparison
question version for political elites: p ≤ .01

involved in the experiment is a modest one—merely a mention that the
Constitution incorporates Aboriginal rights—and hence should be expected
to evoke a proportionately modest response (fig. 5.2A).[5] Second, given the
special tensions surrounding the idea of a set of unique rights, we record not
only the direction of responses but also whether qualifications are spontaneously attached to either support or opposition for special rights for native
peoples (fig. 5.2A).

Looking first at the general population sample and comparing their reactions to the issue of Aboriginal rights depending on whether the Constitution was mentioned or not, we see that their response in the two situations is
virtually identical: approximately one in every two supports the idea that
native peoples should be treated like any other Canadian, and one in every
two favors the idea that the unique rights of native people should be preserved. In contrast, consider the responses of decision makers. Absent any

Figure 5.2 B. Attitudes of Elites toward Unique Rights of Aboriginals (neutral condition)

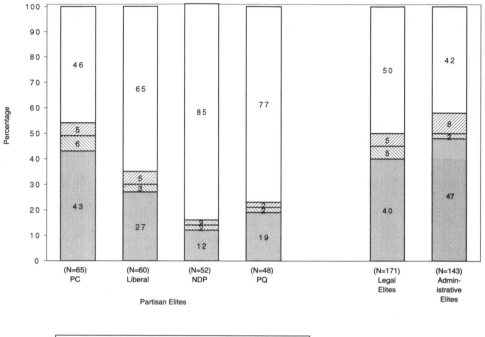

statistical significance of comparison
political elites by party: p ≤ .01; elite groups by sector: p ≤ .01

mention that Aboriginal rights are constitutionally embedded, just under six in every ten favor the preservation of the unique rights of Aboriginals. But if it is first mentioned that Canada's Constitution recognizes such rights, the proportion supporting them goes up to seven in every ten, a difference that easily meets conventional tests of statistical significance. In addition, if qualifications are to be attached to positions on the question of unique rights, they are more likely to be attached to support for preservation of Aboriginal rights than to opposition to them, certainly in the case of decision makers. But the more striking result of the experiment is the demonstration that the Charter[6] serves a springboard function, legitimizing rights in the minds of Canadian decision makers because the Charter asserts it as a right.

Although all the varieties of decision makers are more likely to support the principle of unique rights if they are told it is a constitutionally embedded principle, they are not equally likely to do so. On the contrary, there is a marked variation in support for the idea of unique rights among decision makers (fig. 5.2B).[7] Among legal elites the principle of unique rights has by no means won acceptance as a dominant principle. Absent a reference to constitutional sanction, they are split down the middle, and so it can hardly be said that among those whose profession is the law the notion of special rights—even in the special context of native people—has become the established position. In contrast, the principle of unique rights has patently become the dominant position among partisan elites, apart from one exception. The exception is the Conservatives, who are for all practical purposes evenly divided, half favoring and half opposing the principle. In contrast, a majority in each of the other political parties favors native peoples' possessing unique rights. That majority is sizeable in the case of Liberals (more than two in every three) and still larger among the NDP and PQ. The Conservatives thus most closely approximate the public at large. However, no prize is awarded simply for a party's mirroring the preferences of the public on a given issue; indeed, the question of unique rights for native people is an issue in which the very notion of a majority is misleading, given that approximately as many citizens line up on one side of the issue as on the other. Nevertheless, the party of the right does enjoy an advantage on an issue of equality like this, not because they have the backing of the public for their position, but because they are not locked in to a position on the issue. The Conservatives, by dividing equally themselves, have the luxury of being able to take either side of the issue—or, no less important, of not taking either side; indeed, given their own differences, they have an incentive not to make very much of the issue at all. This option of passing an issue like Aboriginal rights by, of avoiding (in Albert Hirschman's terms) the option of voice, can be of considerable value politically. Consensus within a party can be advantageous; yet there are times when it presents difficulties. The distribution of preferences for parties of the left is one-sided on the issue of Aboriginal rights, anchoring them.

We want to probe further four fundamental dilemmas inherent in the notion of unique rights in a liberal democracy. The first turns around the issue of acceptance. Is a desire to ensure that Aboriginal peoples can enter fully into all aspects of the life of the larger society an act of acceptance? Or will the very act of incorporation serve to extinguish their distinctive identity? The ambiguities of acceptance were a central issue in reaction to Trudeau's policy paper on native people in the late 1960s and remain at the center of Aboriginal rights issues, for acceptance can be double-edged, appearing from one angle as a sign of the larger society's tolerance and openness, from another as a strategy for assimilation to its values and norms. A second dilemma hinges on the uniqueness of Canada's native people. Their claim not only to uniqueness but to unique rights introduces a new card to the political game of rights. It is a card whose value is uncertain at this point and may indeed never be fixed, the result being that whether a claim to unique Aboriginal rights trumps other rights hinges crucially on the inescapable ambiguity of the notion of uniqueness. This ambiguity can be glimpsed once it is recognized that the meanings of uniqueness form a spectrum, running from habits and customs at one pole to fundamental ways of life at the other. The closer the claim of uniqueness is to the habits and customs pole, the lower its value in the politics of rights because other groups are also in a position to make the claim. The more encompassing the claim of uniqueness, the greater its potential value. But the more domains of life the claim of uniqueness takes in, from religion through economics through politics, the greater the difficulty of honoring it; for it amounts to a claim that liberal democracy can and must incorporate not only competing values but a whole way of life that may in some fundamental respects violate the norms of Western liberalism.

The third of the quartet of dilemmas over Aboriginal rights is procedural and hinges on who is entitled to define the issues both of acceptance and uniqueness. Who should decide whether acceptance is an opening up of the larger society to native peoples or an incorporation of them into the larger society? Who should decide whether claims made on behalf of native peoples go beyond the preservation of customs and values and run fully to the defense of whole ways of life that may be antithetical to the way of life prescribed for the larger society and codified in the Charter of Rights itself? If an Indian nation, for example, were to approve of hereditary leadership, would and should this stand?

Again, one can imagine a spectrum of answers. At one pole would fall those who believe that Aboriginals must accept the will of the Canadian majority. In the middle are the partisans of pluralism, taking the position that the place of native peoples in the larger society raises issues of rights and identity that must be decided by the plurality of groups that will be affected. At the other pole would fall exponents of self-determination, arguing that because the crux of the issue is the rights of native peoples and their place in the larger society, the decision as to whether to join the larger society and the terms on which a merger should take place belongs properly to native peoples themselves.

The final dilemma concerning Aboriginal rights to be discussed here is simultaneously practical and moral. The negotiations on land claims highlight a dilemma over whether or not to allow development projects to proceed on lands traditionally occupied by native people before any treaty or land claims agreement is made with them. A strong case for not proceeding with development in the absence of a treaty or a land agreement can be made in moral and legal terms: in most instances, Aboriginal peoples have lived on their lands for countless years, and in many cases they have never surrendered title of that land to anyone. And even when they have, it has often been on grossly unfair terms. To many Canadians it seems morally wrong to develop Aboriginal lands without the agreement of the peoples living upon them; it is also questionable in law. These moral and legal concerns are buttressed by a growing recognition of the Canadian public at large that native Canadians are profoundly attached to their lands. The land is a sacred connection in the circle of life, linking today's Aboriginal people with their forebears and with those yet to be born. And in many instances, these moral concerns are upheld by legal requirements of various stripes to settle any outstanding land claims before proceeding with development projects. Although the case for postponing development has substantial appeal for many Canadians, it does not obscure for others the economic facts of life in a resource-hungry world and a country in which resource development has been the cornerstone of many provincial economies. It may not be an exaggeration to say that Canadian economic development as a whole and Canada's standard of living generally have been realized in large measure through the development of basic resources. The economic outlook, not only for private but also public enterprise, in Canada depends upon the timely development of the resources at the frontiers. Yet the negotiations involved in settling land claims may be extremely drawn out and difficult, often involving several native communities as well as several levels of government, all with their own agendas and timetables. And negotiations over land claims entail more than financial considerations in exchange for rights of access. Inevitably, knotty issues of self-government and the protection of traditional ways of life are involved, stretching negotiations into decades, all the while threatening well-established non-Aboriginal enterprises as well as delaying future development. From this perspective a strong practical case can be made for responsibly proceeding with development while land claims are being negotiated. So on the development issue, we see once more a possible dilemma for many Canadians as well as the potential for conflict over how to proceed.

The politics of Aboriginal rights reveals itself in the reactions of people not only to each of these four issues—acceptance, distinctiveness, self-determination, and development—taken separately but in the deep interplay among them. We want to capture something of this interplay (even if there are obvious limits to the depths we can probe) by reporting the reactions of Canadians to four questions on Aboriginal rights, each reflecting an aspect of the dilemmas presented by issues of Aboriginal rights in Canada (fig. 5.3). The first raises the issue of acceptance in its most provocative form: assimilation. Everyone was asked if they agreed or disagreed with the statement,

"In the long run, it would be best for native people to be completely assimilated into Canadian society."

People are being asked here to engage a moral dilemma, not explicitly to be sure, but implicitly and genuinely all the same. A dilemma represents, of course, a special kind of choice, one requiring a person to choose either between two goods, necessarily sacrificing one, or between two evils, necessarily suffering one. Here, the choice offered is not simply whether to respond to native peoples positively and sympathetically or negatively and mean-spiritedly; rather, the choice poses a genuine question about what constitutes a positive response. Is it not, after all, a worthy goal to have native peoples finally accepted into Canadian society, on an equal basis, no longer sequestered on reservations and shut off from opportunity? But, then again, may this not result in the disappearance of their culture, the death of their way of life? Perhaps because the issues involved are genuinely complex, the most notable feature of responses, certainly among the general public and broadly among elites, too, is the amount of disagreement. The modal position among ordinary citizens, by the slightest of margins, was to agree with the ideal of assimilation, but for all practical purposes, just as many of them disagreed, while nearly one-fifth have no opinion (fig. 5.3A). Much the same is true of Conservatives and, except that the predominant tendencies are reversed, of administrative and legal elites, too. Among Liberals, a majority is opposed to assimilation, but only among the NDP and the PQ is there a decisive consensus in opposition.

The ideal of assimilation exposes the tensions between equality conceived in the light of autonomy and conceived in the light of acceptance. A

Figure 5.3 A. *"In the long run, it would be best for native people to be completely assimilated into Canadian society."*

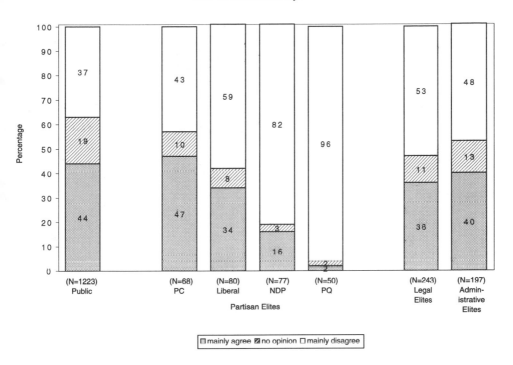

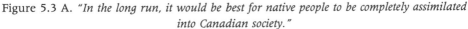

statistical significance of comparisons
public vs. elites as a whole: p ≤ .01; political elites by party: p ≤ .01; elite groups by sector: p ≤ .01

different angle is offered by the principle of self-determination, not because it is free of normative tangles, but because they are less obvious, and responses to the principle can thus illustrate the contingency of judgments of principle as one or another facet is exposed to clear view. To see how people felt about the principle of native self-determination, taken by itself, we asked them if they agreed or disagreed (and how strongly) with the statement,

> "Canadian Indians should be able to decide for themselves their way of life."

So phrased, the principle of self-determination commands majority support, although, tellingly, it does not enjoy strong support as a rule (fig. 5.3B). Thus, almost three in every four citizens agreed that Indians should

Figure 5.3 B. *"Canadian Indians should be able to decide for themselves their way of life."*

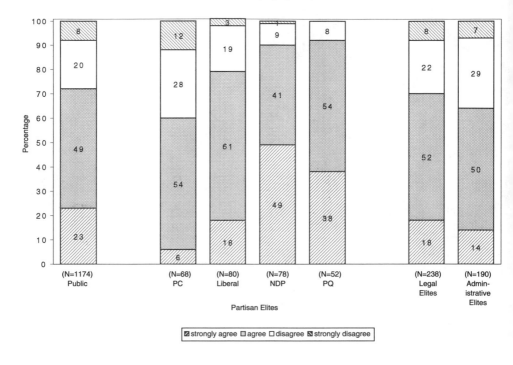

decide on their own way of life, although only one in every four of them strongly agreed with this. The principle of self-determination commands even larger margins of support among political and legal elites (with the exception of Conservatives), but that support is most often not strong (with the exception of New Democrats and the PQ). This observation of majority support for native self-determination across all elite groups calls out for comment. The birth of the 1990s was announced by strife and bloodshed over self-determination at Oka, Quebec. Television news and newspapers presented indelible images of an armed confrontation and standoff between Canadian Forces and Mohawk Warriors, both in full battle dress. In a show of support for the cause of the Mohawks, native peoples across the country blockaded roadways as far away as British Columbia as well as at the Mercier Bridge, a major artery into Montreal. Although the flash point was at Oka-Kahnesatake, this armed standoff was just the most serious and

Figure 5.3 C. *"Native peoples should be able to have a large amount of self-government . . . (1) as long as their system of government conforms with the principles of Canadian democracy; (2) no matter what system of government they adopt."*

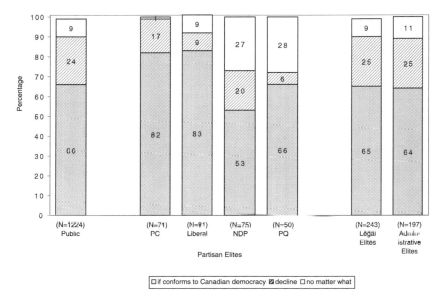

statistical significance of comparisons
political elites by party: p ≤ .01; elite groups by sector: p ≤ .01

most publicized of a series of confrontations between natives and Canadian authorities across the country in recent years. There was also a standoff at Kahnawake, near Montreal, in June 1988 at which armed Mohawk Warriors blocked a highway; armed Ojibwa Warriors seized a park near Kenora, Ontario; native people clashing with Royal Canadian Mounted Police officers and Canadian Forces troops disrupted the opening of Parliament in 1974; the Haida have blocked logging roads in the Queen Charlotte Islands of British Columbia; natives on the Bear Island reserve in Ontario have blocked a logging road in the Lake Temagami area; the Innu have carried on lengthy protests outside the Goose Bay Canadian Forces Base in Labrador; the Lubicon have blockaded a huge tract of land in northern Alberta; most recently we have seen a standoff at Iperwash during the summer of 1995. How is the political, legal, and bureaucratic elites' endorsement of native self-determination to be reconciled with the confrontations with native

Figure 5.3 D. *"Land claims settlements with native peoples . . . (1) should be reached before using their land for economic development purposes; (2) should not be a reason for postponing major development projects."*

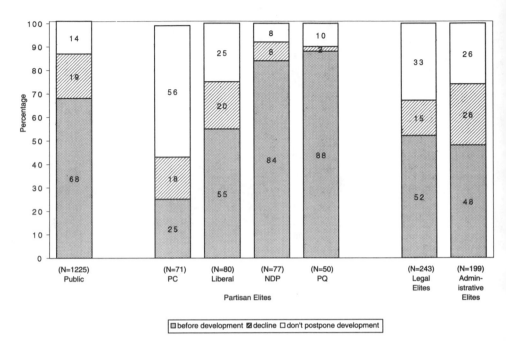

statistical significance of comparisons
public vs. elites as a whole: p ≤ .01; political elites by party: p ≤ .01

peoples in Quebec and elsewhere? Is this but one more episode in the familiar tale of cynicism in which people proclaim their undying support for democratic values in the abstract, then violate them as they are caught up in the heat of political controversy?

Part of the answer is that people do not always mean what they say, but the larger point is that what they say on any one occasion often does not exhaust what they mean. People have more than one attitude relevant to an issue like Aboriginal rights, and focusing on their opinions about only one aspect radically underestimates the range of positions they are prepared to take. Consider, for example, how people react to the principle of self-determination when it is made explicit that self-determination may entail a way of life that stands outside and opposed to the Canadian way of life. We asked respondents to complete the following statement by choosing one of the two alternatives:

"Native peoples should be able to have a large amount of self-government
(1) as long as their system of government conforms with the principles of Canadian democracy
or
(2) no matter what system of government they adopt."

It is one thing to want native peoples to run their own affairs. But what if they elect to run them in a way that is at odds with the basic principles of the larger society? Two in every three Canadians in general support native self-government, but only on the condition that it conform with principles of Canadian democracy (fig. 5.3C). Very few—fewer than one in ten—endorse self-government unconditionally. Popular support for native self-government, these results suggest, is conditional: self-determination for native people may be a value, but it is by no means the highest value, and if self-determination collides with larger, more universalistic criteria, it loses popular support.

This clash of values is by no means hypothetical or abstruse. The particular forms of native self-government advocated under the rubric of an inherent right to self-government have yet to be specified, but they may indeed not always conform with the principles of west European democracy. For instance, recognition of an inherent right to Aboriginal self-government was opposed in the discussions leading up to the proposed Charlottetown Accord when it became clear from the comments of the Grand Chief of the Assembly of First Nations that a right of self-government might be taken to exempt native communities from the guarantees of basic democratic procedures (elections rather than direct democracy and legislatures meeting once a year) called for in sections 3, 4, and 5 of the Charter. Whether ordinary Canadians are likely to see hereditary chiefs or decision making through community consensus rather than elected legislature, for example, as consistent with the principles of Canadian democracy is not at issue here. Public attitudes on these questions, if indeed they ever become matters of public attention, will no doubt be influenced by the reactions of the political elites. Little can be said about the specifics of such debates in advance of the particular moment and occasion when they are conducted, but the reactions of the elites to our question about native self-government and principles of Canadian democracy highlight some of the likely contours of the politics of rights surrounding native self-government. The first thing to note is that majorities in all of the elite groups insist on conformity with Canadian principles of democracy as a sine qua non of native people's self-government. And among Conservative and Liberal political elites this is the overwhelming response, with only very few willing to approve native self-government unconditionally. The legal and executive elites differ principally in that fewer of them are willing to choose one of the substantive options offered. Only a small number of them offer unconditional support for native self-government. The responses of the NDP and PQ are noteworthy in that they alone are divided on this question. Only here do more than a handful of respondents lend full support to native government whatever form it may take, yet even so this is patently a minority position in both parties (fig. 5.3C). A majority of the NDP political elite and the PQ still insist that native self-government take democratic forms. The politics of Aboriginal rights encapsulates some of the antinomies of equality, but perhaps especially so from the perspective of the political left. As we have seen, the PQ and the NDP almost unanimously support the principle of self-determination for native peoples, while by a similar margin (and quite consistently) rejecting the notion of assimilation. The problem, from the perspective of the left, is that the issue of Aboriginal rights has more than one facet, and, crucially, these facets can cut against one another. Thus the very strength of the NDP and PQ elites' commitment to self-determination and of their opposition to assimilation exposes them to difficulty when they find it necessary to consider whether native people's right to self-government is in the end subordinate to the principles of liberal democracy itself.

Lest it seem that the dilemmas of Aboriginal rights and the ambiguities of politics of equality cut only against the left, we turn briefly to the fourth of our dilemmas: conflicts over land claims and resource development. In this instance our question read as follows:

"Land claims settlements with native peoples:
(1) should be reached before using their land for economic development purposes
or
(2) should not be a reason for postponing major development projects."

Roughly two in every three Canadians think that agreements on land claims should be reached with native peoples before development proceeds on their lands (fig. 5.3D). Among elites, the Conservatives are out of line. The majority of them are of the view that development projects should not be set aside until land claims have been sorted out. In contrast, a majority of the Liberal political elite and commanding majorities among both the NDP and PQ take the opposite side. The point that falls out of this, of course, is that a variety of strongly held values may come into conflict with the value of equality, and in this case, the Conservatives' economic views, which we saw working to their advantage in the previous chapter, contribute to their political isolation on this issue. The politics of rights are thus deeply embedded in the interplay of political values, of which equality—even equality variously understood—is only one and not necessarily the most important one.

It is all too common to observe that the abstract principles people profess and the specific political choices they make only imperfectly correspond—and, all too common as well, to conclude that the reason for such incongruence is hypocrisy—as though the difficulty in the politics of rights was a failure to believe sincerely in rights. Without slighting the importance of hypocrisy for a moment, we would suggest that the larger problem is just the opposite: problems in political reasoning over public rights are vexing not because people have no political convictions, but because they have a multitude of them (too many to permit simple answers). Canadians are broadly sincere in their desire that native people should have self-determination and in their belief that they are entitled to their own lands and way of life. Problems arise, however, because Canadians are committed to a variety of other understandings both of equality and of other values. It takes little imagination to scout the opportunities for mischief were native peoples to be severed clean from the rights assured them as Canadians: opportunity abounds for victimization couched in the vocabulary of self-determination. And it would be unfair to impeach the commitment of Canadians, particularly those on the left, to democratic values because of their desire to ensure that native people's way of life be consistent with the dominant society's democratic principles. The difficulties—of favoring unique rights for native peoples, of wanting native peoples to retain not merely the husk but the vital center of their way of life and identity, yet of insisting that the Aboriginal's way of life be consonant with the democratic way of life of the larger society—are there for everyone. And in meeting these challenges, we shall all confront the tensions (and perhaps the limitations) within our own conceptions of politics and democracy.

Section 15 (2): Affirmative Action

We have argued that the politics of equality consists as much in the conflict among competing conceptions of equality as between equality and competing values, and this is illustrated most vividly by the final aspect of the politics of equality and the Charter of Rights that we shall explore, namely, affirmative action. The Charter defines "Equality Rights" in section 15, and the section is set out in two parts:

> 15. (1) Every individual is equal before and under the law and has the right to the equal protection and equal benefit of the law without discrimination and, in particular, without discrimination based on race, national or ethnic origin, colour, religion, sex, age or mental or physical disability.
>
> (2) Subsection (1) does not preclude any law, program or activity that has as its object the amelioration of conditions of disadvantaged individuals or groups including those that are disadvantaged because of race, national or ethnic origin, colour, religion, sex, age or mental or physical disability.

Section 15 (1) expresses the classical liberal theory of equality. The dominating notion is the removal of external barriers arbitrarily imposed: women denied a job because they are women; Jews rejected from medical school because they are Jews; Blacks refused the opportunity to vote because they are Black—all are constitutionally impermissible. No one may be treated as inferior because of his or her religion, gender, or race. The thrust of 15 (2), however, goes in a quite different direction. It favors equality conceived in terms of the standing not only of individuals but also of groups. It aims not at equality of opportunity but equality of outcome. It offers a distillation of Rawlsian equality in which the stress falls on redistribution keyed to the worst off.

The pairing of the two subsections involves precisely an acknowledgment that conflicts among alternative conceptions of equality are irrepressible. But it involves more. What is striking about the pairing of subsections 15 (1) and (2) is the effort to immunize equality conceived as equality of outcome from equality conceived as equality of opportunity. Section 15 taken as a whole was written very much with an eye to the American experience, and in particular, in an effort to ensure that claims on behalf of disadvantaged groups to special treatment cannot be trumped by claims on behalf of individuals to equal treatment under the law. As a matter of principle it was decided that conflicts between these competing conceptions of equality should *not* be adjudicated on a case-by-case basis in the American style. On the contrary, the dominating fear was that absent explicit constitutional sanction, laws enabling preferential treatment for the benefit of disadvantaged groups would be struck down; hence, the explicit assertion of subsection (2) that subsection (1) does not "preclude *any* law . . . that has as its object the amelioration of conditions of disadvantaged individuals or groups."

This need constitutionally to privilege affirmative action is a telling clue to the politics of this form of equality. It bespeaks a concern about the standing of equality conceived in terms of groups, a concern that it might not hold its own if it clashes head-on in the courts with more traditional conceptions of equality. It is this implicit suggestion of a hierarchy of rival conceptions of equality that we want to explore, and the most appropriate terrain on which to examine claims made on behalf of groups rather than individuals is that of claims on behalf of women. In the United States arguments over affirmative action are dominated by race, but in Canada the representations over affirmative action in the drafting of the Charter of Rights were dominated by advocacy primarily by politically organized women on behalf of women and, to a lesser extent, other disadvantaged groups. Accordingly we asked,

> "Do you think large companies should have quotas to ensure a fixed percentage of women are hired, or should women get no special treatment?"

The standing of affirmative action so construed in the public as a whole is one-sided (fig. 5.4; represents those opposing quotas). Ordinary Canadians are opposed to affirmative action quotas in hiring by a margin of two to one—or, more accurately, they are opposed to it by that margin in this instance.

How far is the public opposition to this form of affirmative action shared by elites? Quite far, particularly by legal and administrative elites but also (though more selectively) by political elites (fig. 5.4). Among senior lawyers, for example, three in every four oppose hiring quotas for women in large companies, while a clear majority of administrative elites also oppose it. The balance of opinion among Liberals is closer, but the direction of feeling among Conservatives is one-sided, nearly eight in every ten being opposed. Only among the NDP and the PQ does a majority stand in favor of such affirmative action.

This picture of public attitudes toward affirmative action, the standard one offered in studies of public opinion, summarizes the distribution of preferences accurately enough, but it does not highlight the nuances that

Figure 5.4. Opposition to Affirmative Action for Women in Large Companies

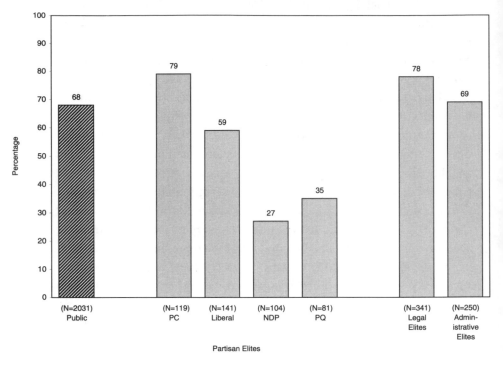

Figure 5.4. Opposition to Affirmative Action for Women in Large Companies

statistical significance of comparisons
political elites by party: p ≤ .01; elite groups by sector: p ≤ .01

give a distinctive flavor to the politics of affirmative action. Consider, therefore, exactly who spontaneously qualifies their support for affirmative action. Spontaneous qualifications are rarely attached to positions on affirmative action by the larger public, and this holds regardless of whether ordinary citizens support or oppose it (fig. 5.5). Moreover, essentially the same is true for legal and administrative elites. Scrutinizing figure 5.5, however, one can see a sector that stands out precisely for its readiness to qualify its position on affirmative action. Consider first the partisan elites who are most likely to support affirmative action, New Democrats. Approximately one in every five of them spontaneously qualifies his or her position and, no less interesting, it is supporters, not opponents, who are more likely to qualify their position. Virtually the identical results hold for the PQ. They are markedly more likely to qualify their positions on affirmative action than either ordinary citizens or elites in general, and when qualifications are attached to

Figure 5.5. Qualified and Unqualified Judgments about Affirmative Action
for Women

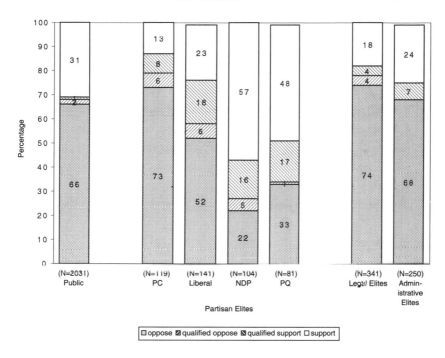

statistical significance of comparisons
political elites by party: p ≤ .01; elite groups by sector: p ≤ .01

their positions on affirmative action they are far more likely to be voiced by proponents than by opponents. And, indeed, if we consider the only other group that offers substantial support for affirmative action, namely, parliamentary Liberals, exactly the same pattern is to be observed.

All of this points to the rather special mood accompanying claims on behalf of equality conceived as equality of outcome. It is quite clear to many, certainly among the politically active and aware, that this conception of equality conflicts with other claims advanced as a matter of right, including other conceptions of equality—among them, the right to equal treatment under the law. But it is not the fact of value conflict that stands out most here—not even awareness of the fact—although conflict of competing claims is the signature of the politics of rights, as we have detailed.[8] In speaking of alternative conceptions of equality and of competing claims to public rights and benefits made on their behalf, there is a great danger of

152 THE POLITICS OF EQUALITY

overintellectualizing the politics of rights, as though it consisted in the clash of pure ideas and the rules of the battlefield were defined by an abstract logic rather than by concrete interests and concerns. The danger of overintellectualization, of making ideas count for too much in politics, is especially acute in the case of equality and affirmative action because of the flood of philosophical treatments of this issue over the last two decades, making it seem as though debate over it was driven by abstract concept and doctrine. But it is a mistake to treat support for affirmative action as though it issues simply from a commitment to a set of abstract ideas. Support for equality of outcome is not a product of fidelity to doctrine, and to represent it as doctrinal is to misunderstand its character and to miss its source of political appeal. It is just such misapprehension that the British historian J. R. Pole, commenting on the American scene, has scented out, observing, "The politics of proportional pluralism did not owe either its inception or its successes to any unified or comprehensive theory" (1993, 418).

But if equality of outcome and affirmative action are not concept and doctrine, what are they? They are methods, means to an end, and the end is to put things right for disadvantaged groups, to see them better off, and to see their chances improve straightaway. There is an array of feelings and ideas commingled under the heading of affirmative action, but what is felt and thought about it can be tied up with what is felt and thought about who is to benefit from it. It is a mistake to suppose that in taking a position on whether quotas should be imposed on hiring, for example, people are expressing only their attitude toward affirmative action, as though it could be abstracted from its social and historical context, and responded to as though it embodied an autonomous idea of fairness. What people think of equality of outcome can be context-dependent.

Just this is the source of both the moral strength and the moral weakness of the idea of equality of outcome, and by way of illustrating this a special experiment was conducted: the quota beneficiary experiment. The logic of the experiment is perfectly straightforward. We asked everyone the same question about affirmative action but randomly varied who was to benefit from it: the beneficiary one-half of the time was French Canadians, the other half of the time women. Specifically, everyone was asked,

"Do you think the government in Ottawa should make sure that a certain proportion of the top jobs in government go to . . . "

Figure 5.6. Quota Beneficiary Experiment: Levels of Support for French Canadians or Women

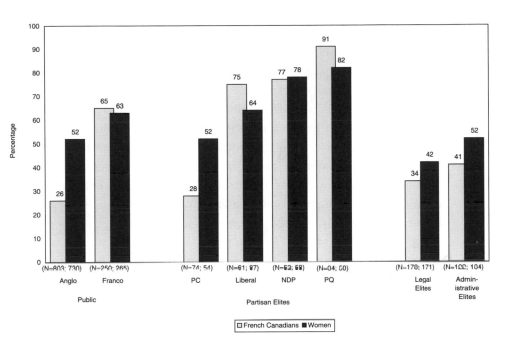

statistical significance of comparisons
anglophone public, question version: p ≤ .01; both question versions, anglophone vs. francophone public: p ≤ .01

the question being completed randomly either by "French Canadians" or by "women." The experiment focuses on government jobs at the federal level and pairs the claims of women to special treatment against those of French Canadians because the effort to open up the national government to French Quebeckers was a key element in Trudeau's vision of a new national federalism.

The differences between the willingness of English and French Canadians to support affirmative action depending on whether the beneficiaries of it are French Canadians or not are striking (fig. 5.6). English Canadians are twice as likely to support affirmative action if the beneficiaries are women rather than French Canadians: 52 percent of them favor a percentage of jobs being set aside for women; only 26 percent, for French Canadians. The reactions of French Canadians are of course rather different: a strong majority of French Canadians favor affirmative action for women—and, not surprisingly, just as strong a majority favor it for themselves.

These data apply to people who see affirmative action from the outside, who are objects of it whether as losers or winners. But it is quite different from those who make the rules for it. Consider the reactions of parliamentary elites. With the single exception of Conservatives, what stands out is their striking support for affirmative action applied to government jobs whether the beneficiaries are women or French Canadians. Perhaps not surprisingly given their concern with political cohesion, so far as there are any differences in their support for affirmative action for French Canadians or for women, it is to the advantage of the former, not the latter. By contrast, nonpartisan elites, resembling the ordinary English Canadian, stand out by virtue of their lack of support for affirmative action whoever stands to benefit from it. The result is a gap, even on this limited conception of affirmative action, between ordinary citizens and their political representatives on the legitimacy of such a policy. Political leaders can commit themselves to it, seeing their stand as evidence of their pursuit of justice, while a majority of ordinary citizens and those charged with responsibility for implementing affirmative action oppose it as unfair.

Equality of outcome embodies systematically conflicting intuitions of fairness. Applied as systematic policy, in private as well as public enterprises and on behalf of a medley of disadvantaged groups and not just women, it tends to engender conflict between groups not simply because some groups are winners and others are losers under a regime of affirmative action, but because of the competing beliefs about fairness that are inevitably implicated. The group that loses from affirmative action sees the special treatment awarded the group that wins as a violation of the norms that everyone should be treated alike and hence perceives affirmative action to be deeply unfair. But the group that benefits, believing it is entitled to the benefit, accepts the benefit as no more than their due while perceiving the resentment of other groups as proof of *their* prejudice and, just for this reason, deeply unfair. Equality of outcome thus generates a dynamic of unfairness, initially among losers, then among winners responding at least in part to the resentment of losers. The losers' feeling of unfairness is not softened by a sense of justice having been done to the winners, and the winners' feeling of unfairness is not softened by a sense of gratitude for the special benefits received from the losers. Affirmative action is thus a conception of social justice that does not win the gratitude of those it benefits even as it earns the resentment of those it offends.

A Final Word

From one angle, the most familiar one, affirmative action and equality of outcome illustrate the Americanization of Canadian politics: political arguments and schemes born out of the uniquely deep, prolonged, and miserable history of American racism brought north and applied to a different place and culture. But from another angle, affirmative action is a specific example of certain distinctive aspects of Canadian politics that have increasingly become crucial to the dynamics of liberal democratic polities around the world. What seems at first distinctive to Canada—the historic clash between French Canadian and English Canadian coupled with the recent innovation of the Charter of Rights and Freedoms—in fact exposes the emerging pattern of democratic politics at the end of the twentieth century: the use of written rules in the form of a constitution to define citizens' rights, to assure equity not simply between individuals but among groups, in order to achieve political cohesion at the level of the nation. This emerging pattern and its dynamics are the subject of the final chapters of this book.

SIX GOVERNANCE AND IDENTITY

A people's political institutions and their political identity are interknit. Some of the threads tying the two together are manifest, but more are subtle. From the common vantage point, political institutions represent not agreement on what choices should be made but agreement on how public choices are to be made; so conceived, political institutions are about means, not ends. Yet, at levels deeper than everyday politics, how a people agree that their choices as a people should be made and the values they as a people honor and defend are connected. It is this connection between governance and identity, at three different levels, that we aim to explore.

The first of the three is institutional. The deepest change in Canadian governance has been that in the balance of power between Parliament and the courts. From its founding until the adoption of the Charter of Rights, Parliament dominated the politics of Canada at both federal and provincial levels. The political party winning the last election, through its control of Parliament, had the ultimate say on the acts that government was obliged to undertake as well as on the actions citizens were entitled to undertake. No court, trial or appellate, provincial or federal, could announce to Parliament that it was obliged to foreswear a course of conduct it had chosen within its sphere of jurisdiction or that it was required to undertake a course of action it did not wish to perform.[1] The Charter of Rights has decisively changed the

balance of power between Parliament and the courts by extending the principle of judicial review: the right of the Supreme Court to scrutinize and,
where it deems appropriate, to overrule acts of Parliament. Is this new
allocation of authority to the courts over elected legislatures legitimate in
the eyes of Canadians? Do they accept this fundamental reworking of political authority? Do they even have a position as a matter of principle on the
role of the Court versus Parliament or are their allegiances to political institutions merely instrumental, a function of whichever decision rule promises
to advance their policy preferences?

The place of the Charter of Rights in the thinking of ordinary Canadians
deserves examination in its own right, and this is accordingly the second
level for exploration. The Charter, after all, is simultaneously the instrument
defining the new relations between citizens and institutions and the symbol
of these relations; its symbolic aspect is arguably as important as its narrowly
instrumental one. The Charter of Rights and Freedoms was devised not to
identify and secure specific legal understandings but to serve as the centerpiece of then–Prime Minister Trudeau's nation-building strategy. Canada,
as he saw it, was riven by regional and linguistic cleavages. The central idea
behind the Charter was to weaken these forces of cleavage within Canada
and strengthen identification with the nation as a whole by emphasizing the
rights and freedoms shared by all Canadians. The Charter thus constitutes a
legal expression of a political theory on the connections between the role of
rights and the identity of citizens in the modern democratic state. From the
perspective of the Charter, the tie that binds citizens is not a shared ethnic or
social background or a common set of cultural, social, or religious values.
Rather, it is a common set of rights, enjoyed by virtue of a shared status as
citizens and guaranteed by a Charter that symbolizes a new covenant.

The Charter of Rights and Freedoms, as envisioned by its proponents,
serves as a primary instrument for the socialization of Canadians as Canadians, instilling in them support for individual rights and in the process
binding them to each other and to the nation as a whole. The political theory
of the Charter as an instrument of national socialization represents, of
course, a bet on its impact over the long run: if the Charter does indeed
establish a shared national identity and erase narrow and divisive linguistic
and regional identities, it will do so through an extended process of political
socialization over a number of generations. But to understand where the
Charter winds up in the thinking of Canadians, it is necessary to know
where it started, the more so as there is a countertheory to the original

argument on behalf of the Charter as a nationalizing, consensus-building instrument. On the countertheory, the Charter is divisive, not solidarity producing, in its impact; divisive because partisan and ideological. From this perspective, the crux of the matter is not necessarily the content of the Charter but its manner of adoption. It was, according to the countertheory, imposed on Quebec, and its privileging of individual rights over provincial rights, especially the right of Quebec's French majority to control cultural policy in Quebec, was antithetical to Quebec's interests. Approved by the other nine provinces but not by Quebec, the Charter has by the manner of its adoption been a source of irritation and disunion. Hence the need to bring Quebec into the "new" Constitution through a series of further constitutional amendments; hence the ill-fated Meech Lake and Charlottetown accords.

Obviously, no one is yet in a position to pronounce on the ultimate consequences of the Charter of Rights, but we can provide the basis for a determination of the role of a symbolic covenant like the Charter in promoting a national political identity. First, we shall show that the balance of the findings runs against the suggestion that the Charter has been a divisive instrument, one that francophones as a whole have felt excluded from or found unwelcome. Second, and indispensable to recognizing the dynamics of a symbolic political covenant, we contrast reactions of ordinary citizens and of the politically engaged and influential. The two do not perceive or react to the Charter in the same terms. The Charter, for the politically aware and active, is a political instrument: political because its provenance was political; and their reactions to it are accordingly political in a sense and to a degree that those of the ordinary citizen are not.

The Charter itself is of course only one element of a larger program of nation-building instruments and symbols launched in the era of political nationalism initiated by Trudeau. The third and final part of our exploration of the connection between governing institutions and political identity explores this larger program, focusing on the new intersection of culture and politics.

Culture and politics have come to meet in a new way. With the rise of Canadian nationalism, it has become a commonplace that a distinctive Canadian political identity requires a distinctive Canadian cultural identity. And this, in turn, has exposed the strategic role of national mass media in nation building. Accordingly, we shall examine the beliefs of Canadians, both ordinary citizens and political and civic leaders, about the place of government regulation of radio and television programming in a liberal society like Canada.

The results we shall report are important in their own right, but we shall also say a word about the deeper pattern running through them. Put in the most straightforward terms, our results show a *consensus among ordinary Canadians*, both francophone and anglophone, on the institutions of governance; at this level, the Charter summarizes (and to a degree symbolizes) a basis for national identity and governance. In contrast, our results also show a *cleavage among political elites*. In part because it is inescapably a political act, the Charter has crystallized deeper lines of political cleavage among precisely those charged with politically representing ordinary Canadians. The contrast between citizen consensus and elite cleavage is, we believe, deeply implicated in the volatile dynamics of Canadian politics since adoption of the Charter.

Parliament and the Principle of Judicial Review: The Politics of "Override"

Constitutional politics consists in deciding how decisions are to be made. A constitution represents a form of metapolitics, summarizing agreements on how agreements are to be reached and enforced. The exceptional politics of constitutions thus bound the normal politics of public policy.

Set against the background of the American and British examples, the Charter of Rights and Freedoms offers an original strategy for the institutional management of political conflict. From a metapolitical perspective, the Charter is defined by three parameters: a constitution—written; a set of representative institutions—parliamentary; and a form of governance—federal. Paradoxically, however, the very institutional parameters designed to conciliate conflict also induce it.

It is easy to anticipate generally forms of conflict: for example, between a written constitution, which elevates the position of those who pronounce on it, the judiciary, and a parliamentary regime, which is accustomed to holding its own pronouncements as the decisions of last resort; and that between authority at the national level, whether constitutional or parliamentary in form, and authority at the level of provinces or states. But these varieties of conflict take on a unique dynamic in Canadian politics because of a crucial innovation embodied in the Charter of Rights.

The innovation is the controversial "notwithstanding" or "override" section, set out in section 33 of the Charter of Rights. Section 33 enables legislatures to ensure, either prospectively or retrospectively, that their policy goals are not frustrated by courts citing the Charter of Rights.[2] In the event that the Supreme Court strikes down a piece of legislation or in the alternative is thought likely to do so, Parliament or a provincial legislature may declare it valid notwithstanding any Court decision against it. This assertion (or reassertion) of validity is in one aspect unconditional, in another not. The law retains all of its standing as an enforceable law, but only for a period of five years: after five years, it must once again be reasserted by the Parliament notwithstanding any judicial decision, or its legitimacy is again open to Court challenge.

The root issue is, Who shall have the final word: the courts, in their role as ultimate authorities on the Charter, or the parliaments, in their role as ultimate representatives of the public? Historically, liberal democracies have given two quite different answers. Regimes following the American model have invested final decision-making power in courts; regimes following the English model have put it in Parliament. What distinguishes the Canadian regime is its deliberate effort to forestall an authoritative answer to the question of who shall have the final word. The Canadian political order invests final institutional power *simultaneously* in the courts, above all the Supreme Court, and in parliaments, both federal and provincial.

From its conception, section 33 has been the subject of debate. To some, it was thought to be incompatible with the very notion of legal guarantees of fundamental rights. And they were accordingly concerned that it might be too often used by legislatures seeking to advance their political agendas at the expense of the rights of Canadians. To others, the override or notwithstanding clause represented a reasonable balance between courts and legislatures in deciding the appropriate bounds of basic rights and freedoms. On this view, parliaments were thought unlikely frequently to override the Charter or to set aside a formal decision of the Supreme Court of Canada.[3]

Subsequent events have done nothing to reduce the controversy over section 33. Then–Prime Minister Brian Mulroney, for example, became sharply critical of section 33's inclusion in the Charter, and former prime minister Trudeau has singled out section 33 as an Achilles heel in the Charter of Rights. On Trudeau's account, when the Supreme Court ruled, in the Constitutional Amendment Reference,[4] that repatriation of the Constitution required substantial assent from the provinces, the override provision quickly became the price demanded by the provinces in exchange for having the Charter apply to both levels of government. Trudeau reluctantly paid that price but only after wringing one further compromise from the provinces. The agreement was to insulate the core rights in Trudeau's constitutional vision, the Charter's language and mobility rights, from the reach of the legislative override. The Charter in its final form, then, and most specifically with the inclusion of section 33, represented an ingenious compromise between two sharply conflicting visions of governance.

How effective was the compromise? As subsequent events have shown, the inclusion of section 33 has placed into the hands of the provincial legislatures a substantial constitutional instrument to counterbalance the nationalizing influence of the powers given to courts under the Charter. The result has been something of a stalemate on questions of both governance and identity.

The National Assembly of Quebec was the first legislature to avail itself of section 33, and it did so almost immediately. Under the leadership of René Lévesque, whose Parti Québécois at that time enjoyed a substantial legislative majority in Quebec, the National Assembly passed Bill 62, which provided for a blanket application of the override to every new and existing Quebec statute. This admittedly symbolic preemptive use of the notwithstanding clause nevertheless had the political effect of seriously questioning the legitimacy of the Charter in Quebec. And thus the override went from a provision that was expected to be used rarely or not at all, and then only with respect to specific pieces of legislation, to one applied *tout court*, with the Quebec legislature invoking section 33 to exempt all of its legislation from judicial review across the board.

Even though the actions of Quebec's National Assembly were ultimately ruled proper by the Supreme Court of Canada,[5] the days of Quebec's ubiquitous override were put to an abrupt end by politics within the province of Quebec. The provincial Liberals in Quebec came to power under Robert Bourassa by defeating the PQ in the provincial election of 1985. Bourassa promptly put an end to Quebec's blanket use of the override. But with an irony not uncharacteristic of the politics of identity, what was given in one political act was taken back in another. The very same party and leader who stopped the blanket use of section 33 soon thereafter provided Canadians with perhaps the most (in)famous instance in which section 33 has been invoked to date. At the end of 1988, after the Supreme Court of Canada struck down the "French only" public sign law provisions of the previous government's Bill 101 as violating the Charter's guarantee of freedom of expression, the Quebec Liberal government made use of the notwithstanding clause once again. This time it was to override the Court's ruling and reinstate a version of the sign laws. Although pleasing many in Quebec, this use of section 33 angered many English-speaking Canadians across the country, straining anew relations between Quebec and the rest of Canada and ultimately contributing to the failure of the Meech Lake constitutional accord.[6]

Section 33 has not been used only to promote the linguistic agenda of successive Quebec governments. Grant Devine's Conservative government in Saskatchewan used the override provision in 1986. Concerned that legislation ordering striking provincial employees back to work might be challenged in court under the Charter's freedom of association provisions, the Conservatives resorted to the section 33 notwithstanding provision to protect its back-to-work legislation against court challenge. Although this action was greeted in some quarters with hoots of derision for both the legislation and section 33, the government's use of section 33 to protect its legislative agenda was both legal and appropriate within the context of post-Charter politics in Canada. Even so, governments outside of Quebec have not been quick to embrace this constitutional device.

The lesson to draw from these events, we are persuaded, is that an account of the override provision must proceed from a quite particular perspective. It is not sufficient merely to determine what citizens think of section 33 taken by itself. It is not that citizens are likely to be bereft of opinions about the override provision in the abstract, not even that their opinions about it would be hollow if they were asked about it in the abstract. The crux of the override provision—whether a parliament or a court should have the last word—can readily be grasped and is likely to be taken as serious, certainly the more seriously people take politics. But the lesson that experience has taught is that what counts is not people's views of constitutional principles in isolation but their responses to the use of constitutional arguments embedded in political arguments.

Our aim is to work through a political theory of constitutional rights, and the proper point of departure, therefore, is to recognize that people may have more than one opinion about the override provision, depending on how it cuts politically on any given occasion. How can one get a grip on the *politics* of the override provision? How can one determine people's reactions to section 33, not in the abstract, but when they are caught up in political clashes? The standard approach is to present respondents with a series of parallel questions, beginning with one about their opinion on the issue of override in the abstract and following with questions on the validity of the override provision in specific circumstances. If the standard strategy has the advantage of being obvious, it has the debilitating disadvantage of obvious-ness: respondents can easily see that the point is to assess their consistency, and, given that people prefer to project an impression of themselves as being consistent, other things equal, they can readily adjust their responses ac-cordingly. To accomplish the objective of assessing people's opinions about the override *in a variety of political contexts*—and without their being aware of this—the principle-policy experiment was carried out.

The principle-policy experiment is designed to assess support for the override provision both in the abstract and in the context of clashes over specific policies—indeed, for the purpose of realism, policies taken from opposing ends of the ideological spectrum, and for purposes of reference, also in one situation in which no legislative goal is supplied. Thus, the issue of override appears in three different guises; but instead of soliciting from each subject responses to all three versions (and thus risking contamination of responses), we administered each version randomly to one-third of the respondents.[7] Because the assignment of question versions is made ran-domly, each third of a representative sample is itself representative. The three versions were as follows:

"When the legislature passes a law . . .
[version A] [no context given]
[version B] for example to control unions
[version C] for example to assist poor people"

Then, the question carried on the same for everyone:

"but the courts say it is unconstitutional on the grounds that it conflicts with the Charter of Rights, who should have the final say, the legislature or the courts?
— Legislatures should have the final say.
— Courts should have the final say."

In the clash between parliaments and courts as the ultimate sources of sovereignty when the issue is put in the abstract, that is, not put in the context of a specific legislative objective, Canadians taken as a whole prefer that courts should have the final say (fig. 6.1A). Indeed, considering how recently the principle of judicial review had been installed, the margin of

Figure 6.1 A. Principle-Policy Experiment, Version A: *"When the legislature passes a law but the courts say it is unconstitutional on the grounds that it conflicts with the Charter of Rights, who should have the final say, the legislature or the courts?"*

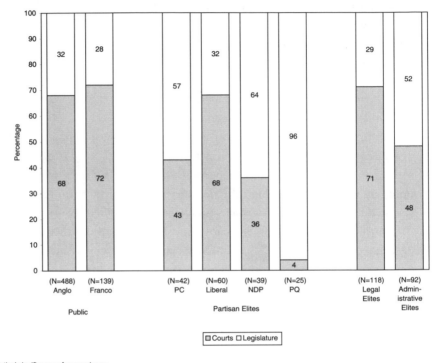

statistical significance of comparisons
public as a whole vs. elites as a whole: p ≤ .01; political elites by party: p ≤ .01

public support in its favor is lopsided: in the public as a whole, Canadians prefer courts rather than parliaments to have the final say by a margin of two to one. What is more, francophones are just as likely as anglophones to support the principle of judicial review (fig. 6.1A), a striking result set against the conventional wisdom that French Canadians see their protection as bound up with the supremacy, or at any rate the autonomy, of the Quebec legislature.

The principle-policy experiment, as noted, is designed to compare citizens' reactions to constitutional principles when taken in the abstract and when embedded in concrete political clashes. Contrasting the reactions of francophones and anglophones at the levels of principle and policy reveals an interesting pattern. On the one side, how the issue of judicial review is framed makes no difference (or next to no difference) to anglophones: a

Figure 6.1 B. Principle-Policy Experiment, Version B: *"When the legislature passes a law, for example, to control unions . . ."*

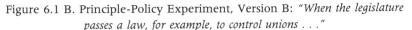

Figure 6.1 B. Principle-Policy Experiment, Version B: "When the legislature passes a law, for example, to control unions . . ."

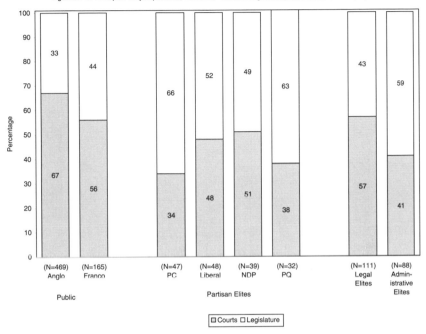

statistical significance of comparisons
public vs. elites: p ≤ .01; political elites by party: not significant

clear majority of them favor the courts having the final say whether the issue is framed in the abstract or embedded in concrete conflict (fig. 6.1B, C). On the other side, when the supremacy of courts over parliament is confronted in a specific case, francophone support for judicial review noticeably slides: rather than an overwhelming majority favoring the supremacy of the courts, as is the case when the issue is put in the abstract, only a bare majority of francophones supports judicial review in the case of a law intended to control unions, and just under a majority favor it in the case of a law intended to help the poor (fig. 6.1B, C).

Without wishing to make too much of this difference—the number of respondents, particularly on the francophone side, tends to be small, hence the estimates tend to be erratic—we do believe that these results suggest a larger lesson in understanding public opinion and the dynamics of politics. Typically, citizens come to deliver a judgment on large principles in politics not in isolation, but only as they confront principles embedded in the details of particular cases. So far as the objective is to understand the dynamics of

Figure 6.1 C. Principle-Policy Experiment, Version C: *"When the legislature passes a law, for example, to assist poor people . . ."*

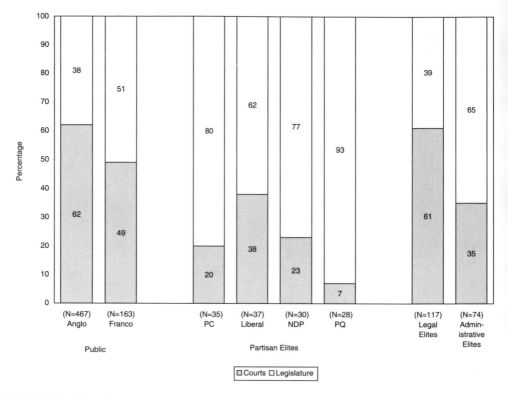

statistical significance of comparisons
public vs. elites: p ≤ .01; political elites by party: p ≤ .05

actual political behavior, the focus must be on responses not to abstract principles but to concrete clashes: not because citizens do not comprehend or care about political principles, but because the logic of political choice requires them to pick from a predetermined menu of alternatives defined by the details of specific conflicts.

The same holds for political elites—except more so. Political elites, by virtue of their political convictions and their political ambitions, understand that constitutional issues do not lie on a separate plane unconnected to actual controversies but are, inescapably and centrally, political issues holding out benefits to some and penalties to others depending on how they are decided. And political elites understand that what gets decided hangs on who gets to decide. Notice the way that political elites, who are, after all, themselves parliamentarians (with one exception, namely, Liberals, which is telling in itself since the Charter is a product of the Liberal party), are far more likely than the average Canadian to believe that parliament should have the final say. Members of the PQ, consistent with their desire to protect Quebec's autonomy, almost unanimously favor parliamentary sovereignty, while a clear majority of both Conservatives and New Democrats, notwith-standing the sharp ideological differences between them, also support it. But the reactions of political elites can hinge on the political complexion of the issue being contested. Thus, the NDP is even more likely to favor parliamen-tary supremacy in the case of a law intended to help the poor (fig. 6.1C), yet more ambivalent in the case of a law intended to control unions (fig. 6.1B). This could be because there are times when it pays for a party to have or to be perceived to have its hands tied[8] or, alternatively, because the memory of the Saskatchewan Conservatives' back-to-work legislation was still fresh in the minds of the New Democrats who have strong ties to labor. Correspond-ingly, as against their views in the abstract, the Conservatives are more likely to favor parliament having the last word in the case of a law intended to control unions, and still more so in the case of a law intended to help the poor.

The reactions of political elites cannot be reduced to a single factor. But their responses reflect a sensitivity to political context. And this is as true for Liberals as for the others. When the principles of parliamentary supremacy and judicial review clash in the abstract, approximately two in every three of them believe that the courts should have the final say. This is not surprising considering that the political sponsor of the Charter of Rights, which re-placed the principle of parliamentary sovereignty with that of judicial re-view, was the Liberal Party under the leadership of Pierre Trudeau. And it was, of course, the provincial Liberals in Quebec that put an end to the PQ's blanket use of the override. On the other hand, when the constitutional principle is embedded in a concrete controversy such as controlling unions, Liberals tend to split more or less evenly between legislatures and courts having the final say in the case of a law to control unions, and even wind up favoring parliamentary supremacy in the case of a law to help the poor. Again, the reactions of political elites cannot be reduced to a single factor, but the balance they want to strike between the claims of legislatures as the privileged institution of popular representation and those of courts as the interpreters of basic rights under the Charter, these results suggest, can hinge on their views not simply of institutions in the abstract but also of the political objectives that may be realized and the strategic choices that need to be confronted.

The Charter as Political Instrument and Symbol

The Charter of Rights sets the context of constitutional politics, privileging courts at the expense of legislatures (Russell 1983). But the Charter is at the same time part of normal politics, and the positioning of some of the principal political actors, and especially the political parties, is bound up with the unfolding of Charter politics. The Charter is thus text and context.

Reactions of Canadians to the Charter at its inception afford not only a view of the politics of national identity, but also more fundamentally a perspective on the vicissitudes of constitutional politics. The tangle of Canadian constitutional politics leading up to and following the collapse of the Meech Lake and Charlottetown accords presents itself as a text to those who would preach a sermon on constitutional politics. And one of the principal sermons preached, notably by proponents of Meech Lake and Charlottetown, concerns the politics of esteem. In this view, not the Charter of Rights but the manner of its adoption, at the insistence of the central government and without the concurrence of the Quebec government, was an insult to Quebec. Technically, of course, Quebec was covered by the Charter. In the Quebec Veto Reference, the Supreme Court had called for only substantial agreement, hence the assent of the nine other provinces was sufficient to include Quebec.[9] Nevertheless, Quebec's National Assembly symbolically signaled that it did not accept the Charter by invoking the blanket override (see above). Negative feelings in Quebec, at some level, over the Charter and other features of the 1982 constitutional changes, such as the new amending formula, which did not give Quebec its historic veto, led the federal government to begin efforts to bring Quebec "back into the constitution."

Quebeckers, on this view, may not have been up in arms protesting the Charter of Rights. Privately, however, they found it an indignity not to have given their consent to a constitutional document whose fundamental purpose, after all, is to express a consensus; a humiliation that eventually and predictably they would protest and attempt to reverse. Hence the importance of conciliation, of drawing Quebec explicitly and freely into the Charter; hence the necessity of the efforts culminating in the Meech Lake and Charlottetown agreements.

Partisan advantage aside, this sermon on the politics of esteem has plausibility. It is easy to imagine the bruised feelings that may have been occasioned by a seemingly arbitrary and coercive imposition of a constitutional order, however fair or even appealing the actual provisions of that order. But surface plausibility aside, is it true? Were French Canadians wounded by adoption of the Charter of Rights? Did they see it as being imposed on them and against them? It is important to gauge the feelings of English and French Canadians about whether the adoption of the Charter of Rights was, taking all things into account, a good or a bad thing for Canada. The question, then, is the role of the Charter as a political symbol. Has it been a unifying symbol, drawing French and English Canadians together in agreement, or a divisive one?

To gauge the feelings of Canadians about the Charter, we followed a two-step strategy. We first took the precaution of asking respondents whether they had heard of the Canadian Charter of Rights or not. Only if they had heard of it did we ask them whether they think the Charter is a (very good or just somewhat good) thing or a (very bad or just somewhat bad) thing for Canada—the precaution turned out to pay an unexpected dividend.[10]

Consider first rank-and-file Canadians (fig. 6.2). Anglophones and francophones alike are overwhelmingly positive in their views of the Charter of Rights. Specifically, 72 percent of anglophones and 62 percent of francophones think the Charter is a good thing for Canada; conversely, only 1 percent of francophones and 6 percent of anglophones think it is a bad thing. In fact, attitudes toward the Charter are remarkably consistent across all the regions of Canada (data not shown), and Quebec is no exception to this national pattern of consensus.[11] There is no evidence of negative reactions to the Charter on the part of any significant number of ordinary Canadians, whether in Quebec or anywhere else in Canada.

In this sense, consensus on the Charter was achieved virtually from the outset. But the results require closer scrutiny. What people do *not* say can count for every bit as much as what they do say. That is why, in figure 6.2, we detail not only the proportions of Canadians who say that the Charter is either a good or a bad thing for Canada, but also the proportion who say that they have not heard of it. The contrast between French and English Canadians is striking. Francophones are far more likely to say they have never heard of the Charter than are anglophones: 31 percent compared to only 11 percent.This one difference should not be overinterpreted because it may reflect not disengagement on the part of the francophone public but simply

Figure 6.2. Attitude and Knowledge Regarding the Charter

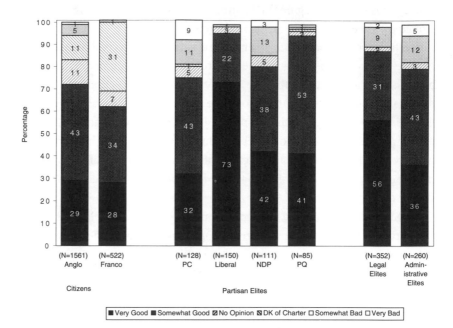

statistical significance of comparisons
anglophone vs. francophone public: p ≤ .01; public as a whole vs. elites as a whole: p ≤ .01; political elites by party: p ≤ .01

the thinner French media coverage of federal constitutional developments.[12] But it should not be overlooked either because it points to a potential for disengagement on the part of French Canadians notwithstanding the
high rates of approval of the charter at the outset among francophones who
had heard of it.

Elite responses toward the Charter are even more positive than those of
the public at large. Overwhelming proportions—84 percent of legislative
elites, 87 percent of legal elites, and 79 percent of bureaucratic elites—rate it
as good or better. Moreover, unpacking legislative elites and examining
them by party further strengthens this picture of the Charter of Rights as a
consensual, not a divisive, political symbol, although it additionally calls
attention to several more specific features of this consensus. The first of these
concerns the distinctive reaction of Liberals. Even against the background of
the highly positive endorsement of elites in general the response of Liberals
stands out. Seeing themselves as the party of the Charter, they are by far its

most enthusiastic supporters. Almost 75 percent of Liberal legislators regard it as a very good thing, and nearly all of the rest of them say it is a good thing. On the other hand, the responses of Progressive Conservatives supply a mirror image expression of the element of strategic electoral competition. Three in every four of them judge the Charter to be a good thing, but a nontrivial fraction, nearly 20 percent, see the Charter as bad or very bad for Canada. This minority, like that in the NDP who similarly see the Charter in a negative light, tend to be members of legislative assemblies from the West. So far as there is a cleavage at all over the Charter, the results in figure 6.2 suggest, it runs between ordinary citizen and elites, whether legislative, legal, or administrative. Elites respond more positively to the Charter than does the public at large, and, still more tellingly, only among the public as a whole, whether anglophone or francophone, are there substantial numbers who have failed to form an attitude and evaluation of the Charter. Finally, and perhaps most important to imprint on the historical record, is the strikingly positive response to the Charter of the PQ: 93 percent say that the Charter is a good thing for Canada, and nearly one-half of them say it is a very good thing. In sum, none of these results give grounds for the now commonly made contention that the Charter, at its inception, was unwelcome in either Quebec or Canada as a whole among the public as a whole or among political activists or even among separatists.[13]

These responses to the Charter, however, are at the level of emotion, of positive feeling toward it. On the plane of beliefs and ideas, the picture of elite consensus and popular reservation changes subtly but significantly. The positive feelings of elites toward the Charter do not, as we shall see, proceed from an agreed theory or understanding of it. On the contrary, elites are deeply divided over some of the most fundamental political consequences of the Charter; and the longer-run dynamics of the Charter as a political symbol cannot help but reflect this absence of an anchoring political theory among elites.

In speaking of political theories of the Charter—even in the case of political elites—we do not mean assemblages of abstract propositions but rather the commonsense intuitions an ordinary person may form about the likely political consequences of adoption of the Charter of Rights. Political theories of the Charter, so understood, have more to do with the way in which the Charter was promoted and criticized than with direct experience or detailed knowledge of it. When the Charter of Rights and Freedoms was proposed, the ensuing debate evoked a train of arguments pro and con, arguments expressing radically different views of Canada. The Charter's proponents, led by Trudeau, envisioned Canada as essentially an association of individuals, each possessing certain basic rights and freedoms. Trudeau, who entered national politics primarily to combat separatist sentiment in Quebec, favored the idea of a common identity for all Canadians as rights-bearing citizens. He argued that a Charter of Rights, applied to both federal and provincial levels of government, might go a long way toward lessening the divisions between francophone Quebec and the rest of Canada. Hence, the Charter, the centerpiece of his nation-building vision, would have a unifying effect on a country beset by conflicting regional identities.

The emphasis on the commonality of individuals throughout Canada as rights-bearing citizens was seen by opponents of the Charter as a threat to the powers of the provincial governments, both in and out of Quebec. Canada, in their eyes, represented an association of provinces; and the nationalizing, centralizing thrust of the Charter threatened the power of the provinces to define public policy as they saw fit within their own boundaries. This led Peter Lougheed, then premier of Alberta, to argue that "the basic unit of federalism is not the individual citizen but the province." Beginning with this premise, Lougheed and others like him argued that the Charter's focus on individual rights that were enforceable in the courts would ultimately weaken the power of the provinces to pursue their own legislative agendas and thus undercut provincial identities.

Constitutional debates are less often about whether to affirm principles than about how much weight to give them. Federalism as a political principle was agreed to by both proponents and opponents of the Charter. What divided them was the balance that ought to be struck between national institutions and identities and provincial (or regional) institutions and identities. From this perspective, the public debate over the Charter came to center on a pair of companion questions: Will the Charter strengthen Canada as a national unit or will it weaken, even threaten, the provinces?

How did the Canadians as a whole see the Charter? Did they see it, consistent with the ambitions of its proponents, as a centralizing instrument, as a device for increasing national solidarity? Did they, consistent with the fears of many of its opponents, perceive it as a threat to the standing of the provinces?

By way of exploring the extent to which Canadians share an understanding of how the Charter will work as a political instrument, and particularly how it may affect the balance between national and political institutions, we asked a (random) half of the sample,[14] "Do you think the Charter of Rights will strengthen Canadian national identity?" To take cognizance of the flavor of their views, rather than simply recording whether respondents answered yes or no, interviewers also took note of whether respondents answered unconditionally in the affirmative or negative or attached a qualification, restriction, or stipulation to their response.

To what extent was the Charter seen, if not by English, at any rate by French Canadians, as a weapon designed to impose a national, supraprovincial identity upon them? To those who take public discussion of constitutional politics as a mirror of the private concerns of individual citizens, it will seem a near certainty that French Canadians, even if they feel positively toward the Charter (as we have seen that they do), will nonetheless harbor reservations about its possible adverse impact. But francophones are just as likely to see the Charter as an instrument of national identity, and as likely as anglophones to do so without qualification (fig. 6.3A). In all, 66 percent of anglophones and 70 percent of francophones believe that the Charter of Rights will strengthen the Canadian national identity. No signs of covert francophone opposition to the Charter are evident here: the perceptions of anglophones and francophones are identical. And, equally important, perceptions of the nationalizing influence of the Charter are markedly associated (Cramer's V = .281) with support for the Charter in both linguistic groupings.

But if the distinctive feature of the responses of ordinary citizens is the absence of disagreement between anglophone and francophone over the political impact of the Charter, it is precisely the presence of disagreement that is the conspicuous feature of the responses of political elites. Among those who are most directly responsible for operating the institutions of politics, whether legislative, administrative, or legal there is simply no agreed-on sense about how adoption of the Charter will affect the institutional landscape.

The reactions of the NDP and the PQ divide virtually evenly in judging the impact of the Charter. One in every two believes that the Charter will strengthen Canadian national identity. Legal elites are also evenly split, while the balance of opinion among administrative elites is still more skeptical that the Charter will achieve its primary purpose, to strengthen a common identity of Canadians as Canadians. So, too, are Progressive Conservatives, although the mood of Liberals, not surprisingly, is even more optimistic than that of Conservatives is skeptical. The point, however, is not

Figure 6.3 A. *"Do you think the Charter of Rights will strengthen Canadian national identity?"*

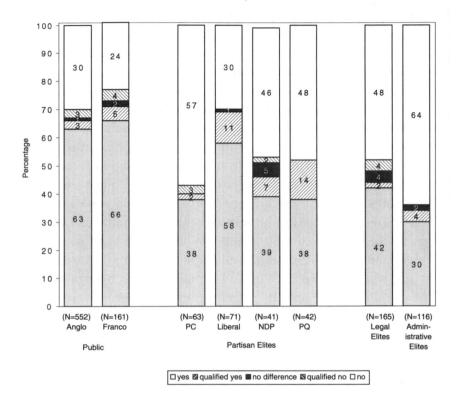

statistical significance of comparisons
political elites by party: p ≤ .05; elite groups by sector: p ≤ .01

that elites are predominantly optimistic or skeptical about the impact of the Charter but rather that they are not predominantly one or the other. They are divided. They do not show evidence of having participated in a thoroughgoing discussion and reached a consensus on the probable consequences of the patriation of a national constitution—including the fundamental issue of whether it will or will not strengthen a national identity.

At least as consequential as whether the Charter will strengthen national identity is the question of whether it will weaken the power of provinces. The two questions, though connected, are logically separable. One can maintain, without contradiction, both that the Charter will strengthen the symbolic ties of unity and identity binding all Canadians and that the provinces will not lose in the future whatever measure of political autonomy

Figure 6.3 B. *"Do you think the Charter of Rights will weaken the power of the provinces?"*

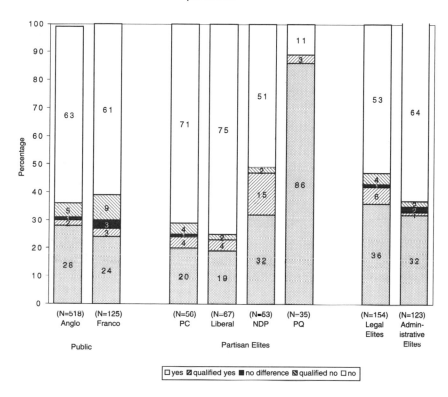

statistical significance of comparisons
political elites by party: p ≤ .01

they enjoy at present. Indeed, it would not be impossible to hold that the essential goal of the Charter of Rights, to strengthen the national identity of Canadians, so far from being weakened by federalism, will be strengthened through the assurance of substantial provincial autonomy under the aegis of the Charter itself.

To find out the bets Canadians are prepared to make on this second dimension of the Charter's future impact, the other half of the sample was asked, "Do you think the Charter of Rights will weaken the power of the provinces?" The responses further illustrate the absence of apprehension or resentment over the adoption of the Charter on the part of the *public* at large (fig. 6.3B). Indeed, most Canadians are optimistic as to both issues of national identity and provincial autonomy. A clear majority of them thus believe that the Charter will strengthen Canadians' national identity *and* that it will not weaken the power of the provinces. Moreover, the French Canadian public is just as likely to take this sanguine position as anglophones, illustrating again the absence of distinctive disaffection, resentment, or even apprehension at the outset of Charter politics on the part of francophones as a whole. The opposite side of the coin, however, can be seen in the replies of the NDP and, still more vividly, of course, in those of the PQ. Thus, close to one in every two in the NDP and nearly nine in every ten in the PQ believe that the Charter of Rights will weaken the power of the provinces. The PQ activists we interviewed were, of course, drawn from much the same group that had formed the government in Quebec in 1982 and the same party that had been shut out of the Constitution at that time; the unanimity of their concern over the Charter undercutting provincial power is impressive.[15]

The full set of results in figure 6.3 raises a basic question about the metapolitics of the Charter of Rights: How far had Canadians arrived at an idea, a common sense, of the likely consequences of the adoption of the Charter— and this quite apart from whether they proved to be right or wrong in hindsight?

Responding in the abstract, one surely would expect political elites to be markedly more likely than ordinary citizens to reach an agreed-on view of the impact of the Charter. After all, political elites distinguish themselves by the amount of time they spend on questions of public affairs and by the effort they expend on reaching an understanding of the most probable consequences of a course of public action. But reviewing the results of figure 6.3, we are struck by the range of views that political elites in particular held about the probable impact of the Charter at its adoption. The adoption of the Charter represents an experiment in politics in Canada on the grand scale; an experiment that can transform the politics of Canada. But these results suggest that the experiment of the Charter was not preceded by agreement among elites on the most probable political consequences of this experiment, not even agreement on the broadest calculations of whether it would strengthen or weaken Canadians' sense of themselves as distinctively Canadian or whether it would give a constitutional protection to or radically undercut the fundamental dynamic of Canadian politics, namely, the competition between the claims of central and of provincial governments.

It makes little sense to tax ordinary citizens for their failure to work fully through a set of expectations about the gains and risks of adopting the Charter of Rights and come to a full consensus. But it surely is not out of place to expect that political elites, those formally charged with responsibility for changing the Constitution, would work through a common set of expectations as to its most likely consequences. But it is just this—common expectations, whether right or wrong—that seems to be lacking among elites, and not merely about concerns that are arcane or remote but about those at the center of the constitutional discussion that preceded adoption of the Charter. The point, of course, is not that there was no discussion by the politically active and influential over the impact of the Charter on Canadian politics (on the contrary, there was no lack of it) but that this discussion never reached anything like the degree of agreement prerequisite to launching a country on a radically new constitutional trajectory. And inscribed in this lack of elite agreement are the very areas and instruments of contention that plague Canada's constitutional developments to this day: continuing conflicts among elites over identity and power, fought even now to the point of stalemate with the tools given to them in the Charter, judicial review and legislative override.

The Autonomy of Culture

Increasingly, a part of the dynamics of the normal politics of liberal democracies has come to include an indeterminacy about the nature of politics itself. The metaconstitutional politics of national identity overlaps and shapes everyday politics. But how far and in what ways do the two overlap and interact?

Politics deals with what is public, not what is private, and so, paradoxically, one way to see the overlap of metapolitics and normal politics is to explore the boundary between public and private. Arguments over the lines that should be drawn—or redrawn—between public and private are part of the stuff of regular politics: but in liberal democracies a new attention to issues of national identity has led to a renegotiation of the boundary between public and private. The demands of identity run deep. And they involve, inevitably, consideration and reconsideration of the reach of politics. In the nineteenth century, the crucial arguments over the border between public and private took place between politics and economics. In the twentieth century, they have increasingly taken place between politics and culture.

Why has the border between politics and culture become so strategic? The fundamental dynamic has to do with national pride and identity, in-

deed, identity as a basis of pride; and this dynamic has been transformed by
the development of transnational mass media. Thanks to these media, the
United States threatens to become a hegemonic culture, and many countries, Canada among them, see themselves as being under pressure to protect their culture from the domination of American culture. John Meisel, an
eminent political scientist and former commissioner of the Canadian Radio,
Television and Telecommunications Commission (CRTC) has stated the common Canadian perception in these terms:

> The greatest threat to Canada lies in the possibility (some might even say
> "probability") that, as a result of the strong presence of American influ-
> ences, our cultural development may be stunted. As I have suggested, U.S.
> styles, ideas and products are never far away. There is, alas, a well-
> grounded fear that as a consequence, our perceptions, values, ideas and
> priorities will become so dominated by those of our neighbors that the
> distinctiveness of Canada will, to all intents and purposes, vanish. The
> danger is greater with respect to anglophones than francophones, but
> even the latter have cause for alarm. (249)[16]

In responding to these concerns, the CRTC, working with the Broadcast
Act, has for more than twenty years set quotas requiring Canadian broadcas-
ters to present Canadian programming for a substantial portion of both their
daily and prime-time evening schedules.[17]

The use of the state, whether for the positive objective of promoting an
indigenous culture or for the negative objective of forestalling an exogenous
one, raises deep issues for a liberal democratic state. For it puts the state in
the business of determining what can and cannot be shown or printed. And
this is doubly consequential, entailing a rethinking not only of where the
boundary between public and private is to be drawn but also of where
responsibility for drawing it is to be lodged.

To explore the legitimacy of the politics of identity, we shall focus on the
use of content regulations in Canadian broadcasting. Specifically, we asked,

> "In order to protect Canadian culture should the government ensure that
> a certain percentage of the programming on television and radio be Ca-
> nadian?
> —Yes, the government should set a certain percentage
> —No, the government should not set a certain percentage."

Consider the opinions of the ordinary Canadian. In politics, the absence
of differences can count for as much as their presence; and, with an eye to
the cleavage that historically has defined Canadian politics, it is worth re-

Figure 6.4. Support for Canadian Content Quotas for Television and Radio

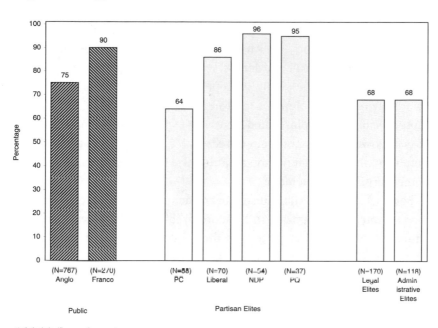

statistical significance of comparisons
political elites by party: p ≤ .01; elite groups by sector: p ≤ .01

marking that French Canadians support media regulation in order to protect *Canadian* culture. Three in every four anglophones believe that it is right and proper for the government to fix a percentage of Canadian content to be seen and heard on television or radio—and, as it happens, francophones are even more likely to concur (fig. 6.4; "Percentage Agreeing" represents those answering in the affirmative). The extension of the role of the state to determine what may be shown as part of an effort to protect the autonomy of a culture is not, the results in figure 6.4 suggest, controversial among the Canadian public. Lopsided majorities among both anglophones and francophones support content regulations for radio and television.

It is perhaps unreasonable to expect ordinary citizens to be sensitive to the vicissitudes of negotiating a border between the public and the private in the modern liberal state. The issue may appear straightforward to them, a matter of ensuring that a public good, the protection of national identity, is accomplished. Surely it cannot be wrong that Canadians should view movies and read books by Canadians; surely it is proper that a certain amount of "Canadian content" in the media is assured; no one, after all, is dictating what particular movies, plays, or books should be commissioned, only what *percentage* done by Canadians should be shown or printed. Such a position has weight. Yet, to the person who has had a deeper experience of government and politics, who has had a more direct appreciation of the vicissitudes of power in liberal democracies the issue ought not to appear so one-sided. Many of the politically sophisticated and active will doubtless favor state regulation of media to protect Canadian "culture." But just because the politically sophisticated have been exposed to the temptations and risks of power, it does not seem unreasonable to expect that a substantial number of them, even if not the majority, will find government regulation of media content problematic.

Some evidence that the issue of government regulation of television and media content is recognized to be more problematic by elites appears in figure 6.4, but the larger pattern of the results teaches a different lesson about the politics of culture. Consider first the views of administrative and legal elites. A clear majority of them favors government regulation but a distinct minority, approximately one in every three, dissents. In contrast, the response of partisan elites, setting aside only Conservatives, is impressive: they are even more one-sidedly in favor of government setting of content regulations than ordinary citizens and in fact are practically unanimous in their support. ,The only legislative party divided internally is the Conservatives, and even a clear majority of them favors quotas to protect culture. Given the depth and breadth of this consensus, it is not surprising that legislative debate over content regulations in discussions of the Broadcast Act featured cross-party agreements, with debate consisting chiefly of Liberal and New Democratic critics urging the then-governing Conservatives to take quotas somewhat further than they had perhaps originally intended. The politics of culture is thus defined by the politics of elite consensus.

What is to be made of this consensus among partisan elites? Why does it occur here and not on the constitutional field? Manifestly, a powerful force is operating to induce Canadians to favor explicit government controls in the name of national or cultural identity; a force that is still more powerful among the politically active and influential. But what is this force? Why are so many Canadians persuaded of the necessity of positive government action to maintain Canadian identity in and through the mass media?

Two alternatives suggest themselves. Support for Canadian content regulations may arise out of a *positive* desire to protect or promote Canadian (or

French Canadian) culture; or it may arise out of a *negative* desire to resist or oppose American culture. It is, of course, quite impossible to estimate the actual weight of the two forces merely by relying on public pronouncements, even pronouncements that candidly acknowledge the possibility that a desire to reject American influence may count as well as a desire to promote Canadian culture. Meisel gave a classic expression to this mixture of sentiments in an essay reflecting upon Canadian broadcasting and the necessity for content regulations: "American popular culture, and particularly, television, are thus an immense Trojan horse enabling foreign concerns and priorities to infiltrate our very minds and beings. Lest the martial metaphor of the Trojan horse give rise to a misunderstanding, I hasten to add that the nationalist, pro-Canadian stance espoused here in no way reflects an anti-American sentiment" (252–53).

Is it true that the negative element Meisel refers to plays no central role in the views of ordinary Canadians on media content regulations? Are Canadians persuaded that government must regulate what may be shown out of a desire to celebrate and conserve the culture and institutions of Canada? Or are the dynamics of political identity adversarial? Do they reflect, at bottom, not a desire of Canadians to preserve their culture so much as to reject and fend off another?

By way of beginning we need to survey Canadians' sentiments, first about Canada, then about the United States. To assess the extent of national identification with Canada among our respondents, we took advantage of two statements (contained in the mailback portion of the study), which ran as follows:

"We must ensure an independent Canada even if that were to mean a lower standard of living for Canadians."

and

"People in the various provinces should put less emphasis on their regional identities and more emphasis on their Canadian identity."

The two statements touch upon somewhat different aspects of national identity; hence, the responses they evoke, though much alike in broad outline, reveal interesting differences in the fine strokes, not least among the legislative elites. Looking first at the willingness to pay a price in order to maintain Canadian independence (figure 6.5A), we find majorities everywhere, among both the general population and elites, in favor of maintaining Canadian independence, even were this to mean lowering living stan-

Figure 6.5 A. *"We must ensure an independent Canada even if that were to mean a lower standard of living."*

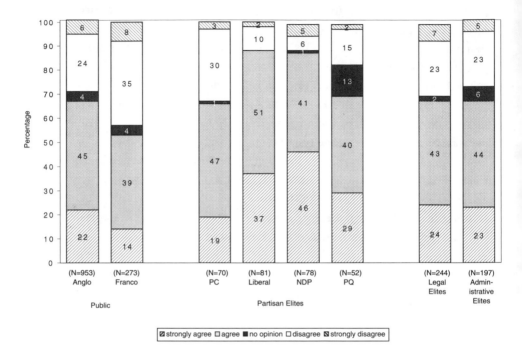

strongly agree ☐ agree ■ no opinion ☐ disagree ◨ strongly disagree

statistical significance of comparisons
anglophone vs. francophone public: p ≤ .05; political elites by party p ≤ .01; elite groups by sector: p ≤ .01

dards. Several differences in emphasis are notable, however. Among the public at large, anglophones are more likely to agree on the importance of ensuring an independent Canada and more likely to feel strongly about it than francophones, although the differences between the two on either point should not be exaggerated. Among decision makers, the Liberals and the NDP stand out as most favoring independence, while legal and administrative elites (along with Progressive Conservatives) tend to be less nationalistic, although a clear majority favor independence. Now looking at responses to emphasizing the national rather than the regional identities of Canadians (figure 6.5B), we again see strong majorities in favor of national rather than regional identification—with a single exception: the legislative elite for the PQ. As an avowedly separatist party based in Quebec, the PQ strongly disagrees (by three to one) with the idea that there should be more

Figure 6.5 B. *"People in the various provinces should put less emphasis on their regional identities and more emphasis on their Canadian identity."*

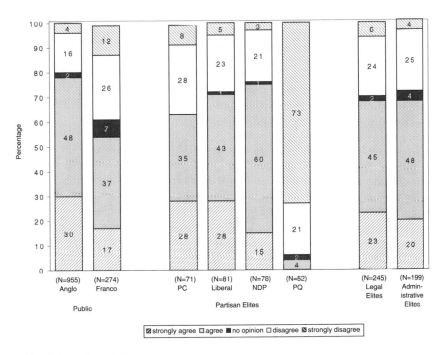

statistical significance of comparisons
political elites by party: p ≤ .01

emphasis on the national and less emphasis on the regional identities of Canadians. But what is worth reflection is the contrast between the responses of the PQ and those of the average francophone. As against the practically unanimous choice of PQ activists in favor of more emphasis on regional identifications, slightly more than one-half of ordinary French Canadians are ready to support more emphasis on a national Canadian identity.

To throw some light on Canadians' attitudes toward the United States we shall draw on three statements, also taken from the mailback questionnaire:

"The Canadian way of life is being influenced too strongly by the United States."

"Canadians benefit a great deal from American investment in Canada."

"Canada should have free trade with the United States."

Respondents were asked whether they strongly agreed, agreed, disagreed, or strongly disagreed with each of the statements; they were also presented with the option of declaring that they had no opinion.

A clear majority of English Canadians and a still larger majority of French Canadians believe that the Canadian way of life is influenced too strongly by the United States (fig. 6.6A). Against this backdrop, the contrasting responses of different groups of elites form a striking pattern. Echoing the popular nationalism are political elites, with one exception only. New Democrats and members of the PQ overwhelmingly and Liberals predominantly agreed that "the Canadian way of life" is being influenced too strongly by the United States. Reacting in the opposite direction are only the Conservatives among the politicians, joined by legal and administrative elites.

The fear of American domination, however, coexists with a belief in the

Figure 6.6 A. *"The Canadian way of life is being influenced too strongly by the United States."*

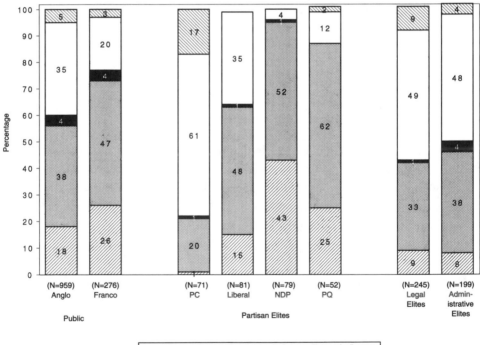

statistical significance of comparisons
anglophone vs. francophone public: p ≤ .01; political elites by party: p ≤ .01; elite groups by sector: p ≤ .01

Figure 6.6 B. *"Canadians benefit a great deal from American investment in Canada."*

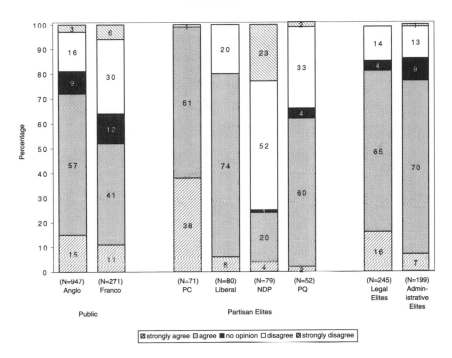

statistical significance of comparisons
anglophone vs. francophone public: p ≤ .01; political elites by party: p ≤ .01

benefits of American economic involvement in Canada, although the detailed results carry a suggestion of the ambivalence that ordinary Canadians
feel toward the United States (fig. 6.6B). Both administrative and legal elites
heavily agreed that Canada benefits from American investment, and members of the two political parties that have formed governments at the national level concur, again overwhelmingly, while a clear majority of ordinary anglophones also positively values American economic investment in
Canada. But although it is true that a majority of the PQ also agrees on the
benefit of American investment, a nontrivial fraction of them explicitly
dissent, and the same ambivalence is apparent among the francophone
public, in a still more accentuated form taking account of the roughly one in
ten who declines to state any opinion, pro or con, on the issue of American
investment. A majority of Canadians thus favor American investment in
Canada, but a nontrivial minority of the public are wary of it, and large

Figure 6.6 C. *"Canada should have free trade with the United States."*

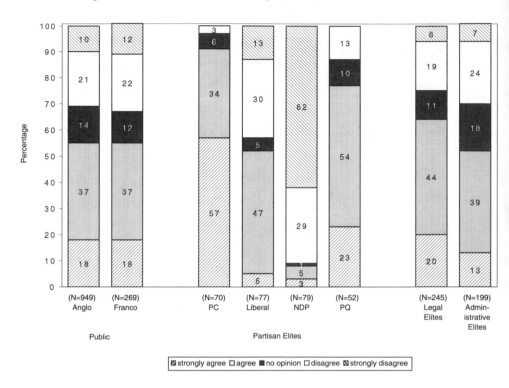

statistical significance of comparisons
political elites by party: p ≤ .01; elite groups by sector: p ≤ .01

numbers of legislative elites (most noticeably among the NDP but also among the PQ) are motivated to resist it.

Finally, Canadian attitudes to a specific policy initiative that has become a central element in Canadian electoral dynamics—namely, free trade with the United States—mirror reactions to American economic investment in general but with the ambivalence of Canadians toward American involvement even more accentuated (fig. 6.6C). Thus, majorities of ordinary Canadians agreed that Canada should have free trade with the United States, but very nearly as many either disagreed outright or decline to take an explicit stand on the issue. Legal elites, although on balance supporting free trade, are by no means as supportive of it as they are of American investment in Canada, while nearly as many administrative elites either reject or fail to take a stand on free trade with the United States as support it. The same

Table 6.1. Correlations of Canadian Identification and Attitudes toward Americans with Support for Canadian Content Regulations

		Anti-Americanism	Canadian Identification
Public	Anglophone	.34**	.09
	Francophone	.05	.00
Partisan	PC	.42*	.31
Elites	Liberal	.51*	.04
	NDP	.43**	.29
	PQ	—	—
	Legal Elites	.39**	.34**
	Administrative Elites	.49**	.08

*: p ≤ .05
**: p ≤ .01

impression of division is apparent among legislative elites, with the exception of the PC and the PQ. Thus, only one-half of Liberals favor free trade, while New Democrats nearly unanimously oppose it. The ground had thus been well prepared for free trade to become a closely contested issue.[18]

Our primary interest, however, is not in Canadians' sentiments toward the United States in their own right but rather in the politics of culture. To what extent is support for government regulations to protect the culture of Canada rooted in a positive identification with Canada? To what extent is it grounded in negative sentiments toward America? To assess the strength of positive identification with Canada, responses to the questions on strengthening national identity in Canada and assuring the independence of Canada (even at the expense of Canadians' standard of living) were combined to form an Index of Pro-Canadian Identification. This index assesses support for a national Canadian identity not in the abstract but when it exacts a cost, either in terms of economic well-being or in terms of the competing value of regional identification. On the other hand, to assess the strength of the desire to resist and to counteract the influence of the United States, responses to the questions on the dangers of American cultural influence, American economic investment in Canada, and free trade were combined to form an Index of Anti-American Sentiment. In table 6.1 we present the correlations between support for government-mandated Canadian content regulations in mass media and the measures of Pro-Canadian Identification and Anti-American Sentiment, respectively.

The results could not be more clear. On the one side, support for content regulations is powerfully and consistently tied to anti-Americanism (with one exception, in itself telling); on the other side, support for content regulations has next to nothing to do with pro-Canadianism, one or two inconsequential exceptions notwithstanding. Consider English Canadians: support for content regulations and anti-Americanism are markedly correlated ($r = .34$). In contrast, the correlation between support for regulations and pro-Canadianism does not differ significantly from zero ($r = .09$). Moreover, anti-Americanism and support for content regulations are even more closely tied together for most elites. Thus, the comparable coefficients for Conservatives, Liberals, and New Democrats are .42, .51, and .43. The alternatives of whether support for government regulation of media is driven by pro-Canadianism or anti-Americanism are not mutually exclusive as a matter of logic. In real life, either (or both) can be important; and indeed, the reactions of Progressive Conservatives and, still more, those of legal elites illustrate this, with support for content regulations among them showing a connection with pro-Canadianism (albeit, even here, a weaker one than with anti-Americanism).

It would be a mistake to take these results to be perfectly consistent, although they are nearly so. Examining the results in table 6.1, one can see at once an exception to the general pattern; an exception, moreover, in its own way strikingly consistent. Among French Canadians as a whole, support for government regulations to protect the Canadian identity is *not* driven by anti-Americanism; indeed, the correlation between the two is essentially zero ($r = .05$). There is reason, then, to take seriously the idea that anti-Americanism does not play the same shaping role in the political thinking of French Canadians that it does in the thinking of English Canadians.

The results in table 6.1 suggest that the politics of culture, in particular the use of government to promote a national identity, need not be based on a positive regard for one's culture but can instead be driven by a negative regard for another's. In Canada, in the specific case of content regulations for the mass media (though no doubt elsewhere and in the case of other policies, too), the motivating spirit behind government control of media content is not a positive regard for things Canadian but an antipathy for things

American. The clouds of noble rhetoric and high intentions hanging over public discussion of Canada's culture obscure this sentiment.

Ironies of Consensus and Dissensus

The Charter of Rights, as we have noted, was conceived as an instrument of solidarity whose purpose was to draw Canadians together in a common, national identity or at least to draw French and English Canadians out of their competing group identities. Yet the mass of specific findings we have surveyed, when viewed as a coherent package, hints at ironies in this politics of consensus.

Viewed institutionally, the Charter of Basic Rights and Freedoms is designed to provide a constitutional fixed point, a set of procedures and norms formally prescribed in the Charter itself and authoritatively interpreted by the Supreme Court. The patriation of the Constitution in the form of a written Charter thus carries with it the new primacy of judicial review over the traditional principle of parliamentary sovereignty, notwithstanding the check of legislative override. Against this background the form of dissensus over the primacy of judicial review is ironic. It would have been perhaps regrettable but understandable if francophones had rejected the principle of judicial review, a principle inherently national rather than regional in character. And francophones, in fact, are not quite as likely to vest final authority in the courts as are anglophones, above all if the constitutional issue is embedded in a specific clash over policy. But the differences between English and French Canadians on this matter tend not to be large and pale by comparison with the differences between parliamentary elites and ordinary English-speaking Canadians on the one side and between parliamentary elites and legal elites on the other. There is, to put the point simply, a profound difference between them over who should have the final say.

We see, of course, only the outlines of a conflict. It is foolish to try to project on any linear basis the impact of ordinary citizens' beliefs on the actual dynamics of constitutional issues; as well, our sample of legal elites consists not of sitting judges but of lawyers, albeit senior lawyers who form the pool of eligible candidates from which federal and provincial judges are selected. Having emphasized these qualifications, however, we believe that the cleavage between legislative and legal elites is worth underlining. The difference between them goes deep just because their constitutional views and their institutional roles coincide. Those whose vocation it is to make laws and those whose vocation it is to interpret them divide over who should have the final say. Parliamentary elites[19] say, "Parliament"; legal elites say, "the courts"—a reminder, if any were needed, that the very effort to achieve a basis of consensus can serve as a source of cleavage.

Yet, at another level, the irony of the politics of the Charter of Rights consists precisely in the fact that popular consensus on the Charter was achieved, among anglophones and francophones alike, in the absence of elite consensus, whether anglophone or francophone. The dynamics of constitutional politics are inevitably and deeply rooted in the dynamics of electoral politics. The Charter was a product of a Liberal government and its improvement the objective of a successor Conservative government, and the argument for change in the second place, as for change in the first place, was grounded in the objective of conciliation, above all, of French and English Canadians. The Charter, it was said, though meant to serve as a basis of consensus, had instead operated as a source of cleavage: not having ratified it themselves, French Canadians felt themselves outside it; they needed to be brought within it. But as we saw, French Canadians who knew of the Charter were as likely to approve of it as English Canadians; as likely also to feel that the Charter would strengthen a national Canadian identity; and finally and most consequentially as likely to *disagree* that the Charter would weaken the power of the provinces. In short, notwithstanding the public argument over whether to have a Charter, our results show that the popular consensus on the Charter itself was as complete among French Canadians as among English Canadians. It remains to be seen whether the consensus that obtained among citizens at the time of the adoption of the Charter will provide sufficient protection against the subsequent efforts of elites to destroy it.

SEVEN **THE POLITICS OF LANGUAGE AND GROUP RIGHTS**

The deepest cleavage in modern Canadian politics has centered on language. Class has counted for less in comparison, ethnicity otherwise understood for still less, and religion, which once seemed the very center of the divide between French and English Canada, has nearly disappeared as an issue in public life. In Canadian politics, language cuts the deepest.

By *language* we mean, of course, not simply the spoken or written word, but all that French and English have come to mean socially, politically, culturally. So understood, language is an aspect of identity, and because claims for a public status have been made on behalf of not one but two languages, Canadian politics has from the outset been organized around a politics of identity.

Public conflict over identity favors a symbolic politics, a style of politics that finds its characteristic expression in public demands for social deference and esteem, and we shall remark upon these themes from time to time. But the instruments and demands of political symbolism are a secondary theme for us. Our overriding concern is the politics of rights—in this case, the rights of Canada's major linguistic groups.

The style of democratic politics has manifestly undergone a change over the past half-century. The idea of rights has been bound up with democratic politics from the outset, but its standing has changed. Traditionally, the vocabulary of political conflict in liberal democracies had been framed in terms of interest and need. The clash of competing claims persists, yet the nature of the claims has subtly but deeply been transformed. As it has become fashionable to observe, rights are now trump. Citizens, it is now routinely claimed, are entitled to services or goods of different sorts, not merely because they need or would benefit from them, but because they are entitled to them as a matter of right.

The notion that citizens, by virtue of citizenship, acquire legally enforceable entitlements to public benefits and government services has reshaped the agenda of liberal democratic politics. Thanks to this new agenda, some issues enjoy a comparative advantage over others in the unending competition for public attention, and language, in the case of Canada, is just the kind of issue to prosper in the new style of politics organized around claims to rights. But the new dominance of the idea of rights is of consequence not only because it influences the standing of issues on the political agenda, but also because it shapes the structure of political conflict. Who must consent, for an issue to be resolved, and how their consent must be obtained depend on how the issue is put; and framing issues in terms of rights takes them out of the incremental give and take of normal politics and imparts more of the transformative potential of constitutional politics.

The dynamics of language as an issue in Canadian politics cannot be understood apart from the special character of language as a right. Rights used to be understood as claims that could be advanced only on behalf of an individual. They are now understood to be claims that can be advanced on behalf of groups. And the politics of language in Canada takes on its special character precisely because the claim to a right to English or to French is made not merely on behalf of individuals, however numerous, but in the name of a group and a way of life.

The claim to language rights is a political claim, and it is accordingly necessary to map the politics of language rights. To what extent does language as an issue divide Canadians, and in what ways? How far does the cleavage run through the larger public, separating French Canadians from English Canadians? Alternatively, to what extent do the lines of cleavage over language divide strategic groups of elites either from the body of citizens generally or from other elites?

The Symbolic Politics of Language

Our objective is to map the patterns of consensus and cleavage over the language rights set out in the Charter of Rights and Freedoms. These sections of the Charter, more than any others, embody the core elements of Pierre Trudeau's vision of Canada. Trudeau believed that to stem separatist nationalism in Quebec a two-front strategy was necessary. On the one hand, francophone Quebeckers must be made to feel at home in the whole of Canada; on the other, English-speaking Canadians must be made to feel welcome in Quebec. Trudeau's political strategy took legal shape first in the Official Languages Act (1969), then in sections 16–23 of the Charter.

Rights may be trump, but not all rights are equal. Of the specific sections of the Charter laying out language rights, four are especially important for our purposes: section 16, which proclaims French and English as Canada's official languages; section 20, which guarantees federal government service in either of the official languages; section 23, which guarantees French and English Minority Language Education Rights; and, finally, section 6, which sets out "mobility rights" intended to ensure that Quebeckers are never effectively locked in their province with everyone else locked out. The special standing of these rights—their central importance to Trudeau's vision of Canada—is signaled by their specific exemption from the override provision contained in section 33 of the Charter.

Our point of departure is the principle of bilingualism. The establishment of French and English as Canada's official languages in the Charter of Rights, quite apart from its narrowly legal consequences, involves a public symbolic assertion of the special standing of French Canadians in Canada; and it is the distinctive forms of conflict evoked by symbolic politics that we want to explore.

Customarily, political conflict is conceived to be polar, taking the form of a clash of factions committed to opposing goals—as proponents of abortion, for example, are committed to "freedom of choice" and opponents to the "right to life." But political conflicts can also be scalar, taking the form not of a clash between proponents and opponents of opposing goals but rather of a cleavage between people for whom an issue matters greatly and those for whom it matters much less or perhaps hardly at all. Conflict over language, as we shall see, tends to be scalar rather than polar; and this, in turn, has much to do with the dynamics of the politics of language rights, with the bulk of anglophones as well as francophones ready to acknowledge the rights of the other when the issue of language occupies a lower place on the public agenda but more reluctant to do so as the issue moves up on the public agenda.

To examine the symbolic standing of bilingualism in defining the official character of Canada, once the interview was under way and had gained some momentum, we asked, "How important is preserving French and English as the two official languages of Canada?"

Figure 7.1A compares the degree of importance English and French Canadians attach to maintaining English and French as "official languages" in Canada. In a clash over political symbolism, relative differences can be as divisive as absolute ones; there is a sizeable split between francophones and anglophones on the importance of bilingualism at the level of principle (fig. 7.1A). Francophones are overwhelmingly likely to see the maintenance of both French and English as official languages as important, and indeed, 80 percent of them see it as very important while hardly any of them feel that it is not important. By way of contrast, only about a third of anglophones believe that maintaining French and English as official languages is very important, while nearly as many believe that it is not important.

For all practical purposes, then, francophones are unanimously agreed on the importance of preserving both French and English as official languages in Canada. But there are marked differences among anglophones over bilingualism, and it is important to identify the factors underlying these differences. Are the differences in support for bilingualism among English Canadians generational? Do they reflect, that is to say, a difference between English Canadians who grew up and learned about politics before bilingualism became a prominent part of the national Canadian life and those socialized after language rights became so prominent in national politics? And beyond this, it is argued that issues of language and national identity are not two-sided, setting Quebeckers apart from other Canadians as the traditional discussion of bilingualism implies, but three-sided, with new Canadians, those neither English nor French in background, forming a distinctive group with a point of view of its own (e.g., Cairns 1988).[1] For that matter, is there not reason to believe that differences among English Canadians in the importance they attach to bilingualism reflect differences not in their social or even economic circumstances but rather in their explicitly political orientations and loyalties?

Figure 7.1 A. *"How important is preserving French and English as the two official languages of Canada?"*

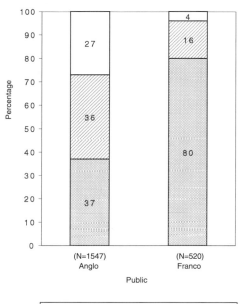

Public

□ very important ▨ somewhat important □ not important

statistical significance of comparison
anglophones vs. francophones: p ≤ .01

Bilingualism is a fairly recent entry to the stock of political principles familiar to Canadians, and it can be argued that its value is most likely to be appreciated by Canadians socialized to politics after, say, the quiet revolution of the 1960s. If this argument is correct (its validity remains to be established), then support for bilingualism will steadily increase as younger cohorts replace older ones. However, young English Canadians are not substantially more sympathetic to the principle of bilingualism than older Canadians; indeed, if anything, they are a bit less enthusiastic (fig. 7.1B). And although better-educated anglophones are likely to rate bilingualism slightly more highly than are poorly educated ones (fig. 7.1C), the difference is modest. Which is to say that the principle of bilingualism, though enjoying substantial support in English Canada, has not yet won for itself status as a

Figure 7.1 B. Cleavages over Bilingualism
by Age (Anglophones only)

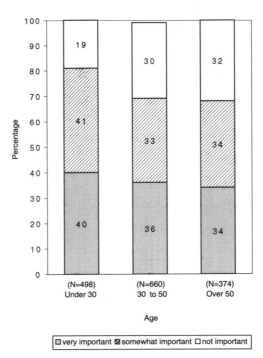

norm: bilingualism is not yet a value that ordinary citizens feel themselves under pressure to approve of or else risk being thought benighted or intolerant.

The results shown in figure 7.1 also throw light on the theme of a "third force" in Canadian politics. The traditional "two-nation" vocabulary of Canadian politics places French and English Canadians at the center of attention. This dualistic focus, it is argued, is out of date. Now, in addition to Canadians who belong to the two founding nations, there is the so-called third force, Canadians who belong to neither of the founding nations. Increasing numbers of Canadians, above all in English Canada, are of neither British nor French descent. But, for this very reason, it is the more important to observe that they do *not* introduce yet another source of cleavage about the status of English and French as official languages in Canada. The views of the third force about the importance of bilingualism are barely distinguishable from those of English-speaking Canadians born and raised in Canada (fig. 7.1D). Moreover, there is no evidence of a class cleavage over

Figure 7.1 C. Cleavages over Bilingualism
by Education (Anglophones only)

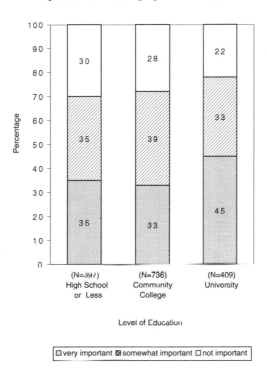

Level of Education

very important ☑ somewhat important ☐ not important

bilingualism: English Canadians making less than $20,000 annually, for example, are as likely to say that the preservation of French as an official language is very important as those making more than $50,000 (fig. 7.1E).

Cleavage in English Canada over whether French as well as English should be an official language, the findings so far suggest, does not have strong social roots. The issue of bilingualism is political, not social. The political character of the issue is suggested by the pattern of differences associated with partisanship (fig. 7.1F). Although the partisan divisions are, as we shall soon see, nowhere near so deeply etched among the general public as they are among the political elite, support for bilingualism is clearly marked out along partisan lines. Liberals are the most likely to attach importance to maintaining both English and French as official languages, PC's the least, with the NDP falling between. Those with another or no partisan attachment are roughly similar to the PC's. Attitudes about language rights among anglophones thus have a decidedly partisan cast that mirrors the

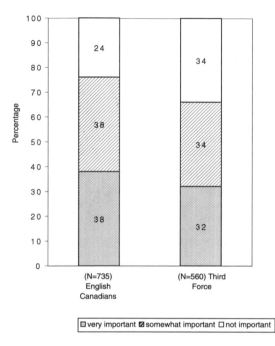

Figure 7.1 D. Cleavages over Bilingualism
by Ethnicity (Anglophones only)

partisan origins in the language policy of the former Liberal prime minister Pierre Trudeau. The politics of language rights, although not reducible to partisan preference, is nevertheless situated in the context of the continuing clash of political parties, which serves as a reminder that in a liberal democracy constitutional politics is inevitably electoral politics.

The dynamics of the politics of language rights, though, are shaped not by the views of ordinary citizens in their own right, but by the *interaction* of popular preferences and elite competition. Partisan elites are divided over bilingualism (fig. 7.2). Liberal, NDP, and PQ elites overwhelmingly regard preservation of bilingualism as very important. (Indeed, they are every bit as likely to do so as French Canadians in general.) Progressive Conservatives, though slightly more likely than the average anglophone to rate bilingualism as important, are very much closer to being the voice of English than of French Canada.

The views of partisan elites are arguably sensitive to the positions of their party's leadership. But the larger question is, Which point of view on bilin-

Figure 7.1 E. Cleavages over Bilingualism
by Partisanship (Anglophones only)

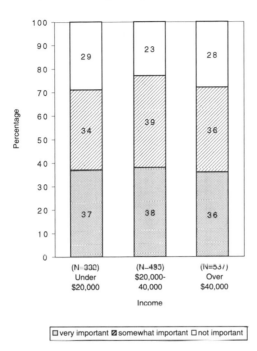

gualism represents the thrust of the larger culture as it is understood by those
best in a position to understand it? Is the relative uniformity of Liberal, NDP,
and PQ positions on this issue evidence that bilingualism has at last become a
fundamental tenet if not of the popular culture, at least of the elite culture?
Or is it, judged in the context of the larger culture of elites (and not merely
political elites), a sign of the compartmentalization of Canadian thinking
about bilingualism?

A partial answer can be gleaned from the attitudes of legal and bureaucratic elites toward bilingualism. Because these elites, by and large, come
from advantaged backgrounds and have extended, often professional, edu-
cations they can serve as a cultural bellwether: if an idea has become a part of
the official culture, if it has become understood that an enlightened and
decently intentioned citizen should back a particular point of view, then
these legal and bureaucratic elites will swing behind it and back it. Legal and
administrative elites may not operate as trendsetters (political elites play the
more conspicuous role here) but they do perform as trend definers, signaling

Figure 7.1 F. Cleavages over Bilingualism
by Family Income (Anglophones only)

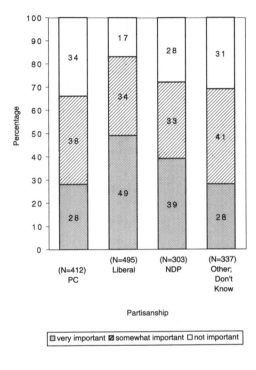

Partisanship

very important somewhat important not important

statistical significance of comparisons
anglophone public by partisanship: p ≤ .01

by their support that an idea has won the broad acceptance of informed
opinion.

What, then, do legal and administrative elites think about the principle of
bilingualism? In both groups about one in every two judges bilingualism to
be very important (fig. 7.2). This, we suggest, is an indication of where the
true center of gravity of the larger culture is located. Parliamentary elites,
Conservatives excepted, are the outliers; the reactions of the legal and bureaucratic elites resemble those of Conservatives and, still more broadly, of
anglophones in general.

What, then, is the symbolic standing of bilingualism? On the one hand,
bilingualism has plainly become a legitimate value throughout the Canadian public in general, and still more so among Canadian elites, above all,
political elites. The measure of its legitimacy is the relatively small propor-

Figure 7.2. Importance of Bilingualism to Elite Groups

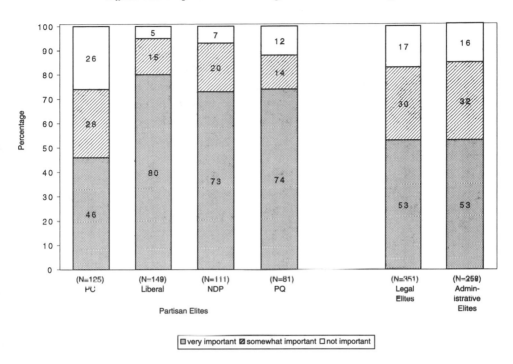

statistical significance of comparisons
political elites by party: p ≤ .01; elite groups by sector: p ≤ .01

tion willing to characterize it as unimportant. At its highest mark, among the English Canadian public, only slightly more than one in every four is prepared to say explicitly that preserving both English and French as official languages is *not* important. On the other hand, there is just as plainly a divide separating English and French Canada in the standing of bilingualism on the public agenda. In French Canada the belief that bilingualism is very important is nearly unanimous; in contrast, in English Canada, far fewer, even at the elite level, take the position that maintaining both French and English as official languages in Canada is very important. Nonetheless, this discrepancy tends to be effectively masked by the pattern of virtual consensus among partisan elites. Huge majorities committed to bilingualism in three of the parties, combined with the commitment of the leadership of the fourth, worked to rule the principle of bilingualism out of court as a subject of debate at the elite level.[2]

Issue Politics versus Symbolic Politics

It is essential to distinguish between two levels at which claims to rights are made. One is the level of symbolic politics, marked by the esteem or deference publicly paid to claims to political rights or to group identities or both; the other is that of issue politics, marked by the levels of support for or opposition to claims to a right. Having charted the level of support for bilingualism as a symbolic principle, we now want to explore the readiness of Canadians to support the specific rights that follow from the principle of bilingualism.

Exploring commitment to a right is problematic—notoriously so. Merely to say that one favors a value is not the same thing as actually favoring it: people are prone if not to present themselves in the best light, then to avoid letting themselves appear in the worst. Asked whether they favor a goal that is socially desirable, they may well say they do even if they do not. An English Canadian is unlikely to say that French Canadians do not deserve to be treated well, even if he or she is perfectly willing for them to be treated ill, and vice versa. Moreover, our interest is not in how English Canadians *feel* about French Canadians, or vice versa. Without minimizing the importance of social feelings—of trust, respect, sympathy, or of resentment, contempt, or indifference—our aim is to gain an understanding of how Canadians construe rights one is entitled to on the basis of language and culture; of what they are prepared to take as legitimate claims, to be enforced by the state both against their fellow citizens and, if necessary, against the state itself.

What does it mean to favor a right? Sometimes, to favor a right is to endorse a claim to act. Free speech is the classic example. To favor freedom of expression is to favor a right that is conditional across situations (no one has the right falsely to shout, "Fire!" in a theater) but unconditional across citizens. In a liberal democracy it is never supposed, for this class of rights, that one set of citizens is entitled to exercise freedom of speech while a second set as fully members of the political order as the first is not entitled to do so. On the contrary, we are accustomed to thinking of rights, whether as claims to obtain benefits or freely to engage in (or to refrain from) a course of action, as something held universally and equally by members of a political community merely by virtue of their membership in the community.

For some, language rights correspond to this classic conception of rights, according to which the identity of the claimant is irrelevant to the judging of the legitimacy of the claim (as long as that person satisfies the requirement of membership in the political community). But for others, what distinguishes the politics of language rights is that *what* may be done is inextricably linked to *who* may do it.

Why is the identity of the claimant relevant to the legitimacy of the right to express a particular thought in one language rather than another but irrelevant to the right to express the thought itself? Because, it is argued, language rights are a quintessential example of a group right. The justification for a language right, for example, the right of francophones to receive their schooling in French or the right of an anglophone to address and be addressed by a government official in English, has nothing whatever to do with either the qualities that set each of them apart uniquely, as individuals, or those that they share universally, as a member of the political community like every other member. Rather, the right to the use of language, in Canadian politics, is bound up with one's collective identity as a French or English Canadian, that is, one's association with one or the other of the so-called founding nations.

So far as language rights are group rights, it cannot be said that people favor such a right in the abstract: to favor a language right is, at the same time, to favor its exercise by a particular group. More exactly, because two groups, English and French Canadians, claim rights to their language under the Charter, what counts are the rights to which each thinks itself entitled as compared to those each thinks the other is entitled. This duality of us and them and what we as opposed to what they are entitled to is at the heart of the special dynamics of a group right like language. As judgments of equity, group rights carry with them a premise of symmetry and reciprocity. If French Canadians outside Quebec are entitled to a right, then English Canadians inside Quebec are entitled to it also; and if French Canadians declare that English Canadians are not entitled to it, then English Canadians will declare that neither are French Canadians, and vice versa. A group right thus distinctively blends strategic and normative considerations. We are more willing to grant them a right that we ourselves want and believe we are entitled to exercise, and still more willing if our exercising it is contingent on their possessing an equivalent right. On the other side, we are, if anything, still more ready to deny them a right if we believe they are prepared to deny it to us.

But if *who* exercises a right is so intimately bound up with *what* is to be construed as a right, then how can it be determined whether Canadians genuinely favor any particular language right? How can it be determined whether English Canadians favor not only English Canadians' exercising of the rights awarded them under the Charter of Rights but French Canadians' exercising their rights as well, and vice versa? Standard practice—asking, first, whether English Canadians should have a right to educate their children in English, then asking the same question substituting only French Canadians and French—will not work. The English Canadian who says, in response to the first question, that English Canadians have a right to an education in English if they live in Quebec would then be under pressure to say, whether really believing it or not, that French Canadians who live outside Quebec should have a right to an education in French. The pressure people feel to be consistent is not the least reason they are insincere. And just for this reason, the level of English Canadian support for French Canadian rights will be exaggerated, and vice versa.

Our study, taking advantage once again of computer-assisted interviewing, randomly selects subsets of the sample as a whole, including both French and English respondents, and asks them questions about language rights identical in every respect except that the beneficiary in one case is French Canadian and in the other English Canadian. If either group, whether English or French Canadian, offers more support for a language right when it is to its benefit rather than the other groups', then this is proof positive of a double standard; proof positive because the subsets of the sample, being randomly selected, are otherwise alike in every relevant respect (chance differences aside).

Rights radiate from core to periphery, and at the core of language rights, entrenched in section 23 of the Charter of Rights and Freedoms, is the right to education in one's own language. Section 23 of the Charter guarantees the two principal language minorities the right to be educated in its own language. Children of French-speaking parents who live outside Quebec accordingly have a right to receive schooling in French; children of English-speaking parents who live in Quebec to receive schooling in English.[3] It is easy to see why the right to schooling in one's own language is at the core of language rights. For language rights are not about words; they are about identity. When the distinctive identity of a group, its traditions, norms, and customs, is both rooted in and buttressed by a distinctive language, the survival of the group hinges on the survival of its language. The right to an education in one's own language is thus a classic example of future generational rights: a right the present generation can demand on behalf of the next.

The recent politics of minority language education rights in Canada have for the most part been focused upon the restrictions on English-language education under Quebec's language law, Bill 101 (also known as the Charter of the French Language). One of the Supreme Court's earliest Charter decisions dealt with the conflict between section 23 of the Charter and Bill 101.[4] The language laws brought into force by the PQ government of René Lévesque to protect the French character of Quebec provided that "instruction in the kindergarten classes and in the elementary and secondary schools shall be in French, except where this Charter allows otherwise." English instruction was permitted in certain cases, the most important of which was the case of a child whose father or mother received his or her elementary instruction in English in Quebec. This meant that the children of English-speaking citizens moving to Quebec from other provinces were not entitled to English-language education. The Supreme Court held that the Quebec language education provisions in Bill 101 (insofar as they affected English-speaking Canadians moving to Quebec) were inconsistent with section 23 of the Charter and did not constitute a justifiable limitation on the Charter's guarantees. Although the Supreme Court's decision in this case was bitterly resented in some quarters, the government of Quebec had little recourse because the minority language rights provisions of the Charter are insulated against the notwithstanding clause in section 33.

How are Canadian attitudes toward minority language education rights to be construed? We shall focus on the terrain contested in the Supreme Court case, the right of Canadians to educate their children in English or French when moving in and out of Quebec. To assess Canadian attitudes toward rights to education in one's language, two versions of a primary question were administered:

"Now I would like to ask your views on some issues affecting families and schooling.
[version A] Should French Canadians who move out of Quebec to . . .
[version B] Should English Canadians who move into Quebec from . . .
. . . another province have a basic right to have their children taught in . . .
[version A] . . . French?
[version B] . . . English?"

All respondents were then presented with two choices: Yes, (the group in question) should have a right (to have their children taught in their own language), or No, they should not have such a right. With an eye to the common criticism of public opinion surveys that, by requiring respondents to select from fixed answers, they do a poor job in capturing the nuances of public opinion, once more we noted whether respondents, in choosing one of the predetermined answers, qualified their answers. It is, as we shall show, crucial to take account of the element of qualification to see the dynamic of claim and counterclaim, for even though a claim to a right tends to be unconditional, acknowledgment of it can be conditional.

Comparing the views of English Canadians about the rights to which they are entitled as against the rights to which French Canadians are entitled, we see a double standard (fig. 7.3). Only about six in every ten anglophones (taking the maximum estimate of support) believe that francophones moving out of Quebec are entitled to education in French (fig. 7.3A). By contrast,

Figure 7.3 A. Attitudes toward Minority Language Education Rights, Version A: *"Should French Canadians who move out of Quebec to another province have a basic right to have their children taught in French?"*

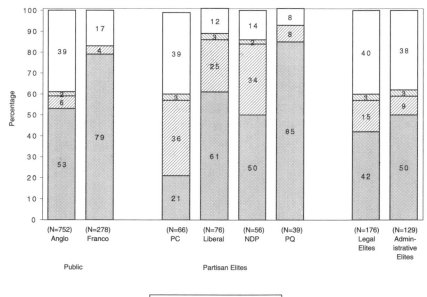

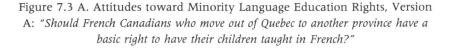

statistical significance of comparisons
anglophone vs. francophone public: p ≤ .01; political elites by party: p ≤ .01; elite groups by sector: p ≤ .01

Figure 7.3 B. Attitudes toward Minority Language Education Rights, Version B: *"Should English Canadians who move into Quebec from another province have a basic right to have their children taught in English?"*

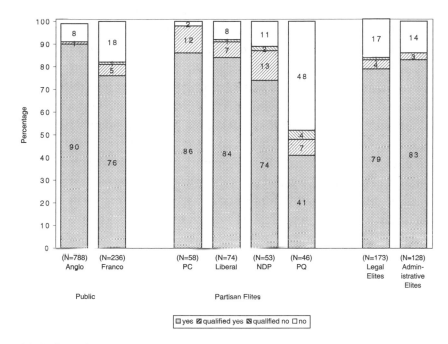

statistical significance of comparisons
anglophone vs. francophone public: p ≤ .01; political elites by party: p ≤ .01

nearly all of them, slightly better than nine in every ten, believe that if they move to Quebec their children are entitled to education in English (fig. 7.3B). Furthermore, this double standard is one-sided. Francophones do not favor themselves over anglophones as anglophones favor themselves over francophones. On the contrary, about eight in ten support the idea that French Canadians who move outside Quebec have the right to have their children educated in French, and by exactly the same margin they support the right of English Canadians who move to Quebec to have their children educated in English. There is thus an asymmetry in the willingness of francophones to grant to anglophones language rights as compared to that of anglophones to grant to francophones the same rights.[5]

Consider now the responses of elites, beginning with the main federal parties. Although there are differences among them, roughly eight in every ten of the PC's, Liberals, and NDP support the *right of anglophones* moving to

Quebec to have their children educated in English (fig. 7.3). Contrast this pattern with the reaction of elites, particularly partisan elites, to the parallel question of whether French Canadians who have moved outside of Quebec should have the right to educate their children in French. On the one hand, it is true that a clear majority of these same legislative elites support the right of French Canadians who move outside Quebec to have their children educated in French. On the other hand, aside from the overall lower levels of support generally, another striking aspect of their responses is the frequency with which they qualify their support for French Canadian language rights. These partisan elites, if they support the rights of francophones to have their children educated in French, are roughly four to five times as likely as ordinary Canadians to qualify their support; when this is taken into account, it is by no means obvious that the legislative elites of any of the three federal parties offer a markedly firmer basis of support for the rights of French Canadians than does the ordinary English Canadian.

It might be argued that these legislative elites more often qualify their support for language rights not because they are being careful to hedge their commitment on the issue of language, but because they are more likely to appreciate nuance and complexity and hence more likely to give qualified rather than unconditional answers to any given issue. If they are qualifying their response because of the complexity of the issue, however, they should be equally likely to do so whether they are responding to the claim of anglophones to have their children educated in English or to that of francophones to have their children educated in French; plainly they are not (fig. 7.3). Moreover, even if one were tempted to argue that the claim of francophones is intrinsically more complex than the claim of anglophones —say, because it involves claims that could be cashed in across the nation rather than in just one province—examination of the responses of legal and administrative elites suggests that an appreciation of this complexity is unlikely to be the reason that legislative elites more often qualify their support for French Canadian language rights than for English Canadian language rights. Like legislative elites, they tend to be more aware of the complexities of issues, better educated, more politically sophisticated, and better informed than the ordinary citizen. They are more likely than ordinary citizens to attach qualifications to their support of language rights, but only slightly, whereas legislative elites are strikingly more likely to append qualifications to their support of language rights.

The double standard that anglophones practice toward francophones is reason enough for concern, but even more distressing is the readiness of anglophone political elites to qualify their support for the language rights of francophones. According to the thesis of democratic elitism, ordinary citizens support basic rights and freedoms superficially and back away from them in concrete, controversial cases; in contrast, elites (especially political elites) serve as the guardians of civil liberties, by no means perfect in their protection of them but far more so than the public at large. Earlier we examined this argument with respect to classic individual rights; now we want to consider whether it applies to the politics of language rights, arguably the most volatile issue in Canadian constitutional politics.

The thesis of democratic elitism maintains that, political elites offer more, and more reliable, support for political rights than ordinary citizens do. But look first at the views of ordinary English Canadians and compare them with those of legal and executive elites (fig. 7.3A). For all practical purposes, there is nothing to choose between them. Senior lawyers are no more supportive of the rights of French Canadians to have their children educated in French than is the ordinary English Canadian. Neither are officials in the ministries of Justice or the offices of the attorney general.

Beyond this, there is a suggestion of a potentially provocative difference between political parties (fig. 7.3A). The majority of Progressive Conservatives support language rights in this instance, albeit with qualifications, but all the same, nearly four in ten of them rejected, *without qualification,* the proposition that French Canadians who move outside Quebec have a right to have their children taught in French. As a glance at figure 7.3A will show, the level of opposition among Conservatives is approximately three times as high as among Liberals and New Democrats and parallels almost precisely the levels of opposition among ordinary English Canadians and legal and bureaucratic elites. It accordingly cannot be said that, on the issue of education and language, elites (political and otherwise) had formed at the time of our study a distinctive consensus to buttress language rights entrenched in the Charter of Rights.

The lack of elite consensus is underlined by the responses of the PQ to the two versions of the minority language education rights question. Virtually all of them support education rights for French-speaking children outside of Quebec. But in responding to the version of the question asking about English-speaking children moving into Quebec, PQ activists are sharply split. Unlike the ordinary francophone, who heavily supports language rights for English Canadians who move into Quebec, the PQ is split in half over the issue; a split that is the more telling in the face of the clear guarantees of the Charter, as explicitly enforced by the Supreme Court of Canada.

The politics of rights hinges not on claims made in the abstract and independent of any other consideration, but on the clash of competing values
when claims to specific rights are advanced. It is essential, it follows, not just
to examine attitudes toward language rights considered in isolation, but also
to explore what happens when a claim to a language right collides with a
claim to some other social or political value.

Pliability of Support for Language Rights in Education

To throw some light on the clash of competitive claims over language rights,
we shall again take advantage of the counterargument technique. Many
people do not make unconditional commitments to the positions they take
on political issues, and for at least two quite different kinds of reasons. They
may, in the first place, have adopted the position primarily because they
guessed it was the side of the issue they were supposed to take, and once
they find out, in the course of ordinary conversation, that their guess was a
bad one, they are naturally inclined to give it up. But they also may initially
and sincerely have favored *that* side of the issue, but again, as the natural
interplay of a conversation develops and their attention is called to additional considerations to which they did not initially attend, they may genuinely change their mind. From a political point of view, however, what
matters is less why citizens may change their mind on an issue and more that
citizens on one side of a particular issue are more likely to change their mind
than are those on the other side.

Consider the extent to which Canadians can be talked out of their positions on language rights in education. Following the counterargument paradigm, everyone who took the position that a French Canadian living outside
Quebec was entitled to have their children educated in their own language
was then asked,

> "Would you feel that way even if it substantially increases the amount of
> taxes people have to pay over and above what they are paying now?
> Yes, feel the same.
> No, feel differently."

The proportion of English and French Canadians changing their position in
the face of this counterargument is set out in the left-hand columns of
figure 7.4.

In view of the evidence of a double standard on language rights favoring
English Canadians, it is important to focus on the dynamics of support for
language rights for French Canadians. And numerically the most obvious

Figure 7.4 Pliability of Support for Minority
Language Education Rights

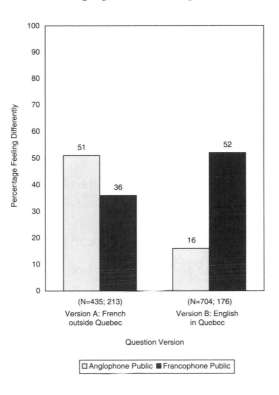

Question Version

☐ Anglophone Public ■ Francophone Public

statistical significance of comparisons
both versions, anglophone vs. francophone public: p ≤ .01

(and politically the most consequential) result is this: even though proportionately fewer English than French Canadians support French Canadian
language rights, large proportions of English Canadian supporters of French
Canadian rights can readily be talked out of their support: one in every two
English Canadians backs away from supporting French Canadian language
rights if assurance of these rights carries with it the price of higher taxes (fig.
7.4).

What should one make of this? Does it mean that the English Canadian
commitment to French Canadian rights is meaningless? Does it demonstrate
that English Canadians are not only distinctively less likely to approve of
French Canadian rights than French Canadians are to approve of theirs, but
that they are distinctively more likely to be hypocritical in the bargain?

It means, certainly, that the commitment of English Canadians to the
language rights of French Canadians is conditional; conditional in ways that

elected politicians must attend to: very large numbers of anglophones are prepared to withdraw their support of bilingualism if they must pay higher taxes, which means that, in an era of economic austerity and government deficits, there is an inherent volatility to support for bilingualism. But this result is by no means evidence of a distinctive hypocrisy on the part of English Canadians: substantial numbers of French Canadians are just as prepared to withdraw their support for French Canadian language rights when faced with higher taxes (fig. 7.4). To be sure, they are not as likely as English Canadians to do so: 36 percent of francophones say that they feel differently about French Canadians living outside Quebec being entitled to educate their children in French if it means higher taxes, as compared to 51 percent of anglophones; but the number of French Canadians prepared to retract their support for fellow French Canadians is impressive by any reasonable standard. Beyond this, the appropriately symmetrical test is to determine the pliability of French Canadian support for bilingualism stated in terms not of the rights of French Canadians living outside Quebec, but of the rights of English Canadians living inside Quebec. To assess this, all supporters of the rights of English Canadians living in Quebec to educate in English were asked,

> "Would you feel that way even if it threatens the right of Quebec to be a predominantly French-speaking community?
>> Yes, feel the same.
>> No, feel differently."

Now, as the right-hand side of figure 7.4 shows, the positions of anglophones and francophones are reversed; it is the latter, not the former, who are more easily talked out of their position: specifically, one in every two French Canadians—virtually the same proportion of English Canadians talked out of their support for French Canadian rights by a reference to higher taxes—say they would feel differently about English Canadians living in Quebec having the right to have their children be educated in English if doing so threatens the French character of Quebec; in contrast, only a relative handful of English Canadians—less than one in every six—want to rethink their position in consequence of this threat. What this signals, of course, is that should the French-speaking character of Quebec appear threatened, francophones might no longer be willing to support the language rights set out in the Charter for English Canadians moving to Quebec. The provisions of Bill 101 in this regard may be gone, but they are not forgotten.

It could be argued that this finding of symmetry is more apparent than real. For an English Canadian to be talked out of supporting French Canadian rights by the prospect of higher taxes is not in the same league as a French Canadian being talked out of supporting English Canadian rights by the specter of the dissolution of Quebec as a French-speaking community. But whether English Canadians *should* attach differential importance to higher taxes and to the integration of French Canadians is not the issue: politically, what counts is the extent to which Canadians, English and French, can be talked out of their positions in favor of bilingualism by politically credible threats.

To see the dynamics of bilingualism more clearly, it is necessary to see not only how pliable support for bilingualism is but also how firm the opposition might be. On first blush, it might seem that those who oppose bilingualism might be very firmly dug in. But is this impression that it is difficult to talk English Canadians who oppose French Canadian language rights out of their opposition a reflection of the strength of their opposition to those rights or, alternatively, an indication of the weakness of the counterarguments deployed against their position? Moreover, might it be difficult to talk opponents of French Canadians' having language rights out of their position because of the strength of their feelings against French Canadians or, alternatively, because opposition to claims of this kind, whether on behalf of francophones or anglophones, is difficult to overturn?

To gauge, first, the depth of resistance to French Canadian language rights, we randomly divided into two sets all respondents who were opposed to French Canadian families that live outside Quebec having a basic right to have their children taught in French. Each was then exposed to a counterargument, but the particular counterargument differed. Half the time it was

> [version 1] "Would you feel that way even if, as a result, French Canadians feel less at home in Canada and separatism is strengthened?"

and half the time it was

> [version 2] "Would you feel that way even if, as a result, parents don't have the right to educate their children in the language of their choice?"

Responding to the first counterargument, most anglophone opponents of French Canadian language rights are not moved to reconsider their opposition by an appeal to the risk of separatism (fig.7.5). But is this because English Canadians who oppose French Canadian language rights simply do not care how French Canadians feel? Hardly; they are, if anything, even more likely to maintain their position in the face of an appeal to the right of parents to have their children educated as they want (fig. 7.5). Faced with a

Figure 7.5. Pliability of Opposition to Minority
Language Education Rights

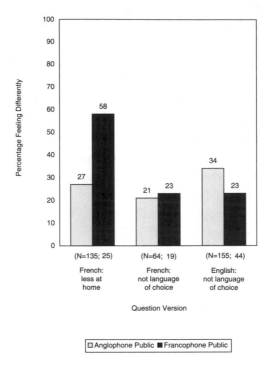

counterargument directing attention to the risks of separatism, 73 percent of
anglophones continue to oppose francophone language education rights;
faced with an argument centered on the rights of parents, 79 percent of
anglophones continue to oppose francophone language rights.

Is it difficult to persuade English Canadians to change their position on
French Canadian language rights because of what they think about the issue
of language rights or because of how they feel toward French Canadians?
Some light can be shed on this question by considering those English Canadians who believe that English Canadians, moving to Quebec, do not have a
basic right to have their children educated in English and those French
Canadians who take the equivalent position with respect to French Canadians who moved outside Quebec—some light, we say, because given the
politics of the issue relatively few anglophones or francophones wind up
objecting to language rights being assigned to their fellow anglo- or franco-

phones. Notice their reaction when presented with an appeal to change their position out of respect for a parent's right to have their children educated as they judge proper. The pattern is essentially the same as for anglophones who object to the rights of francophones: it is just about as difficult to talk them out of their position, though it is hard to be precise about this, given the sparseness of the cases (fig. 7.5).

Public Funding of Religious Schools

The story of Canadian politics, from the outset, has been a story of the intersection of the claims of citizenship and community, and just because of the centrality of this intersection, education has, also from the beginning, been both a constitutional and a political issue.

One of the central compromises that made Confederation possible in 1867 took the form of an agreement over religious education. Lower Canada was predominantly Catholic; Upper Canada, predominantly Protestant. A bargain was therefore struck, an exchange of rights assuring publicly funded schools for the Protestant minority in Quebec and for the Catholic minority in Ontario. The bargain, however, came unstuck: Quebec honored its commitment to the full, but Ontario refused to extend public funding of Catholic schools beyond the second year of high school.

The politics of rights in liberal democracies is driven by the political dynamics of electoral competition; issues of education in general, and of public funding of religious schools in particular, are no exception. Catholics, once largely confined to Quebec, now make up a politically significant segment of the electorate outside Quebec: Indeed, in our general population sample, fully 30 percent of respondents outside Quebec (and of course very nearly 87 percent of those inside it) classify themselves as Catholic. A bloc of votes this size can be expected to catch the eye of politicians, above all those willing to run the risk of alienating their traditional supporters or of having their successors do it for them. In 1984, just prior to resigning as leader of the Ontario Conservatives, Premier William Davis suddenly broke with long-standing party policy and announced an extension of public funding of Catholic schools to the senior grades of high school. In spite of sharp criticism by public school boards, their teachers, the Anglican Archbishop of Toronto, and the press, Davis's successor and the leaders of the other political parties decided not to discuss the issue in the provincial election campaign of 1985, tacitly committing themselves to full public funding as well. As it turned out, the Conservatives lost the Ontario election, owing perhaps in part to the public funding issue. The Liberals, with the support of the NDP, succeeded in forming a minority government and, realizing that the whole issue was a political hot potato, referred it to the courts. The Ontario Court of Appeal split 3–2 in deciding to support the extension of public funding. The Supreme Court of Canada upheld the privilege of the Catholic schools over other religious schools.

The issue of public funding of religious schools belongs, at one and the same time, to the worlds of normal politics and of constitutional politics. Thus, it frequently is argued that public funding of Catholic schools is inconsistent with section 15, the Equality Section of the Charter, which gives every individual the right to equal benefit of the law without discrimination based on religion. So viewed, the provision of public funds to Catholic schools breaches the equality provision by providing "benefits on the basis of religion to one religious group only and is therefore in direct conflict with [the equality] right." But it can be and judicially has been argued in response that public funding of Catholic schools, so far from conflicting with the Charter, is provided for in the Charter, specifically in section 29. This section, another of the saving provisions of the Charter, states that "nothing in the Charter abrogates or derogates from any rights or privileges guaranteed by or under the Constitution of Canada in respect of denominational, separate or dissentient schools." In the Supreme Court of Canada, section 29 has so far played a pivotal role, the Court ruling that it protects the rights flowing from the religious schooling agreement reached at Confederation from the equality rights of the Charter.

It is, obviously, inappropriate to expect ordinary citizens, even thoughtful and attentive ones, to be able to unravel the tangle of conflicting legal, political, and constitutional considerations, the more so as the legal place of religion in public education is so uncommonly complex and variable across the country. So we shall instead take them through the process of considering the issue, starting with a presentation of the fundamental public choice, then unfolding a background of historical and political considerations, and concluding by examining the extent to which acknowledgment that a group has a right tends to provide a ground for extension of the right to other, similarly situated groups.

By way of beginning, every respondent was asked, "Should there be public funding for religious schools?" Public opinion is deeply split over this issue (fig. 7.6A). The reactions of the public at large exhibit a deep cleavage between English and French Canadians. A clear majority of English Cana-

Figure 7.6 A. Support for Public Funding
of Religious Schools

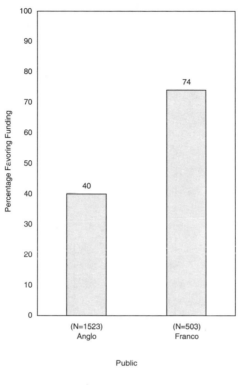

statistical significance of comparison
anglophone vs. francophone public: p≤ .01

dians, six in every ten, oppose public funding of religious schools, while a
still larger majority of French Canadians, nearly three in every four, favor it.

What is the reason for this cleavage? Is it proof of the depth of the division
between French and English Canada? Or evidence of a quite different form
of cleavage: of a difference of opinion about the politics not of language but
of religion?

Two characteristics of Canadian citizens, the language they speak and the
religion they practice, tend to overlap; indeed, so much so that, in the case of
Quebec, because the proportion of people living there who are both Catholic
and French-speaking is so high, the impact of religion and of language on
political thinking, at the level of data analysis, is indistinguishable.[6] Just for
this reason, we have compared only Catholic and non-Catholic Canadians
outside Quebec (fig. 7.6B). There is a marked divergence between Roman

Figure 7.6 B. Support for Public Funding of Religious Schools (Catholics and non-Catholics living outside of Quebec only)

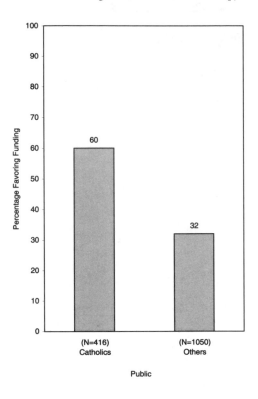

statistical significance of comparison
Catholics vs. others: p ≤ .01

Catholics on the one side and Canadians who belong to other religions (including those Canadians who choose to belong to no religion) on the other. Sixty percent of Catholics favor public funding of religious schools, while 68 percent of non-Catholics oppose it. The issue of public funding of religious schools is, in this sense, primarily an issue of religion, not language.

But regardless of whether the root motive for support of public funding of religious schools is religious rather than political, religion and language are politically intertwined. It is therefore worth carrying further our exploration of beliefs about schools and public funding, and we shall do so by getting beyond people's first reactions to the issue and seeing how they respond when the issue is put in its genuine political and historical context.

Ordinary citizens may not know that a claim to a right—in this case, a right to public funding of religious schools—is historically grounded. Asked their view, they respond, viewing the claim in a political vacuum, unaware that it is a link in a chain of promises. We want to see whether they will, once made aware of the historical rationale, concede the right. All respondents who said that they opposed public funding of religious schools were, upon declaring their opposition, given, as it were, a brief history lesson: "Since Canada was formed, our Constitution has recognized a special right of Catholic minorities outside of Quebec, and the Protestant minorities inside of Quebec, to have public funding for their schools." This lesson having been delivered, they were then asked, "Do you think public funding for these groups should continue or should public funding not continue?"

The willingness of opponents of public funding of religious schools to reverse their ground is registered in figure 7.7A. But even though our focus is exclusively on those whose first reaction was to oppose public funding,

Figure 7.7 A. Pliability of Opposition to
Public Funding of Religious Schools with
Reminder of Historical and Social Context

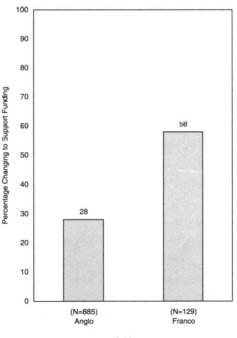

statistical significance of comparison
anglophone vs. francophone public: p ≤ .01

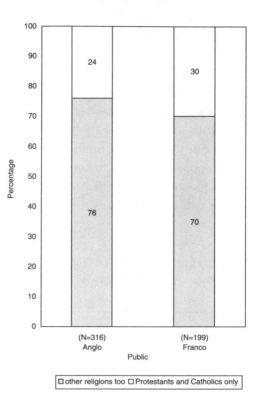

Figure 7.7 B. Support for Public Funding
of Religious Schools Other than Protestant
and Catholic

whether they are anglophones or francophones, again the reactions of French and English Canadians differ markedly. French Canadians are approximately twice as likely as English Canadians to reverse their opposition in the face of the history lesson: six in every ten French, compared to only one in every four English. In short, the contrast in the responses of English and of French Canadians, who started off holding to the same position and who each heard exactly the same history lesson, confirms the depth of the disagreement between them.

But what about those on the other side of the fence? Do people who support the public funding of Catholic and Protestant religious schools generalize the principle and believe that schools for other religions are also entitled to public funding? Do they take the view that history is, as it were, what happened *then,* or are they inclined instead to view it as an unfolding process?

A powerful process of generalization is at work in liberal democracies, whether fueled by equality as a societal idea, as Tocqueville believed, or driven by consistency as a political principle, as we suspect. So far as this tendency to generalization holds, to declare that any given group (say, Catholics) has a right to government support of religious education is, in the process, to legitimize the idea that other groups similarly situated have a right to government support.

To throw a little light on this, we treated all respondents who said that they favored religious funding of public schools to a special history lesson of their own, which ran as follows: "When Canada was formed, this right was established in the Constitution only for Protestant minorities in Quebec and for Catholic minorities outside of Quebec. Do you think that's acceptable today, or should there be public funding for other religions too?" The right to public funding of religious schools, respondents were thus reminded, was originally restricted to the two founding nations, and it is not unnatural for the question therefore now to arise whether this should remain restricted to them or, alternatively, be extended to religions across the board. By way of making clear what an extension of funding can concretely entail, one-half of the respondents (randomly selected) received the history lesson with one crucial variation, being asked, "Should there be public funding for other religions too, *for example, for Jews*?" (italicized words added in experimental variation).

The proportions saying that funding should be extended to other religious groups—separately calculated for the two experimental groups, one exposed to a specific reference to Jews and the other not—are reported separately. The largest proportion of respondents, having already said that they favor public support for religious schools, go on to say that there should be public funding of religious schools other than Protestant and Catholic ones (fig. 7.7 B). Moreover, pointing out explicitly that to do so will entail public funding of Jewish schools, at a minimum, does not undercut public support for funding religious schools (fig. 7.8).

Having observed this, however, we are struck by the sizeable fraction of citizens—in the neutral version, one in every four—who say they are opposed to public funding of religious schools other than Protestant or Catholic ones. To be sure, this is a minority: but a sizeable one considering the specific circumstances. After all, these respondents have already said that there should be public funding of religious schools; they have, so to speak, just put themselves on record as favoring public funding. No doubt many of them,

Figure 7.8. Support for Public Funding of
Religious Schools Other than Protestant and
Catholic, with Specific Reference to Jews

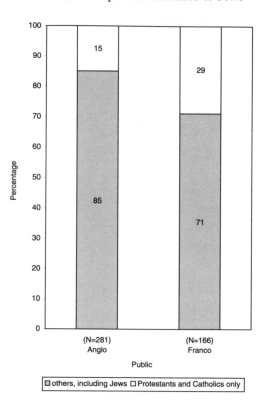

whether Catholic or Protestant, simply assumed that the schools belonged to
the two principal Christian denominations. Yet, given the logic of conversations, having just said that they favor government funding "for religious
schools," they are now under pressure to show they meant what they said—
even though when they said it, they might have meant something else. And
it is in the light of this implicit commitment that the figures reported in figure
7.8 deserve to be read. Had the initial commitment not been made, we
suspect that significantly more would have opposed extending public funding to schools other than Catholic or Protestant ones. And, even if only a
relatively small number were, so to speak, to reverse their ground, the effect
would be to cement the majority *against* public funding of religious schools
in English Canada and come near to undermining the majority *in favor* of it
in French Canada.

To put the point more broadly, the results in figures 7.7 and 7.8 are evidence that sizeable chunks of the public are willing to move from one to the other side of the issue of public funding of religious schools as competing considerations are called to their attention. What makes the politics of this specific issue—and, indeed, the contemporary politics of rights more broadly—so potentially volatile is the swing in support possible if citizens were to take part in a discussion of the issue and take in the pros and cons on both sides. There is, given this swing, both the potential to form a winning coalition on behalf of public funding of religious schools (when available to all religions), coupled with the risk that opponents can put together a commanding majority against it. But that swing is just the point to underline in a consideration of the politics of rights. Politics is dynamic. People are not fixed in the positions they take on major issues, and not simply because some of them have only superficial commitment to these positions. More fundamentally, even citizens with quite genuine preferences, who align themselves pro or con sincerely, often do not commit themselves unconditionally. As we noted earlier in this book, they can be persuaded, if their attention is called to competing considerations, to qualify their initial position or to reverse it entirely. And by directing attention to the pliability of public preferences on issues of rights as well as by disclosing the kinds of considerations that induce citizens to reconsider their positions on Charter issues, we have intended to underline the potential for swings. In politics, majorities are made—and unmade.

Mobility Rights

The mixture of motives that drives the politics of rights can vary not only with the passage of time but also with the context of the political actor; and the politics of mobility illustrates this variability both with respect to time and perspective.

The issue of mobility—of the free, unimpeded flow of Canadians across Canada not only to live but more especially to work—was from the beginning an important item on the nationalizing agenda of Pierre Trudeau and the constitutional architects of the Charter of Rights. To promote a sense of national identity, Trudeau sought to ensure that Quebeckers could migrate out of Quebec and other Canadians could migrate into Quebec. Mobility, so understood, may seem a right to which no one would object, but it is precisely the signature of the politics of rights that claims to a public benefit excite counterclaims, and therefore require elites, if not citizens, to decide not whether they favor a right considered by itself, but whether they favor it in preference to a counterclaim made against it.

The right to mobility, when first asserted, excited several counterclaims (Greene 1989, 45–47). Most obviously, the politics of mobility and of language were intertwined nearly at once: Quebec has since 1977 endeavored to maintain its distinctively French character by requiring newcomers to send their children to French schools and to speak French before becoming an accountant or other professional. But provincial opposition to transprovincial mobility rights was broader still. There was thus a fear in the richer provinces that disadvantaged Canadians from the poorer provinces would flock to theirs to take advantage of their more ample social and health benefits. And, where appropriate, the other provinces (Newfoundland, for example) responded in kind, attempting to see to it that their own residents profited the most from the economic opportunities that lay immediately ahead.

The dynamics of mobility rights reflect this web of competitive fears and desires. The right to live and work anywhere in Canada is, at one level, an individual right; that is, it hinges on a claim to a public benefit that individuals may choose to exercise, on their own initiative and for their own benefit. But, at another level, mobility rights are group rights and the rights of groups of a special kind, namely, provinces.

What difference does it make that mobility rights involve claims that one province can make against another? Because the relevant groups in terms of which mobility rights are defined are provinces and because every one of our respondents is a resident of one of the provinces, the structure of conflict over mobility rights is Janus-like. Claims to mobility rights present themselves to Canadians in two mirror-image contexts. They may involve presenting a claim on behalf of people who reside in another province in support of their right to live or work in the province in which an individual currently lives; alternatively, a claim may be presented on behalf of people who reside in an individual's own province in support of their right to live or work in another province.

Mobility rights thus have a built-in "we–they" structure, with conflict accordingly defined in two contrasting ways: (1) rejection of claims of residents of *other* provinces to the jobs and benefits of *one's own* province; and (2) acceptance of claims of residents of *one's own* province to the jobs and benefits of *other* provinces. But an additional dimension requires consideration. It is an ironic aspect of the contemporary idea of equal rights (we offer this as merely a factual statement, not as a value judgment) that at the elite level it can encompass both a claim that a member of group *X* is entitled to be treated the *same* as a member of group *Y* and a claim that he or she is entitled to be treated *better* than a member of group *Y*. It is surely of interest to see the extent to which the terms of a claim to a right like mobility rights are couched—as a claim to equal or to preferential treatment—as well as on whose behalf the claim is made—to benefit a resident of one's own province or that of another—shape the willingness of Canadians to honor the right to mobility.

A norm of reciprocity tends characteristically to be a central, if implicit, consideration in judgments about group rights. A French Canadian may honor an English Canadian's claim to language rights not out of a specific concern that she should be able to have her children educated in English, but rather out of a parallel concern that French Canadians, similarly situated, should be able to have their children educated in French. Analogously, an English Canadian may reject a French Canadian's claim to language rights not out of an opposition to French education for French minorities outside Quebec, but out of a sense of grievance arising from the failure (as he or she sees it) of French Canadians to do the same for English Canadians in Quebec. Given this norm of reciprocity, it follows that respondents who declared themselves in favor of the right of others who live in their province to live and seek work in other provinces will be under pressure, if then asked whether those who live in other provinces should be able to seek work in their province, to declare themselves in favor, whether they favor it or not; and vice versa.

To get around the problem of a response to one version of mobility rights infecting responses to others, we again resorted to an experiment. Four distinct versions of a question on mobility rights were prepared, and each administered to a randomly selected one-quarter of the respondents, relying on our computer-assisted facility both to randomize and to customize the version of the question. In all, the question ran as follows:

[version 1] "I have some questions about issues relating to jobs and work that I would like to ask now.

What if jobs open up in other provinces of Canada, should people who live in [respondent's province] be allowed to compete equally for those jobs?"

[version 2] "I have some questions about issues relating to jobs and work that I would like to ask now.

What if jobs open up in [respondent's province], should people who live in other provinces of Canada be allowed to compete equally for those jobs?"

[version 3] "I have some questions about issues relating to jobs and work that I would like to ask now.

What if jobs open up in [respondent's province], should people who live in [respondent's province] get preference over Canadians who want to come from other provinces to get those jobs?"

[version 4] "I have some questions about issues relating to jobs and work that I would like to ask now.

What if jobs open up in other provinces, should people who live in those provinces get preference over Canadians who come from [respondent's province] to get those jobs?"

How does the identity of a beneficiary—whether the person to get a crack at a job is one of us, a resident of one's own province or one of them, a resident of another province—interact with the character of the claim for equal treatment or for preferential treatment?

Take as a baseline reactions to claims to the right of mobility, made on behalf of one who is like oneself, in terms of being treated like others. So construed, support for the right to mobility is virtually unanimous (fig. 7.9, version 1). More than nine in every ten anglophones and an equal proportion of francophones agreed that people in their home province should be able to compete equally for jobs in other provinces. Of course, in this situation both the identity of the beneficiary—that a person is from one's own province—and the terms of the right—that it involves equal treatment—work to favor support for mobility rights. What happens, though, if one or both of these elements change?

In the case of "outsiders" claiming a right to compete, on an equal basis, for jobs in a person's own province (version 2), intriguingly, a cleavage begins to be evident in the responses of anglophones and francophones. Anglophone support for mobility rights, though dropping slightly, remains quite high, eight in every ten supporting the right of residents of other provinces to compete, on an equal basis, for jobs in their provinces; francophone support drops sharply, from the 93 percent who believe that Quebeckers should be able to compete equally for jobs in other provinces to the 65 percent who believe that residents of other provinces should be able to compete equally for jobs in Quebec. Group rights thus *invite* normative

Figure 7.9. Support for Mobility Rights

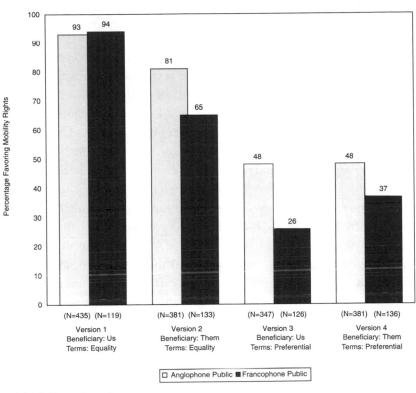

statistical significance of comparisons
anglophone vs. francophone public, version 1: not significant; version 2: p ≤ .01; version 3: p ≤ .01; version 4: p ≤ .05

asymmetries, with different standards of judgment being applied depending upon whose ox is being gored, ours or theirs. But, as these results make plain, it is essential to understand in exactly what sense normative asymmetries are invited. A normative asymmetry, that is, a different standard of judgment according to whether another person is a member of one's group or not, is not impelled by an immanent logic. Framing a right at the level of a group rather than of an individual permits rather than requires normative asymmetries. And the severity of the asymmetry accordingly can vary markedly depending on the norms of the group itself.

To illustrate how group norms help define what is perceived to be fair, consider the final pair of situations. It is not difficult to understand why residents of a province should feel that fellow residents should get preference if jobs open up in their province over people who live in other provinces (version 3); not difficult, and not on its face especially interesting because it appears to illustrate only a garden variety form of in-group favoritism, albeit one more commonly found among francophones than anglophones. Consider, however, respondents' reactions when they are asked whether people who live in other provinces should get preference over people in that other province if jobs open up in those other provinces (version 4). The shoe, so to speak, is now on the other foot. Rather than their fellow residents getting preferential treatment for jobs in their own province, the issue is whether people living in other provinces should get preferential treatment for jobs in *their* province. Yet, strikingly, this makes no difference for anglophones and very little difference for francophones. Both react similarly to a claim for preferential treatment on behalf of an outsider as to one on behalf of a fellow resident,with just under one-half favoring mobility rights, illustrating an interesting aspect of the problem of equitable treatment. The notion that "we" deserve special treatment when it comes to opportunities arising from "our" group need not violate the standard of equal treatment because it paradoxically can carry with it the presumption that "they" similarly deserve special treatment when it comes to opportunities arising out of "their" group. And this swirl of responses supporting mobility rights in some circumstances and opposing them in others illustrates yet again our larger theme of the interdependence of abstract claim and specific context in the politics of rights.

The Dynamics of Language Rights

The dynamics of the politics of language rights are shaped partly by the fact that a claim to a group right can evoke different responses depending on whether it is made on behalf of a group of which a person is a member or on behalf of one of which he or she is not a member. But if the issue of *who* claims a right matters, so does the question of *when* a claim to a right is made.

The lability of support for a language right according to time and circumstance is, from our point of view, the very core of the politics of rights; and by way of illustrating this, we want to take up the specific case of the use of English in Quebec. To assess attitudes on the issue, both within and outside Quebec, we posed the following statement: "To preserve French culture the use of English in advertising should be prohibited in certain parts of the country." Everyone was asked to indicate both whether they agreed or disagreed with the statement, plus the strength of their feelings, pro or con.

Figure 7.10 A. *"To preserve French culture the use of English in advertising should be prohibited in certains parts of the country."*

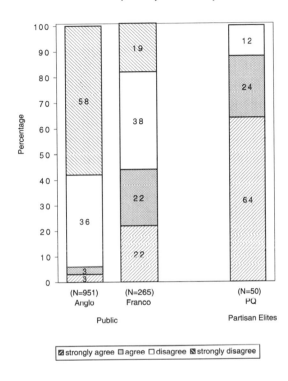

Public   Partisan Elites

☒ strongly agree ☐ agree ☐ disagree ☒ strongly disagree

statistical significance of comparison
anglophone vs. francophone public: p ≤ .01

The pattern of cleavage between English and French Canadians is described in figure 7.10A, and for purposes of comparison, the responses of PQ activists are also shown (other elites overwhelmingly disagreed with a prohibition on the use of English in Quebec). Consider first the contrasting reactions of English Canadians and the PQ. They lie at nearly opposite ends of the spectrum. Nearly all English Canadians disagreed with prohibitions on the use of English in Quebec, most of them strongly. In contrast, most of the PQ agreed with such prohibitions, most of them strongly. The cleavage between the two could not be sharper or deeper.

It may seem obvious this should be so: that on the issue of the hegemony of French in Quebec anglophones and francophones will inevitably and overwhelmingly wind up at opposite ends of the spectrum. Which is all the

Figure 7.10 B. *"A business in Quebec
should . . . (1) have the right to put whatever
language it wants on signs outside a
building; (2) accept that Quebec is basically
French and put only French on signs outside
its building."*

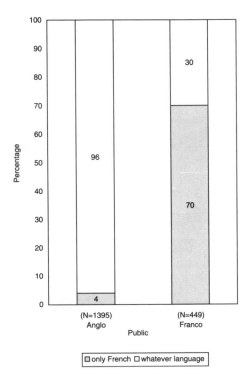

Source: 1988 Canadian National Election Study
(1989 mailback questionnaire)

more reason to weigh the reactions of ordinary francophones. They were
very far from universally committed at the time of our study to the prohibition of English in Quebec (fig. 7.10A). To be sure, a substantial number of
them favored it. But more did not.

What does this tell us about the structure of conflict over group rights? It
may seem self-evidently true that members of a group on whose behalf a
claim to a right is being asserted will back the claim. But, these findings
suggest, the politics of rights can take opposing forms: claims may be made
not only as to what French Canadians may do, but also as to what English

Canadians may not do; and French Canadians as a whole are ordinarily more likely to rally around the first type than the second. And just so far as this holds, a line of cleavage between the politically engaged and the larger public is likely to open up *within* Quebec—as the contrasting reactions of ordinary francophones and PQ activists illustrate. But—and this is just the point of underlining the dynamics of language rights—this cleavage is not frozen. It can grow larger or, as we mean to illustrate, shrink with the play of politics.

The dynamic character of attitudes on language rights was illustrated in late 1988 when on December 15 the Supreme Court of Canada struck down another section of Quebec's Bill 101. This time the Court declared its "French-only" commercial sign law provisions to be inconsistent with the Charter of Rights freedom of expression provisions. Many ordinary Quebeckers were outraged, and the nationalists made the most of it. Public rallies were held demanding that the provincial Liberal government of Robert Bourassa act decisively to protect the French commercial face of Quebec signs. Bourassa, who only three years earlier in the midst of a provincial election campaign had promised to permit bilingual signs, emerged on December 18 from a weekend-long huddle with his advisors to announce that he would use the override provision in section 33 of the Charter of Rights to require that outdoor commercial signs be in French.[7] Indoors, bilingual signs would be permitted. This bit of political compromise got the government past the immediate crisis, but it pleased few. Indeed, the political fallout of the Court's decision and Bourassa's reaction to it was very substantial. In Quebec, popular attitudes shifted sharply in favor of restricting English signs, while outside of Quebec these events signaled the beginning of the end for the Meech Lake Accord. At the elite level, the provincial Conservative government in Manitoba, led by Gary Filmon, who had vigorously fought bilingualism in the province through filibuster and an election campaign, withdrew the accord from legislative consideration. And at the level of the larger public, political attitudes on language rights became, if anything, less accommodating.

We have evidence of these changes thanks to a happy accident of timing in the scheduling of the mailback portion of the Canadian National Election Study (CNES) of 1988. In that study, a random sample of Canadians were interviewed by telephone during the course of the federal election of 1988 and again immediately thereafter. Subsequently, a mailback questionnaire was sent to respondents beginning early in 1989, just after the Supreme Court's ruling in December and the events in Quebec. Although the wording of the cnes item differs from that in our Charter of Rights Project in that it asks more directly about the policy announced by Bourassa, it offers an important point of comparison with our measurement, also by means of a mailback, in mid 1987. The wording of the cnes question was,

> "A business in Quebec should:
> (1) have the right to put whatever language it wants on signs outside a building
>
> or
>
> (2) accept that Quebec is basically French and put only French on signs outside its building."

The responses to this item are reported in figure 7.10B. When we compare these data with the results of the Charter Project signs question, reported in figure 7.10A, we find a strong pattern of continuity in anglophones and a dramatic pattern of change among francophones. Thus, among anglophones, we see again an almost uniform opposition to French-only sign laws. In contrast, however, among francophones, we see marked change: the distribution of opinion on French-only signs goes from something like 55 percent opposed to 70 percent in favor. Differences in wording and formatting warn against exact comparison, but the center of gravity manifestly has shifted and over a strikingly short time frame, on the one hand markedly narrowing the gap between French Canadian political activists and French Canadians as a whole and, on the other hand, markedly widening the cleavage between English Canadians and French Canadians.

Precisely this kind of swing seems to us the mark of the politics of group rights. The willingness of members of one group to acknowledge that members of another group have the same rights that they believe that they are themselves entitled to is inherently volatile. It is volatile because the principle of reciprocity that underlies it—"they" are entitled to be treated as "we" are entitled to be treated—can easily be seen to be violated. And once "they" are perceived to be refusing to acknowledge "our" rights, then the force of exactly the same norm of reciprocity reverses itself, now undercutting rather than shoring up the willingness of members of one group to acknowledge the rights of members of another group. Legitimacy must thus be time-subscripted: a readiness to respect claims to rights—and perhaps particularly to group rights—is a variable, not a constant.

Reprise

The politics of language rights is carried on at a symbolic level and also at the level of definable rights spelled out in specific sections of the Charter of Rights and Freedoms. And the cleavages and tensions over language take different shapes across the levels of symbolism and right.

At the level of symbolic politics, the fundamental cleavage is between English and French Canadian, with political elites, whether English or French, playing a role of conciliation by lining up with the French Canadian perspective. At the level of the politics of rights, patterns of cleavage and consensus are more complex, nuanced, problematic. Judged by the side of the issue on which they come down, English Canadian parliamentary elites overwhelmingly support the claims of French Canadians to education in their own language. Judged by the frequency with which they spontaneously attach qualifications and conditions to their support for this right, however, their commitment is more contingent.

The politics of language rights is, moreover, volatile in a special way. It turns on the readiness of members of one group to grant to members of another a right to which it believes it is itself entitled. It does not follow, and this deserves emphasis, that just because members of a group believe that they are entitled to the right that they are willing to extend the same right reciprocally to members of another group. There is, we suspect, a built-in asymmetry to reciprocity in rights. A political minority has a stronger interest in acknowledging that the majority is entitled to a right that it wants itself to exercise than the majority has in acknowledging that a minority is entitled to a right that *it* wants to exercise.[8] Just such an asymmetry is evident in the markedly greater willingness of French Canadians to support the rights of English Canadians under the Charter than English Canadians show in supporting the rights of French Canadians under the Charter. And, considering French Canadians now not as a minority in the country as a whole but instead as a majority in their province, just such an asymmetry is evident in the propensity of French Canadians to declare that they are entitled to benefits and rights in Quebec that English Canadians living in Quebec are not—just as (with respect to mobility rights, for example) English Canadians return the compliment. But if a group's desire to exercise a right is only imperfectly translated into a willingness to allow members of another group similarly situated to exercise an equivalent right, its willingness to withdraw support for another group's claim to a right is more closely tied to its perception that members of the other group are unwilling to acknowledge *its* claim to the right. Reciprocity is a social norm: but its negative cycles tend to be more rapid than its positive ones; hence the inherent fragility of group compacts on parallel group rights.

EIGHT VALUE PLURALISM

Pluralism has been the figure in the carpet—pluralism of ideas, of institutions, above all, of values. It is time to pull together the threads of the argument. Our argument, put in the broadest terms, is that conflicts over democratic rights are inescapable, not simply because many citizens do not understand what the values of a democratic politics require in practice, but because many of these values clash with one another, and some of them even clash with themselves.

In its modern dress, pluralism entered empirical democratic theory as a theory of political power. Examined close-up, public decisions turned out to be made by different hands from one issue area to another, and political influence, though not unrelated to economic advantage and social standing, was reducible to neither of these taken individually nor both combined (Dahl 1961; Polsby 1980; Wolfinger 1974). Our interest, in contrast, is with pluralism as a theory of democratic values.

Two Theories of Disagreement over Democratic Rights: Error and Contestability

A prime question—indeed, arguably the prime question—for empirical democratic theory is why people disagree over claims to democratic rights.

Two theoretical approaches have been staked out. The first, featured in previous studies of civil liberties, treats disputes over democratic rights as rooted in a failure to understand the foundational values of a liberal democratic political culture; the second, emphasized in our study, treats these disputes as driven by the inherent contestability of democratic values. The two theories of democratic dissensus—error and contestability—are not mutually exclusive[1]—but they are patently distinct.

In the classic study launching the empirical analysis of public opinion and civil liberties, Stouffer (1955) called attention to the connections between support for freedom of expression and an array of personal and social factors, central among them the amount of formal education people have had, the number of years they have lived, the breadth of their exposure to different places and points of view, and the size of the community in which they live. A miscellany of factors at first glance, but a common thread can be picked out on closer inspection. Why does schooling foster support for freedom of speech? Because it "puts a person in touch with people whose ideas and values are different from one's own."[2] Why does living in a large city encourage support for freedom of assembly? Because "the citizen of a metropolitan community is more likely to rub shoulders with a variety of people whose values are different from his own and even repugnant to him than is the man or woman in a village."[3] And why is the older generation less supportive of liberty? Because their mental outlook is narrower, more rigid, less accepting of diversity and heterogeneity.[4] In sum, any factor that enlarges citizens' mental horizons, exposes them to a wider range of ideas, experiences, and people, overrides an inclination to simplistic thinking and dividing the world into us and them promotes a willingness to accept the political rights of individuals and groups whose point of view or background is unfamiliar, controversial, or threatening. Conversely, a failure to uphold democratic values reflects a narrowness of experience, a parochial background, an unwillingness or inability to make complex and nuanced judgments, a susceptibility to oversimplified, rigid, dichotomous judgments.[5] Democratic dissensus is thus assimilated to social prejudice, with disagreement over civil liberties belonging to a larger domain conceived as encompassing religious, racial, *and* political tolerance.

This straightforward insight—that a value like liberty is not naturally and effortlessly acquired but requires critical thinking and complex standards of judgment—has provided the basis for arguably the most systematically developed account of commitment to democratic values: the so-called social learning theory. Social learning theory holds that support for democratic rights is a function of the extent to which citizens have been exposed to the norms of the culture, understand them, and are motivated to accept them.[6] A failure to adhere to democratic values in the heat of a controversy represents a form of error: if citizens understood better the values of liberty and due process, they would be more willing to accept, for example, that people accused of a crime have a right not to incriminate themselves.[7] Conflict over democratic rights represents, at its heart, a clash between those who understand what the norms of a democratic polity require and those who, for whatever reason, do not.

By contrast, conflicts over democratic rights can be viewed as rooted in the inherent contestability of democratic values. On this second view, it is essential to appreciate that the political culture of liberal democracy, including the high or official or elite version of liberal democracy, does not speak with a single voice. It necessarily incorporates a multiplicity of values, and these different values unavoidably cut in different directions, sometimes strengthening, sometimes cutting across, a claim to a right. It follows that merely to say that learning the values of the political culture of liberal democracy strengthens commitment to democratic rights does not say nearly enough. Disagreement over claims to democratic rights cannot be reduced simply to a failure of learning and judgment, important as ignorance and ill-considered judgments are in political affairs. Claims to democratic rights are inescapably contestable because the values on which they rest inevitably collide.

The two theories—the error interpretation, which treats opposition to democratic rights as rooted in a failure to understand the norms of the political culture, and the contestability interpretation, which views disagreement over democratic rights as driven by the conflict of values—are not mutually exclusive. Both have a measure of validity. Proponents of the error interpretation, which has been the dominant theme from the start of systematic studies of public opinion and civil liberties, have themselves acknowledged from the start that collisions between competing and equally legitimate values can generate disagreement over claims to democratic rights. But their emphasis falls overwhelmingly on the limits of citizens' understanding of democratic values. Disagreements over the most disparate of issues, for example, freedom of speech and the press, protection against self-incrimination, involvement of prisoners in medical experimentation, symbolic speech, civil disobedience, the right to abortion, and a host of other issues involving privacy and differing life-styles, are treated as though they hinge on essentially the same conflict: between those who understand rightly what the values of a democratic society call for and those whose understanding is, for whatever reason, muddled.[8]

So one-sided an emphasis has given an almost content-free flavor to accounts of disagreement over democratic rights. Every disagreement, viewed from this perspective, tends to be like every other. From an explanatory point of view, what is at issue in the question of whether police can search a car they have stopped for a traffic violation is essentially the same as what is at issue in the question of whether a teenager can have sewn onto the back of his jacket the message, "Fuck the draft" or even burn a cross on the lawn of a Black family. Conflicts over democratic rights, regardless of their specific content, reduce to disputes between those who know the right answer (because they understand the core values) and those who do not.

We disagree. To recover the real character of conflict over political rights, it is necessary to begin by appreciating that democratic values cannot be immunized against political challenge. Different democratic values, however, are not necessarily contestable in the same way.

Contesting Liberty

It is common practice to speak of the value of liberty as though it can be conceived in distinct ways, each legitimate, yet each conflicting with the others. Liberty conceived as negative freedom has thus been famously distinguished from liberty conceived as positive freedom, and much of the history of politics in advanced societies since the eighteenth century, it has been suggested, can be read as the record of the clash between the two. As against this, Isaiah Berlin has argued for the singularity of liberty as a democratic value:

> What troubles the consciences of Western liberals is not, I think, the belief that the freedom that men seek differs according to their social or economic conditions, but that the minority who possess it have gained it by exploiting, or, at least, averting their gaze from, the vast majority who do not. . . . Liberty is not the only goal of men. . . . But nothing is gained by a confusion of terms. To avoid glaring inequality or widespread misery I am ready to sacrifice some, or all, of my freedom: I may do so willingly and freely: but it is freedom that I am giving up for the sake of justice or equality or the love of my fellow men. I should be guilt-stricken, and rightly so, if I were not, in some circumstances, ready to make this sacri-

fice. But a sacrifice is not an increase in what is being sacrificed, namely freedom, however great the moral need or the compensation for it. Every thing is what it is: liberty is liberty, not equality or fairness or justice or culture, or human happiness or a quiet conscience. (1969, 125)

Whatever its fate at the level of normative political theory, Berlin's argument on the singularity of liberty as a democratic value has force at the level of empirical democratic theory. We can offer no evidence for rival ideas of liberty, whether conceived in terms of a commitment to a realization of self or of society, held by either ordinary citizens or the politically influential and sophisticated. For both, liberty means the right to say and do what you want, to say what you think about public issues, to join with others and promote a point of view.

That the meaning of liberty is essentially immediate, and agreed, is of primary importance. It allows ordinary citizens to make a genuine commitment to liberty. If what was required was that they first master a set of abstract political doctrines, then by a process of logical deduction identify the appropriate position on a live issue of democratic rights, ordinary citizens could hardly adhere to the value of liberty. The results we have reported both here and elsewhere,[9] however, suggest that when citizens are asked to judge a claim to liberty, they summon to mind a vivid example, or prototype, of what freedom involves—What is liberty? It's being free "to say and do what you think"—then make judgments of similarity, favoring the claims of liberty the more similar the specific controversy is to their prototype of freedom, opposing it the more dissimilar it is. On this natural category approach, special powers of cerebration on the part of the average citizen need not be assumed. On the contrary, citizens learn to apply the category of liberty the same way they learn to apply a wide range of "fuzzy set" natural categories to other complex, ambiguous, real-world events: on the basis of rapid-fire intuitive judgments of similarity. In a word, they learn to apply the category of liberty the same way they learn the category of yellow as a color.[10]

But if there are not mutually conflicting conceptions of liberty in general circulation, then what does it mean to say that it is contestable? It is true to say that liberty as a value is exposed to challenge by its conflicts with other values; true but not nearly instructive enough, for liberty is subject to challenge in at least two quite different ways. The first and archetypal form of conflict consists in collisions between liberty and competing values on the right, including securing the country against external threats, safeguarding individuals against crime and violence, maintaining respect for tradition and common practice, and ensuring the effective operation of government—the overall set of which we call, for convenience, the politics of order. The second and more recent type of conflict involves a clash between liberty and competing values on the left, most notably, a variety of claims made in behalf of tolerance, particularly in the last half-century, of religious, racial, and ethnic minorities.

Consider the issue of whether a protest demonstration should be allowed to proceed or whether it should be prohibited as a threat to public safety. In a situation like this, it is customary to speak of a clash between liberty and order, but reflect upon the choice from the perspective of a person asked to make it. He will favor allowing the protest demonstration insofar as he places a high value on liberty, favor prohibiting it insofar as he places a high value on order; but, what is crucial, he will be more likely to do the former insofar as he is unlikely to do the latter, and will be more likely to do the latter insofar as he is unlikely to do the former. In any given situation, then, the claims of liberty and order can *logically* clash, in that honoring one means rejecting the other; yet for any given person, in deciding which claim to honor in that situation, there need not be intense *psychological* conflict because the empirical results, others' as well as ours,[11] make plain that the more importance people attach to the value of liberty, the less they tend to attach to that of order, and vice versa. Indeed, just insofar as political values like liberty and order do matter to citizens or political decision makers, they minimize the likelihood that they will find themselves having to choose between them by ensuring that their positions on the two values are politically consistent, that is to say, negatively correlated.[12]

A distinct form of value conflict is represented by the clash of liberty and racial tolerance; distinct because the structure of conflict is quite different. Support for liberty and order, as we remarked, tends to be negatively correlated: the more importance that people (whether citizens or decision makers) attach to one, the *less* they attach to the other. Support for liberty and tolerance of minorities, in contrast, tends to be positively correlated: The more importance that people (whether citizens or decision makers) attach to one, the *more* they attach to the other. Having to choose between liberty and tolerance thus can represent a dilemma in a way that having to choose between liberty and order need not.[13] In either case, however, the choice is not simply which abstract principle to prefer. As we have shown in chapter 2, the specifics of the claim to rights can make a big difference. The responses of both citizens and elites differ markedly depending upon who wants to hold a public rally or whom the government seeks to wiretap. Thus support for civil liberties can depend to a substantial degree upon whose rights are at stake. And in this respect politics are front and center.

Liberty, then, is contestable in different ways, and the differences matter politically. Specifically, we have illustrated connections between the structure of value conflict and the role of political elites in buttressing democratic rights. The accepted position, as we detailed in chapter 2, has been that political elites in democratic polities provide a bulwark for essential democratic rights, including freedom of expression and assembly, due process, and privacy, and that they do so by the strength of their commitment to essential rights when they are translated from abstract principles to specific claims in controversial situations. By contrast, ordinary citizens, though endorsing democratic rights unanimously at the level of principle, fall far short when they confront specific claims in threatening or controversial situations. Political elites, it is accordingly argued, provide a special measure of steadiness and fidelity to democratic principles when political passions are excited. It is the singular strength of the commitment of elites to democratic principle *and* practice, coupled with the special influence they enjoy by virtue of their uncommon engagement in politics and public affairs, that allows them to play a strategic, steadying role.

In support of this argument, which we and others have called the thesis of democratic elitism, every large systematic study of the views of political elites and of ordinary citizens (including our own past work) has found elites to be more supportive of civil liberties and civil rights than the general public. Our view, nonetheless, is that the role of political elites is more problematic than the standard presumption of an elite-grounded consensus allows. It is more problematic, to the extent that one focuses on the clash between liberty and order, because the role of political elites and the nature of value conflict need to be set in an institutional context. As we have argued at length, it is misleading to contrast ordinary citizens with political elites taken as a whole. Political elites tend to seek out and to be welcomed into political parties made up of people of broadly sympathetic views. Under the pressure of shared values and in response to electoral incentives, political parties tend to diverge in the positions they take on a range of issues and in the emphasis they place on an array of political and social values, including those bearing on claims to individual rights. This tendency of political parties to diverge ideologically tends to be checked in some degree by counter-pressures to obscure their programmatic commitments in order to maximize their vote share, and so is variable in both degree and salience depending on time and circumstance. Yet acknowledging this, taking advantage of direct evidence in Canada and indirect evidence in the United States, we have seen marked differences between the preferred positions of competing political parties on key issues of civil liberties.

The original argument for democratic elitism is, in retrospect, quite remarkable. It hinged on the contrast between the views of ordinary citizens and those of the politically active and influential stratum, a notion that can be traced back at least to the groundbreaking work of V. O. Key.[14] The politically active stratum, in study after study, showed themselves to be more committed to democratic rights than the general public, and although disagreement has been expressed from time to time about why this is so,[15] every major study has found it to be so. But the notion of a politically active stratum was itself understood in curiously apolitical terms, as though it could be located and representative participants in it could be identified outside of the institutional context of politics and, above all, independent of the party system. Yet it is precisely the party system that gives not only institutional but also ideological form to the competition between elites for authoritative control. The dynamics of the beliefs and values of the *political* elite cannot be grasped outside their competitive struggle for political power, a struggle that differentiates them into organized groups representing distinctive political tendencies. To focus on the preferences of political elites taken as a whole and without regard to political party is to focus on a mythical political tendency. It is necessary, on the contrary, to focus on the distinctive commitments of political elites, organized into political parties competing for political power. It matters who wins the election. And the overlooking of political institutions and, above all, of the party system in promoting systematic differences in commitment to civil liberties *between* competing sets of elites organized around political parties has been a long-standing, albeit unsuspected, failing of the thesis of democratic elitism.

The thesis has a second failing, one that has disclosed itself only recently and, paradoxically, only as a function of a movement to a more tolerant outlook in contemporary democracies. Judged from any angle, the largest normative movement in public opinion in liberal democracies like the United States and Canada has centered on racial tolerance. Race prejudice has not disappeared, of course, but the objective record of trend studies registers a profound attenuation of explicitly racist sentiments[16] over the past forty years, while studies of political tolerance (including but by no means limited to ours)[17] demonstrate that the group now most disliked by citizens, again both in Canada and the United States, is racists. The movement toward racial tolerance is a principal component of a larger spirit of tolerance that has become a visible feature of liberal democracies in the late twentieth century and that shows itself in gains across a broad front. The promotion of tolerance, that is, assuring that a number of groups once treated as second-class citizens are treated fairly, has become a prominent theme of contemporary politics.

It would be wrong to suggest that each aspect of this larger program is interchangeable with the others, and just for this reason we have in our detailed analysis considered the distinctive character of the choices each poses. Here, however, we want to address a primary source of their common trajectory: the contemporary concern over racism. The last twenty-five years have seen a quickening of the desire to end racial discrimination and victimization, and it should not need saying—but it does—that the gathering campaign to combat racism represents a remarkable argument on behalf of liberal democracy. The movement away from prejudice and the emergent pressure to combat discrimination, taken just by itself, epitomizes the capacity of democratic citizenship to enlarge its understanding of fundamental values.

Yet, our fundamental theme is the irreducible pluralism of values, hence the unavoidable contestability of all values, including, it must now be acknowledged, liberty and racial tolerance. The clash between liberty and tolerance is reshaping the politics of elite and mass publics in liberal democracies. As we have seen, political elites taken as a whole have formed a consensus supportive of freedom of expression, and not merely as an abstract principle but as a claim contested in actual political controversy. But this elite consensus breaks down when applied to the problem of racism. Political elites are, to be sure, more likely to support the right of racists to freedom of assembly than are ordinary citizens, but little comfort is to be taken from that because the crucial point is that the consensus in favor of freedom of expression is fractured. On the issue of whether a group said to be racist has the right to hold a rally, elites are divided down the middle, as many opposed to freedom of expression as in support of it.

Looking forward, without, of course, being able to foretell the detail and circumstance of the specific clashes that will be carried out over the immediate years ahead, we suspect that liberty will be even more heavily contested. More heavily contested because subject to challenge now from two politically opposing directions: from the right, in the name and on behalf of order; from the left, in the name and on behalf of tolerance.

Contesting Equality

Liberty is contestable because it unavoidably collides, when specific choices must be made, with other values. In contrast, equality is contestable both for this reason and also because different conceptions of it unavoidably collide. Equality is itself a plurality of values, inviting not merely different but conflicting understandings. Equality, in consequence, is a chameleon value politically: it is perhaps the most formidable weapon of the left, yet it can also be just as sharp a sword for the right.

A proper appreciation of political ironies begins with consideration of equality as a symbolic value. At this level, equality is taken to be a defining value of popular political culture, but in a paradoxical way. On the one side, the trademark of American popular culture is egalitarianism, while Canadian popular culture is, by comparison, organic, corporate, hierarchical; on the other side, just because the Canadian culture is organic and communitarian compared to the American, it can be collectivist, even socialist in a way the American cannot. Hence the paradoxical representation of Canadian popular culture as both more elitist, hierarchical, and deferential and more egalitarian and collectivist. But the lesson of our findings is not paradox but irony. On comparison after comparison, equality as a symbolic value has a similar, not a distinct, standing in the two cultures: ordinary Canadians and Americans are, although not identical in every respect, very much alike.

Equality is a chameleon value, varying in both its appearance and political trajectory across levels and contexts. As a symbolic value, equality has a high standing particularly in the popular culture, but pitched in terms of economic equity it has a quite different standing. It is not merely that the idea of equality, understood as equivalency of income if not of wealth, is rejected both by the public at large and by elites taken as a whole. Rather, the point to emphasize is the positive legitimacy of inequalities of economic rewards, and not merely at the periphery of the culture but at its center. Moreover, there is a cleavage within the elite culture, legal and administrative elites giving equality as a symbolic value a markedly qualified backing while political elites themselves divide over equality along ideological lines.

The notion of acceptable inequalities is most often taken to be a contingent feature of liberal democracy, not an essential one, best understood as a by-product of the historical conjunction of capitalism and democracy. Our findings suggest, however, that the notion is more deeply rooted psychologically. What is involved is not merely a passive acceptance of income inequalities that result inevitably but unintentionally from equality of opportunity, but an active belief that the chance to do better than others can shape and strengthen people's character, teaching them the value of hard work and personal achievement. Yet, to put matters this way, though true enough, obscures a telling asymmetry in public opinion that normative theories of distributive justice obscure. Economic success and failure, conceived by libertarians as the product of individual choice and conduct, are mirror images: the qualities of initiative and effort that mark success are, by their very absence, what distinguish failure. Conversely, economic success and failure conceived in more Rawlsian terms as the results of a lottery independent of considerations of personal merit offer not just mirror but identical images, both reflecting arbitrary initial assignments. By contrast, popular ideas about success and failure are asymmetrical: there is a greater willingness to give credit for success, to see it as crowning individual desert, and at the same time a greater reluctance to stigmatize for failure, to see it as proof of the absence of individual merit.

Ideas of individual merit and desert supplied the core of individualism as a political value, and individualism was the form that egalitarianism took in both popular and elite cultures in the nineteenth century; it remains a central expression of egalitarianism, at any rate in the popular culture, in the twentieth century. It is, all the same, inherently difficult to characterize the standing of individualism: difficult because pluralism is a condition of values, not only in the sense of their being multiple values, but also because of the multiple conditions under which citizens make choices about values. Thus, the common practice is to speak as though citizens affirm or reject individualism as a value, in varying degrees to be sure. So viewed, the popular image of individualism appears wildly inconsistent: some expressions of it, for example, the notion that people should stand on their own two feet rather than depend on government, are overwhelmingly popular; others, for example, the notion that government should "look after" citizens, which appear to be contradictory, are comparably popular. Some part of this is no doubt attributable to the loose-jointedness of ordinary citizens' political thinking in general, but not very much in this instance because the pattern is the same for even the most sophisticated legal and political elites. As the full array of our results drives home, people do not just strike up a position with respect to a value like individualism in the abstract. Their feelings, the stance they take and not merely the degree of enthusiasm they express, depend on the problem context. Values like individualism have a symbolic status and evoke responses for and against in their own right, but more often and more deeply, with the exception of the ideologically anchored, people respond to a value like individualism not as free-floating and considered in itself, but taken as a (possible) solution for a particular problem engaging them. Hence the diversity of their evaluative responses: it is not that their view of individualism, taken by itself and abstracted from concrete circumstances, has necessarily changed. It is rather that they contemplate the specific problem before them, recommending a course for public action by relying in part on internalized values and preconceptions about politics and society and in part on the salient features of the specific problem context. In a word, the specific problem they confront supplies the context defining the value of individualism.

The politics of liberal democracy is, to a greater extent than is ordinarily appreciated, concerned not just with who gets what but with who *should* get what, and this applies not merely to the judgments of ordinary citizens but also to those of political decision makers seeking public power. It is, of course, perfectly understandable that other approaches to an understanding of politics give short shrift to the role of values, accentuating instead the extent to which both individuals (particularly people running for public office) and organizations (particularly political parties) act to maximize their advantage. It would be unconvincing to any seasoned political observer, and in any event quite unnecessary from the point of view of a rounded theory of politics, to minimize the role of political self-interest. What is no less clear, however, is the extent to which, precisely among those most successful in the struggle for political power, political parties, if not particular individuals, stake out ideological ground, then hold on to it even if it manifestly is not in their immediate electoral interest to do so. As we have seen, political parties advertise commitments to conceptions of equality that it would pay them electorally to obscure, if not to abandon.

Put this way, there appears to be a paradox. Political parties, by design bent on winning political power by winning over electoral majorities, are locked into positions appealing to electoral minorities. The air of paradox arises chiefly through the implicit presumption of dichotomous thinking: parties must choose their positions to maximize either their electoral advantage or to be true to their value commitments. But this sort of either/or thinking—this presumption that a theory of politics, if cast in rational choice terms, cannot accommodate the impact of values in politics or, if it acknowledges the formative role of values, cannot accommodate the role of political self-interest—is mistaken. It is mistaken if only because of the role of ideology as selective incentive for political parties as organizations: parties dedicate themselves to some points of view that may not pay electorally partly because they need to maintain the internal strength to compete for external support. And just for this reason, equality is an ideological sword that cuts both ways: it can be used both for and against the political left.

It is, however, necessary to push deeper to understand the dynamics of the politics of equality. Political power is not won or lost in debates over equality, considered as a value and isolated from competing considerations, but in electoral arguments over public policy, arguments over what the government is specifically allowed or obliged to do.

A concern with equality at the level of policy rather than principle begins properly with redistribution. The enduring and until recently the central core of equality and public policy has been to attenuate differences in income and life chances between the best off and the worst off. Equality, contrasted with elitism, conveys the sense of equal standing. Alternatively, contrasted with individualism, it conveys the sense of collectivist or activist governance. Attending to this duality has a double payoff, for it clarifies, on the one hand, the meaning of pluralism as a political theory of democratic values and, on the other, the distinctive dynamics of redistributive politics.

If one accepts pluralism as the starting point for a political theory of claims to public benefits, what does it mean to say that equality can be construed in different ways? The underlying notion, sometimes made explicit but more often left implicit, is that the same person endorses contrary notions, for example, supports equality in the sense of equal standing but opposes it in the sense of activist governance; and this endorsement of alternative conceptions of equality is evidence of "ambivalence" toward equality as a value. Notice that the notion of ambivalence implies that people are in a state of conflict regarding equality, seesawing between opposing conceptions of equality. As against the idea of ambivalence, however, it is useful to counterpoise the notion of a belief repertoire, that is, of an array of beliefs that people may hold simultaneously; beliefs that, though pointing in politically opposing directions, they may entertain without being inconsistent precisely because specific problems, even within a common area of policy, need not be of a piece. From this perspective, part of the point of underlining the diversity of conceptions of a value like equality is precisely to call attention to the diversity of problem-situations subsumed under the heading of equality. People have available more than one evaluative belief to guide a response in a particular situation because they have to deal with more than one kind of problem-situation, even within a common field of concerns like equality, and so can make use of a repertoire of coping responses. So viewed, the variety of their responses to redistributive politics represents in part the diversity of policy issues bundled up under the heading of equality.

Several lines of evidence are consistent with this argument, particularly the similarities between elites and ordinary citizens, although it would go too far to suggest that it has been conclusively demonstrated. Given what is at stake normatively, the alternative interpretations deserve clear statement. On the one hand, the ambivalence interpretation, although emphasizing the multiple responses that citizens may make potentially to a value like equality, takes the fact that they give different responses as evidence that their thinking is conflicted or muddled and lacking in consistency. On the other hand, the belief repertoire interpretation treats the diversity of responses citizens can give to a common class of issues as evidence that their thinking is acute; acute, moreover, in the specific sense of being responsive to the actual diversity of problem situations lumped by convention under a common heading. To be sure, the two interpretations are not mutually exclusive. Although both may possess a measure of validity, it makes a good deal of difference which carries greater explanatory weight. Consider a pair of redistributive issues we examined: the universality of benefits, that is, whether benefits from social insurance programs such as old age pensions should be means-tested; and health care extra-billing, that is, whether under government-sponsored medicare doctors and hospitals should be allowed to charge more than what government health plans pay them. The question is not whether citizens respond quite differently to this pair of issues, notwithstanding that both are patently redistributive; it is whether, in responding differently, they are giving evidence of being inconsistent or of being discriminating in their judgments.[18]

This issue aside, equality under the description of redistributive politics has not lacked for attention, either normative or empirical; indeed, so unceasing has been the attention awarded it that the politics of equality has sometimes been very nearly equated with issues of redistribution. But the politics of equality—this goes to the heart of our interest in pluralism as a theory of democratic values—has assumed new forms; new forms generated, above all, by claims to rights and benefits made on behalf not of individuals but of groups.

It is by now wearyingly familiar to remark on the clash of group and individual rights, but the impression of familiarity is potentially deceptive. The issue of group rights has perhaps been too often debated in the specific context of affirmative action, and although the issues under debate here go deep, they have been stamped by the American dilemma of race. Our concern, however, is the dynamics of liberal democracies, not just of American democracy, and so it is important to place the issue of group rights in a fresh context.

That context is the claim of Aboriginals—or, colloquially, Indians—to be bearers of rights under a constitution and also holders of rights outside it. A claim to unique rights advanced on behalf of native people, who are uniquely situated by virtue of both treaty commitments and constitutional undertakings, exposes a number of new dilemmas in the idea of group rights, dilemmas brought to light by the special position of Indians, but not unique to it. Does a desire to ensure that Aboriginal peoples can enter all aspects of the life of the larger society represent a move to accept or, ironically, to extinguish their distinctive identity? To what extent does making a claim to unique rights based on unique group experiences represent a new card introduced into the political game of rights, a card that can disrupt the whole game by introducing a competition not simply between conflicting values but between conflicting ways of life? And supposing these dilemmas are real and not merely conjectural, a still larger dilemma supervenes: how, as a matter both of practice and of political sovereignty, are they to be resolved? Who is to arbitrate between acceptance and uniqueness? Who can? Who has a right to?

Affirmative action, of course, represents a now familiar territory on which the claim of group rights is encountered, although given the one-sided concentration on the American experience, it is a territory less well-reconnoitered than may be supposed. Given our own interest in a political theory of rights, the perspective we have taken on affirmative action may appear paradoxical. The principal pitfall, in our view, is to suppose that the questions driving the argument over affirmative action are, at their core, matters of political theory. What is at issue is not so much a theory of justice, new or old. Fairness is *the* issue, but it is fairness defined in a context. Who has suffered what? Who has profited at another's expense? How can jobs and opportunities be redistributed?

The contemporary vocabulary expresses claims to public benefits in terms of rights, and the idea of group rights under affirmative action is no exception. But if the question is, Who should get what? then the paramount point to understand is that in liberal democracies, where the identity of the collectivity clashes with the identities of groups, the *who* dominates the *should* and the *what*. To exaggerate, in this political context, group rights are about groups, not rights, and this applies both to those who favor them and those who reject them. Their natural effect, therefore, is to sharpen cleavages between groups, whether one has in mind the group that loses under them or the group that benefits from them. The quota beneficiary experiment discussed in chapter 5 randomly varied whether the group benefiting from quotas assigning top government jobs was French Canadians or women. English Canadians, not surprisingly, were markedly more likely to favor affirmative action for women than for French Canadians, French Canadians just as likely to favor it for French Canadians as for women. It is, to be sure, not difficult to imagine why a French Canadian should find it fair for French Canadians to be given preference over English Canadians when governmental jobs are given out; neither is it difficult to imagine why an English Canadian should find this unfair. Two additional features of the politics of affirmative action, however, give it a quite distinctive trajectory. On the one side, the deepest cleavage over affirmative action is between those who make the rules, particularly political elites, and those who live under them, namely, ordinary citizens. By any standard, support for affirmative action, whether to benefit French Canadians or women, is far higher among political elites than among the public at large. On the other side, although it is palpable that groups benefiting from affirmative action believe their present benefits to be fair because they had previously been treated unfairly, there is no evidence to show, and much reason to doubt, that their benefiting from affirmative action eradicates their feeling of having been (and continuing to be) treated unfairly. More needs to be done to pin this down, but it is not unreasonable to suggest that affirmative action may distinctively generate resentment among both those who lose and those who win from it: most obviously, from the losers because they are losing and are manifestly suffering from a double standard; less obviously, from the winners because the very benefits they receive strengthen their sense that they were and continue to be treated unfairly.

Contesting Legitimacy

The political game of rights consists, at one level, in competing to make effective claims to primary political values like liberty and equality. It consists at a different level in determining the rules governing the competition to make effective claims to political values. Deciding both who has a right to decide and how they must go about making a decision raises the most fundamental issues of governance and legitimacy.

Arguments over governance—disputes about the legitimate role of political and parapolitical institutions—manifestly throw light on the politics of liberal democracy generally. But they take on a distinctive dynamic in the context of each country's specific experiences and immediate horizon of expectations. Although issues of governance may often be entangled with the specifics of national identity, our arguments on governance should not be read as specific to the Canadian experience. Issues over governance are often interwoven with broader issues of freedom and equality, illuminating features of democratic politics that go beyond the distinctive Canadian context. For example, the Quebec sign laws not only brought to a head an issue of governance but also threw the clash of liberty and tolerance into sharp relief.

From a North American perspective, arguably the most decisive change in governance in Canada has been the effort to find a *tertium quid* to the problem of institutional supremacy. Until now, authority in liberal democracy has taken one of two forms. Liberal democracies could be organized on the American model, with a Supreme Court having the final authoritative say on how public decisions about rights are to be made. Alternatively, they could be organized on the British model, with a parliament having the final say on all questions. But it had to be the one or the other. The choice between judicial review and parliamentary sovereignty was mutually exclusive. It is, however, precisely one of the principal claims to constitutional innovation made on behalf of the Canadian Charter of Rights that through the notwithstanding clause a third way has been found. On the one hand, the Supreme Court has the right to strike down legislation at either the federal or the provincial levels inconsistent (in its view) with the Charter. On the other hand, Parliament, again at either the federal or provincial levels, has the right to declare the offending legislation valid notwithstanding the Court's decision, at which point the law retains all of its standing as an enforceable law for five years, after which Parliament may reassert its validity (again for a five-year period) notwithstanding any judicial decision.

Our interest is in a political theory of rights. Our concern, therefore, is not the balance that ordinary citizens or even political decision makers believe should be struck between parliamentary sovereignty and judicial review in the abstract, although we are interested in the degree of consensus that obtains among both citizens and decision makers on what the right balance is, whatever it happens to be. What is of more importance to us, given our desire to take both politics and political argumentation into account, is the extent to which people's judgments on metapolitical issues like judicial review and parliamentary sovereignty are driven by their views on the issues of the day. The principle-policy experiment discussed in chapter 6 was designed to determine the extent to which both ordinary citizens and decision makers would take a different tack on the principle of judicial review depending on whether they confronted it in the abstract or in the context of an issue of importance to either the political right or left. There is, in our detailed empirical findings, suggestive evidence that ordinary citizens may take into account *what* is being decided when they themselves decide *how* it should be decided—that is, whether the courts or parliaments should have the final say. But the sharp contrast is between ordinary citizens and political decision makers. On the one side, political decision makers are markedly more sympathetic to the principle of parliamentary sovereignty in the abstract—not surprisingly considering that they are parliamentarians. On the other side, again quite fittingly considering that they are parliamentarians, when they confront the principle of parliamentary sovereignty in the context of a specific issue, political decision makers show a noticeable sensitivity to the politics of the issue in deciding whether the final decision should be made by the courts or parliament. Politicians are in the business of politics, and we think it therefore of some interest—and possibly of some amusement, too—that parliamentarians can react discriminatingly to the principle of parliamentary sovereignty, sometimes rallying around the principle in order to be able to take control of the final choice, sometimes tempering their support of it precisely in order to be able to say that they did not have the final say.

It would, however, be a mistake to focus only on the principles and processes set out in the Chapter of Rights, important as they are. For the Charter, considered by itself, is both instrument and symbol in Canadian politics, and the reactions of Canadians to it, particularly their reactions at its inception, are a vital part of the story of the future of Canadian politics whatever that future turns out to be. This contrast—between the place of the Charter in Canadian politics at its adoption and the state of Canadian politics, say, in a quarter-century—will almost certainly prove to be a wellspring of irony. But given the fissures between the politically engaged in Quebec and in the rest of Canada, the dominant irony may well be this. It is now commonly claimed that the feelings of French Canadians were wounded by the establishment of the Charter of Rights, not because they disagreed with the fundamental political principles it espoused, but because they objected to the manner of its adoption: by the other nine provinces, plus the federal government, without the express approval of Quebec. Indeed, as we noted, the presumption that the Charter had itself provoked anger and resentment among Quebeckers was precisely the reason given for the ill-fated Meech Lake and Charlottetown accords. But notwithstanding the wide circulation that has been given to the charge of French Canadian anger at the mass level, we can find no evidence to support it. French Canadians were somewhat less likely to have heard about the Charter than English Canadians, but if they knew about it, they were just as likely to have a positive view of it. To be sure, political elites in Quebec, and above all those sympathetic to an independent Quebec, recognized from the outset that the Charter might have a centralizing, nationalizing impact on Canadian politics, weakening the autonomy of the provinces and their own political power. But this recognition notwithstanding, *they*, just like ordinary French Canadians, had an overwhelmingly positive view of the Charter of Rights. Whatever subsequently happens in Canadian politics, and whatever is said about the adoption of the Charter having aggravated French Canada's feelings of betrayal and injustice, the truth of the matter is that the Charter, considered as a political symbol in the general public at the time of its adoption, was consensual, not divisive.

Yet if the dominant note with respect to the Charter as a political symbol is agreement, the dominant note with respect to it as a political instrument is disagreement. To be sure, it is not surprising that ordinary citizens might not have worked out and reached agreement on the likely impact of adopting a written constitution for the first time—and one, moreover, written in just the way the Charter was. It is, however, instructive, whether surprising or not, that political decision makers should be at sixes and sevens about what was likely to happen, politically and institutionally, if the Charter was adopted. It is a fact worth remembering, precisely because the future of Canada itself is now uncertain, that at the time of the Charter's adoption, political decision makers had failed to reach agreement even among themselves about the probable consequence of the patriation of a national constitution, including the altogether fundamental issue of whether it would strengthen a national identity.

The issue of national identity dominates Canadian politics, and the form that it takes is the special rights and status that French Quebeckers may claim by virtue of being French Quebeckers. From one angle, the clash between French and English Canada epitomizes a conflict peculiar to Canada. From a more inclusive perspective, it represents a paradigm of the kind of conflict that increasingly defines the politics of contemporary liberal democracies. This kind of conflict is new not by virtue of centering on claims to public benefits presented in the language of political rights, but by virtue of centering on claims presented on behalf not of individuals qua individuals but of groups qua groups. A claim made on behalf of an individual or of a group of individuals can of course be seen to benefit some more than others and just for this reason be sharply contested. Nonetheless, the premise on which a classic claim to rights rests is universality. A claim to a right such as freedom of speech may, at a particular historical moment, be pressed on behalf of a particular group. All the same, it is and is understood to be a claim to a right that is held universally and equally by every member of the political community merely by virtue of their membership in the community. By contrast, a group right represents a claim that is inherently particularistic, and particularistic, moreover, in a specific way. A duality of "we" and "they" is built in to group rights. When groups like English and French Canadians or blacks and whites or Israelis and Palestinians claim rights on behalf of their groups, what counts are the rights to which each thinks itself entitled, as compared to those each thinks the other is entitled to. This comparison of what we are entitled to from them and they correspondingly are entitled to from us is fundamental to claims to group rights. Obviously, some correspondence is required between what each acknowledges that the other should be allowed to do; and this requirement of correspondence means that a claim to a group right, inevitably and distinctively, blends normative *and* strategic considerations. We will grant them a right we ourselves want; still more important, we will deny them a right we believe they will deny us. What we are prepared to do thus hinges on both what we believe should be done *and* what we believe they believe should be done.

The claims advanced, whether on behalf of language rights, mobility rights, schooling, or jobs, will naturally vary from one political order to another and, for any given political order, from one historical juncture to another. But the defining feature of claims to group rights—their we–they character—imparts a generic dynamic of fundamental importance. This dynamic is general, but it is vividly illustrated by the clash of English and French Canadians; indeed, so much so that the uncertain fate of Canada has itself become a parable of the vulnerability of contemporary liberal democracies.

The lesson the parable teaches, as conventionally interpreted, is this. Contemporary liberal democracies are inherently vulnerable to the politics of group rights. Canada is facing the most profound challenge ever to its survival, a challenge driven by the refusal of English Canadians to concede the rights that French Canadians claim as French Canadians, and the lesson this drives home is the inescapable limits on liberal democracy imposed by group-based demands of citizens. After all, Canada is one of the longest-standing democracies. It is affluent, enjoying a developed economy. Its citizens are not only well off, whether judged in absolute or in comparative terms, but well educated, and free (so far as any are free) from the threat of external attack. Yet, the constitutional crisis is at its most critical point, a crisis driven fundamentally by an inability or unwillingness of people who speak one language to get along with those who speak a different one.[19] If all the advantages Canadians as a whole enjoy—safety, affluence, education, the institutions of a liberal society—if all of these, taken together, cannot hold in check group rivalry and resentment, then what can? If pluralist democracy is not secure in a country like Canada, in what country is it secure? In the end, the lesson to draw may be that ordinary citizens are always susceptible to the irrational passions of group identity and rivalry, however advantaged and educated they may be taken one by one.

We agree that liberal democracy is vulnerable to the politics of group rights, but where the conventional interpretation goes wrong, we believe, is in viewing the actions of ordinary citizens in a vacuum. Contrary to the popular image that French and English Canadians would not respect each other's rights, our results demonstrate that a working consensus supporting each other's rights had been achieved. A majority of English Canadians had recognized and supported the special rights of French Canadians under the Charter of Rights, and a still larger majority of French Canadians recognized and supported the special rights of English Canadians. The difficulty is that a consensus of this kind rests on a presumption of reciprocity. If we agree that members of your group should have certain rights, then you are under an obligation to agree that members of our group should have comparable rights. Notice that it is not simply a matter of being in your interest to reciprocate: you are under an obligation to do so. Breeches of reciprocity are accordingly taken not merely as mistakes in judgment but as violations of a norm, hence as unfair, even immoral.

But the presumption of reciprocity is inherently vulnerable. We perhaps can be induced, as members of one group, to uphold your right, as members of another (and in some sense opposing) group, if we are persuaded that you will support our rights. We will, however, willingly uphold your right only so long as we believe you are willing to uphold ours. The difficulty is this. Suppose that I am a French Canadian and you are an English Canadian. As an ordinary citizen, you cannot tell directly what French Canadians taken as a whole think; you must infer it from what publicly visible French Canadians think, and so when you learn through the media that French Canadian partisan elites assert that English Canadians in Quebec should not have their language rights under the Charter, you are disposed to think that this is what most French Canadians think too—even though, purely as a matter of fact, through most of this period they did not. However, believing they do, your response is one of resentment, which in turn offers an opening for English Canadian elites to exploit. So a cycle starts: ordinary English Canadians lose faith that French Canadians want to accept their rights under the Charter, not because of anything French Canadians as a whole think or do, which English Canadians in any case are in no position to know, but because of public claims of partisan elites claiming to represent French Canadians as a whole. Reciprocally, ordinary French Canadians lose faith that English Canadians want to accept their rights under the Charter, not directly because of anything English Canadians as a whole think or do, which French Canadians in any case are in no position to know, but because of public claims of partisan elites claiming to represent English Canadians as a whole. And just for this reason, the politics of group rights is subject to a special volatility.[20]

A Final Word

A generation ago, concluding his classic work *Who Governs?* Robert Dahl remarked,

> I want to propose an alternative explanation, namely, that democratic beliefs, like other political beliefs, are influenced by a recurring *process* of

interaction among political professionals, the political stratum, and the great bulk of the population. The process generates enough agreement on rules and norms so as to permit the system to operate, but agreement tends to be incomplete, and typically it decays. So the process is frequently repeated. "Consensus," then, is not at all a static and unchanging attribute of citizens. It is a variable element in a complex and more or less continuous process.[21]

The foundation role of democratic values—of the commitment of both ordinary citizens and the politically active to fundamental rights—has traditionally been well recognized. But the role of values has been cast in static terms, as though normative commitments quite literally served as a foundation for politics in the same sense that cement can serve as a foundation for a building, providing support and thereby stability. By contrast, Dahl's emphasis on process seems to us fundamental to a properly political theory of democratic politics. What requires understanding, if genuine understanding is to be achieved, is the dynamics of democratic values. The traditional image of democratic values as foundational in the way cement is foundational is too inert. Values like liberty and equality play a far more active, far more dynamic and fluid role than this suggests. They are not the only agents of change, but, over extended intervals, they can be among the most potent.

When we began our study, we shared the orthodox belief that a principal source of democratic instability was a superficial, shallow understanding of the central ideas of democratic governance, particularly among ordinary citizens. It is a mistake to underestimate the power of ignorance in human affairs. It is, however, a still greater mistake to underestimate the power of principle. Political conflict is as deeply rooted in a commitment to values as in a failure to understand them. Above all, it is the very quality that constitutes liberal democracy—the public contest for government power between partisan elites, organized into competing political parties, pledged to inevitably conflicting values—that ensures its inherent and inescapable volatility.

Appendix: **Study Procedures**

The data for our study are drawn from interviews with a sample of citizens as well as from samples of decisions makers representing the legislative, executive, and judicial branches of government.

The sample of the general population was drawn from Canadians eighteen years and older living in a household in one of the ten provinces. The sample was weighted by province in such a way as to permit regional comparisons.[1]

Respondents in the general population sample were identified through a two-stage selection process. In the first stage a modified Random Digit Dialing technique using blocks of valid household telephone numbers was used to select households to be contacted.[2] In the second stage, an eligible respondent within each household was selected by enumerating the members of the household and making a random selection (Kish 1949). The overall response rate for the general population sample was 63.5 percent, which is typical for telephone surveys conducted by academic survey units (cf. Shanks, Sanchez, and Morton 1983). Approximately 3 percent of the respondents were unable to complete the survey owing to language problems, illness, or not residing in the household contacted at the time of data collection.

The resulting national sample (N = 2,084) closely matches basic demographic breakdowns available from Statistics Canada on the 1986 Census population. For example, the sample does not differ from the population as a whole in terms of age, sex, language, or income. Thus, the mean age of adult Canadians, according to the Census of Canada, was forty-two; in the general population sample the mean age of respondents is forty-three. Similarly, the proportions of women and men in the sample match their respective proportions in the population as a whole (51–49). The matches on employment and marital status are also very close, with only a slight underrepresentation (29 percent, not 31) of those not in the workforce and again of those who are separated, divorced, or widowed (11 percent, not 13). Moreover, as is often the case, our sample slightly overrepresents the most educated, those with university degrees, but the difference between population and sample is modest (10 percent compared to 15). However, there is no underrepresentation of the least-educated segment of the population: those with a high school degree or less make up 55 percent of the population and 56 of the sample.

The decision makers interviewed in the study (N = 1,348) were selected through nonprobability samples of decision makers in the civil liberties area. Individuals were selected to represent the legislative, executive, and judicial branches of government. The overall response rate was 64.2 percent.

The first component of the decision-maker sample was drawn from the legislative branch of government. Members of federal and provincial parliaments elected between 1979 and 1986 as listed in the *Canadian Parliamentary Guide* formed the population from which we drew our samples. This population was stratified by party affiliation and a systematic sample was drawn for each party.

The executive or administrative component of the decision-maker sample was itself composed of two parts. The first consisted of officials from the federal ministries of the Solicitor General and Justice as well as their provincial equivalents. Respondents were systematically selected from lists drawn from the *Corpus Administrative Index*, 1986, and the *Canadian Law List* and *Canadian Legal Directory* for the same year. The second part of the executive component of the decision-maker sample consisted of crown attorneys from across the country, who were identified and drawn from the *Canadian Law List*, 1986.[3]

A legal component of the decision-maker sample was drawn from the population of lawyers in Canada who have been before the bar for more than ten years but less than thirty. This is the population from which judges are drawn. It was deemed both impractical and ethically questionable to solicit the views of sitting judges because many of the civil liberties issues touched upon in our survey were likely to come before the judges for adjudication in the wake of the approval of the Canadian Charter of Rights and Freedoms. Accordingly, the population of senior lawyers was used as a surrogate. Senior lawyers in Ontario and Quebec were enumerated through the computerized data bases of the Law Society of Upper Canada (Ontario) and the Barreau du Québec and in the remainder of the country through the *Canadian Law List*, 1986. Respondents were weighted by province, and a systematic sample was drawn.

The same questionnaire and interviewing procedures were used for each of the samples. The telephone interviews with the general population, however, averaged about thirty-three minutes in length while those with the decision makers averaged twenty-nine minutes, owing primarily to the omission of items on party identification and political participation at the close of the interview.

At the end of the telephone interview, all respondents in both the general population and decision-maker samples were asked if they would complete a self-administered written questionnaire. Eighty-three percent of the respondents in the general population sample and 93 percent of the respondents in the decision-maker sample agreed to do so and provided us with a mailing address. Approximately 75 percent of those in each sample who were sent the mail questionnaire completed and returned it to us, yielding a mailback sample size of 1,250 respondents for the general population and 936 for the decision makers.

A comparison of those in the citizen sample who completed both surveys with those who completed only the telephone survey turns up some differences. In percentage terms, however, the absolute differences are rather modest: those who answered the mailback are very slightly older (mean difference is +2.25 years), a bit more educated (on average 13.12 versus 12.66 years) somewhat more Protestant (+6.7 percent) and less Catholic (−7.6 percent); they are more English and less French (±7.2 percent), more likely to be married (+9.4 percent), and of slightly higher income. However, both groups come from the same size communities and are equally likely to have been born in Canada and to be employed. Finally, there are no differences in either sex or party affiliation. Overall, it is striking how closely the mailback sample duplicates the phone sample, that is, those who participated in the phone interview but failed to return the mailback questionnaire.

This study was carried out with a grant from the Social Science and Humanities Research Council of Canada (SSHRCC). Together with SSHRCC, we selected the Institute for Social Research at York University in Toronto (Institute for Social Research, 1987) to collect the data. The telephone interviews were conducted in the spring and summer of 1987, using the CASES computer-assisted telephone interviewing (CATI) system.[4] The mailback questionnaires were completed and returned in the summer and fall.

Telephone interviews were conducted in either English or French, depending upon the preference of the respondent. The mailback was also prepared in both official languages. The translation of the survey instruments into French was undertaken by a professional, academically accredited translator. The translation was then subjected to reviews by a Quebec francophone professor, enjoying complete autonomy. After changes from this review were incorporated into the questionnaire, a pretest of the French and English questionnaires was carried out. Finally, the translation was reviewed by French speakers from Quebec as well as English speakers on the Institute for Social Research's interviewing and supervisory staff. The response rates for English and French interviews, moreover, were virtually identical: 63.8 percent and 62 percent, respectively.

Illustrations

Notes

Chapter 1. Introduction

1. Henkin and Rosenthal, eds., *Constitutionalism and Rights*.
2. Canada. *House of Commons Debates*, 23 March, 1981, 8519.
3. Russell, *Constitutional Odyssey*.
4. In Canada's first ten years under the Charter its Supreme Court has decided more than two hundred cases dealing with Charter claims. F. L. Morton, Peter Russell, and Troy Riddell, "The Canadian Charter of Rights and Freedoms: A Descriptive Analysis of the First Decade, 1982–92," *National Journal of Constitutional Law* 5 (1994): 1–60.
5. Lipset, *Continental Divide*.
6. Horowitz, "Conservatism, Liberalism, and Socialism in Canada."
7. See, for instance, Engelstad and Bird, eds., *Nation to Nation*.
8. Wheare, *Federal Government*.
9. Details of sampling are described in the Appendix.
10. Comparisons both of the telephone sample with official census figures and of the mailback with the telephone sample are set out in the Appendix. All figures are presented with the data weighted to adjust for response bias. In fact, the weights are light, usually making a difference of only a percentage point or two.
11. These examples are taken from McClosky and Brill, *Dimensions of Tolerance*, Appendix B.

Chapter 2. The Thesis of Democratic Elitism

1. Our argument is illustrated in the intellectual evolution of arguably the most prominent political theorist of this century: contrast John Rawls, *A Theory of Justice* and *Political Liberalism*.
2. See Dahl, *A Preface to Democratic Theory.*
3. For a recent review and synthesis, see Lipset, "The Social Requisites of Democracy Revisited."
4. Stouffer, *Communism, Conformity, and Civil Liberties*, 43.
5. For example, see McClosky, "Consensus and Ideology"; Sullivan, Piereson, and Marcus, *Political Tolerance and American Democracy*; Nunn, Crockett, and Williams, *Tolerance for Nonconformity*; McClosky and Brill, *Dimensions of Tolerance*; McClosky and Zaller, *The American Ethos*.
6. For a review of public opinion bearing both on the classic theme of minimalism and on recent revisionist responses to it, see Sniderman, "The New Look in Public Opinion Research."
7. In speaking of "the thesis of democratic elitism," we follow common usage and are in no way asserting or implying that scholars who have taken it to be an approximately correct description of political reality favor elitist values, political or otherwise.
8. Schattschneider, *The Semi-Sovereign People.*
9. We are, of course, following the lead of Sullivan, Piereson, and Marcus, who developed this measurement strategy. See *Political Tolerance and American Democracy*.
10. One group, racists, has been set aside, to be examined in chapter 3.
11. It is worth underlining that racists are excluded, and, as chapter 3 will show, they are a prime target of the NDP and PQ, among others.
12. The exact text of the question is, "Do you think members of extreme political groups should be allowed to hold public rallies in our cities, or should not be allowed to do so?"
13. The exact text of the question is, "Now I am going to read you a statement about [name of group most disliked by respondent]. I would like you to tell me whether you strongly agree, agree, are uncertain, disagree, or strongly disagree with the statement. The statement is: [Name of the group most disliked by respondent] should not be allowed to hold public rallies in our city."
14. Schumpeter, *Capitalism, Socialism, and Democracy*, 269.
15. See, for example, Stouffer, *Communism, Conformity and Civil Liberties*, table 4, 55.
16. Commission of Inquiry (McDonald Commission), *Second Report: Freedom and Security under the Law.*
17. Borovoy, *When Freedoms Collide.*
18. To discipline our assessment of issues of wiretapping, the justifications are

drawn from the enabling legislation, the Canadian Security Intelligence Service Act, 1984.

19. The author of this suggestion, if memory serves, is David Northrup of the Institute of Social Research, York University.

20. Borovoy, *When Freedoms Collide,* 1.

21. We ignore the situation of coalition and minority government.

22. The parallels between the attitudes we capture and actual behavior in the October Crisis are impressive.

23. Hewitt, "The Dog That Didn't Bark."

24. Here we align ourselves with classic theories of cognitive consistency. See Festinger, *A Theory of Cognitive Dissonance,* and Abelson et al., *Theories of Cognitive Consistency.*

25. Equally misleading, we should add, would be to imply that the *same* preference is necessarily shared among the four of us.

26. McClosky and Brill, *Dimensions of Tolerance,* 434.

27. The federal election of 1992 reduced the New Democrats and Conservatives to nine and two seats, respectively, in the 295-member House of Commons. The governing Liberals are now challenged by the separatist Bloc Québécois (the official opposition) and the western-based, right wing Reform Party.

28. The test must be indirect because McClosky's data are not available for analysis.

29. See McClosky, Hoffman, and O'Hara, "Issue Conflict and Consensus among Party Leaders and Followers"; Kirkpatrick, *The New Presidential Elite;* and Miller and Jennings, *Parties in Transition.*

30. Dahl, *Who Governs?,* 320.

Chapter 3. The Contestability of Rights

1. The sentimentalist may be forgiven for supposing we have revived Stouffer's original framing of the issue. On the contrary, we have reproduced the text of the *contemporary* construction of the issue in the General Social Survey.

2. For the record, francophones are less likely to pick the KKK than racists, most likely because of language exposure.

3. McClosky, "Consensus and Ideology."

4. Dworkin, "Two Concepts of Liberty."

5. See Hogg, *Constitutional Law of Canada,* 40–47.

6. [1990] 3 S.C.R. 697.

7. In a related case, *Can. v. Taylor* [1990] 3 S.C.R. 892, the Court again split in the same way in upholding a ban on hate propaganda over the telephone.

8. [1992] 2 S.C.R. 731.

9. We are aware that there is a historical context that is relevant. Far more

than a century ago, women claimed many rights in disputes with their husbands. More broadly, arguments over the extension of what is political are not new, nor are they surprising, because many aspects of the "private sphere," as feminists (among others) have argued, are intensely political and always have been.

10. MacKinnon, *Only Words*; For an opposing view, see Dworkin, "Two Concepts of Liberty."
11. [1992] 1 S.C.R. 452.
12. Section 163 (8).
13. A classic study, canvassing many aspects, is McClosky and Brill, *Dimensions of Tolerance*.
14. E.g., McClosky and Brill, *Dimensions of Tolerance*.

Chapter 4. Equality: A Chameleon Value

1. Tocqueville, *Democracy in America*. See also Mandel, *The Charter of Rights and the Legalization of Politics in Canada*, and Knopff and Morton, *Charter Politics*, esp. chap. 9.
2. Horowitz, "Conservatism, Liberalism, and Socialism in Canada." See also Forbes, "Hartz-Horowitz at Twenty: Nationalism, Toryism and Socialism in Canada and the United States."
3. See, for example, Lipset, *Continental Divide*.
4. The American data are drawn from the National Election Study (NES) of 1986. It should be noted that in the American survey, respondents were given an explicit "neither" option whereas Canadians were offered only the two substantive options.
5. The Canadian questions match precisely the American ones in wording, formatting, and mode of collection (mailback). We follow McClosky's lead, summing the "neither" and "undecided" into a "decline" category.
6. Respondents were offered not only the two substantive replies but also the options of "neither" or "undecided."
7. The 1988 Canadian National Election study also used this question and found that about 65 percent of Canadians chose the "hard work" response. The difference, modest as it is, is most likely a reflection of sampling error. For a further discussion, see Fletcher, "Canadian Attitudes toward Competitiveness and Entrepreneurship."
8. The American data are, in this instance, taken from a study of the Oakland-San Francisco Bay Area. See Sniderman and Piazza, *The Scar of Race*.
9. *Brown v. British Columbia* (1990), 19 A.C.W.S. (3d) 216; *Haig v. Canada* (1992), 94 D.L.R. 4th 1.
10. The full results are reported by Sniderman, Wolfinger, Mutz, and Wiley, "Values under Pressure."
11. Cairns, "Political Science, Ethnicity, and the Canadian Constitution."
12. See especially, Sniderman, Northrup et al., "The Psychological and Cultural

Foundations of Prejudice," on the relation between conformity and anti-Semitism in Quebec.

13. Equally important, our data show that compared with the attitudes of the general public, the attitudes of police officers toward immigrants on these questions are not at all out of line with overall societal norms. See Fletcher, "Policing, Police Culture and Race."

Chapter 5. The Politics of Equality

1. Kymlicka, *Liberalism, Community and Culture*.
2. Hochschild, *What's Fair?*; Feldman and Zaller, "The Political Culture of Ambivalence"; Tourangeau and Rasinski, "Cognitive Processes Underlying Context Effects in Attitude Measurement."
3. There was, however, considerable opposition to the Conservative policy of clawing back Old Age Security.
4. Of course this right was not very strong in that the sovereign could force the Indians to cede away title to their land on unfavorable terms.
5. Grouping of the elites provides a reasonable chance to meet conventional tests of statistical significance, although it should be emphasized that exactly the same pattern of responses is found for each set of decision makers taken separately.
6. We suspect that for most Canadians the Constitution is thought to be the same as the Charter of Rights. Of course, the Charter is a part of the Constitution.
7. The figures are taken from the neutral condition, although the pattern is the same in the Constitution-mention condition.
8. See Fletcher and Chalmers, "Attitudes of Canadians toward Affirmative Action," on this point.

Chapter 6. Governance and Identity

1. The exceptions here were in the areas of language and denominational education rights, which were already entrenched in sections 133 and 93 of the Constitution.
2. Technically, section 33 permits an override only of section 2 and sections 7–15 of the Charter. These sections contain the basic freedoms of conscience, religion, expression, association, and assembly as well as the Charter's legal and equality rights provisions. The voting, mobility, and language rights of sections 3–6 and 16–23, in contrast, are exempted from the override provision.
3. The two sides of the argument are set out in Whyte, "On Not Standing for Notwithstanding"; and Russell, "Standing Up for Notwithstanding."
4. Reference re Objection to a Resolution to Amend the Constitution, [1982] 2 S.C.R. 793.

5. *Quebec v Ford* [1988] 2 S.C.R. 712.
6. For further details on these events, see Russell, *Constitutional Odyssey*.
7. The versions of the questions were created in early 1987. Thus, in addition to the abstract formulation of the question, the variations of the questions were developed with the facts of the Saskatchewan override in mind as well as a desire to assure a rough ideological balance. Had we the opportunity to add a version about who should have the final say on something like the sign laws case of 1988, we would also expect the politics of rights to make a difference in the answers of English-speaking and French-speaking respondents.
8. This speculation gains in weight once one sees the unpopularity of unions among the larger public.
9. The court's decision was about political convention, not law—and, in effect, can be overturned by the course of politics. See Russell, *Constitutional Odyssey*, 129.
10. The rating of the Charter proceeded in two steps: respondents first answered whether they thought it a good or a bad thing, then answered how good or bad a thing they thought it. We thus put into one display (fig. 6.2) the answers to three questions.
11. We should perhaps note here that nearly all of our francophone respondents are from Quebec and few of the anglophones are from Quebec. Hence we sometimes equate francophone respondents with Quebeckers. One might argue, of course, that some proportion of francophones, in answering that the Charter is a good thing for Canada, also think that it is a bad thing for Quebec, or at any rate for the autonomy of Quebec. This interpretation is difficult to sustain, however, in light of the data presented later in this chapter, and in particular in figure 6.5B, which show that a majority of francophones want less emphasis on regional identities and more emphasis on a national Canadian identity.
12. A more recent poll carried out by Environics shows that by mid-1991, 6 percent of anglophones compared with 12 percent of francophones report not having heard of the Charter. Thus awareness has increased in both linguistic groups, and the gap between them has narrowed substantially, although it seems that francophones nonetheless remain less aware of the Charter than anglophones.
13. Survey data collected by Environics Research Group in July and August 1991 indicate that respondents in all provinces continue to hold the Charter in high esteem and that many more Canadians see it as having a positive rather than a negative impact on their rights and those of other Canadians generally, including minority groups. These findings also hold for supporters of the Bloc Québécois. See the *Focus Canada Report, 1991–1993*, Environics Research Group.
14. This question and the subsequent one were, of course, asked only of those who had heard of the Charter.
15. An analysis of Charter decisions made by the Supreme Court of Canada suggests that these concerns are realistic because the legislative agenda of

Quebec's National Assembly has suffered more policy vetoes than any other province at the hands of the Court. See Morton, Russell, and Withey, "The Supreme Court's First One Hundred Charter of Rights Decisions.

16. See Meisel, "Escaping Extinction."
17. "It is probably no exaggeration to say that the most powerful factor in the back of the CRTC's mind has been the need to protect the Canadian element in our broadcasting system." Ibid., 257. For an extended justification of Canadian content regulations in the context of the tradeoff between the values of free choice and protection of Canadian cultural autonomy, see Freiman, "Consumer Sovereignty and National Sovereignty in Domestic and International Broadcasting Regulation."
18. See Johnston, Blais, Brady, and Crete, *Letting the People Decide*.
19. A majority of Liberals, to be sure, favor judicial review when the issue is stated in the abstract, but at a minimum, a clear majority in favor of the courts having the final say is lost, even among Liberals, whenever the question of who has the final say—Parliament or the courts—is put in terms of a specific political issue.

Chapter 7. The Politics of Language and Group Rights

1. Cairns, "Political Science, Ethnicity and the Canadian Constitution."
2. Of course, our survey was conducted before the electoral breakthrough of the Reform Party in late 1993.
3. Technically, in Quebec it is only the children of English-speaking parents who received their English education in Canada who qualify for this right.
4. *Attorney General of Quebec v. Quebec Association of Protestant School Boards et al.,* (1984).
5. And these results are not confined to this one particular language right. The same pattern and the same asymmetry appear when claims are made, under section 20, for government services to be available in either founding language. See Sniderman et al., 1989b.
6. In fact, language has clearly taken over as the primary source of cultural identity in Quebec. See Taylor, *Reconciling the Solitudes*.
7. The override could be used here because the Supreme Court case was based on freedom of expression, *not* language rights, which are protected from the override.
8. See Sniderman et al., "Strategic Calculation and Political Values."

Chapter 8. Value Pluralism

1. For an original and uncommonly helpful discussion, see Mason, *Explaining Political Disagreement*.
2. Stouffer, *Communism, Conformity, and Civil Liberties*, 127.
3. Ibid.

4. Ibid., 95 ff.

5. Stouffer's analysis is strikingly consistent with the psychodynamic interpretations of intolerance advanced by Adorno et al., *The Authoritarian Personality*, and both the more ego-psychological account of Sniderman, *Personality
and Democratic Politics*, and follow-up work within the cognitive style tradition of Rokeach, *The Open and Closed Mind*, and Tetlock, "Cognitive Style and
Political Belief Systems" and "A Value Pluralism Model of Ideological Reasoning."

6. McClosky and Brill, *Dimensions of Tolerance*; McClosky and Zaller, *The American Ethos*; Sniderman, *Personality and Democratic Politics*.

7. The "least-liked" model of political tolerance (Sullivan, Piereson, and
Marcus) thus belongs to the "error" perspective; for its central point is
precisely that people who would otherwise approve of a fundamental right
are deflected in specific controversies by the intensity of their dislike or fear
of a particular group.

8. McClosky and Zaller, for example, distinguish consensual and contested
norms, recognizing there can be disagreement about the latter even in the
elite culture. But this disagreement, they suggest, is temporary, lasting only
until there has been an authoritative pronouncement—in the form, for
example, of a Supreme Court decision—about what is congruent with the
core norms of the official culture, after which the core norms point in only
one direction.

9. Sniderman, Tetlock, Glaser, Green, and Hout, "Principled Tolerance," 133.
This argument draws heavily upon cognitive psychological work on natural
categories (Rosch, "Natural Categories;" Tversky, "Features of Similarity."

10. Cf. Quine, "Natural Kinds," 122.

11. See McClosky and Brill, *Dimensions of Tolerance*; McClosky and Zaller, *The
American Ethos*.

12. This argument draws on psychological theories of cognitive consistency in
choice situations (Abelson, "Modes of Resolution"; Festinger, *A Theory of
Cognitive Dissonance*). Confronted by conflicting values, many people cope
by "denying" the value linked to the rejected option and by "bolstering"
the value linked to the accepted option. In this theoretical scheme, the
more frequently and conspicuously the values "clash" in public debates,
the more negatively correlated the importance rankings of the two values
will become among citizens—an effect that may be even more pronounced
among elites.

13. From a cognitive consistency perspective, such intense (inside-the-head)
value conflict should be short-lived as attentive observers of politics cope by
denying one of the competing values and bolstering the other, making the
choice progressively easier by "spreading of the subjective values of the
alternatives." Such simple modes of inconsistency resolution may not, however, always be feasible (e.g., if one belongs to a political party strongly
committed to both values). Here the predictions of the value pluralism

model become engaged (Tetlock, "A Value Pluralism Model"; Tetlock, Peterson, and Lerner, "Revising the Value Pluralism Model"). We should expect high-value-conflict respondents to resort to more complex methods of coping with dissonance, including evaluative differentiation (identifying conditions when one or the other value should prevail) and conceptual integration (identifying rules or schemata for trading off one value against another).

14. Key, 1961.

15. Jackman, "Political Elites, Mass Publics, and Support for Democratic Principles."

16. Schuman, Steeh, and Bobo, *Racial Attitudes in America.*

17. See Sullivan, Piereson, and Marcus, "An Alternative Conceptualization of Political Tolerance."

18. The conceptual issues at stake should now be familiar ones to most political psychologists. For any given style of thinking, it is possible to attach strikingly different value judgments. Simple principled reasoners, who do indeed deduce policy conclusions from abstract premises, will strike some observers as inflexible, dogmatic, and oblivious to nuance but strike other observers as consistent, rigorous, and insightful. Complex pluralistic reasoners, who respond in superficially contradictory ways to policy questions, will strike some observers as confused, vacillating, and even incoherent but strike other observers as thoughtful, sophisticated, and nuanced (Tetlock and Mitchell, "Liberal and Conservative Approaches to Justice"). We suspect that, in the domain of empirical democratic theory, investigators have been too prone to view deductive syllogistic reasoning as a normative ideal and apparent departures from it as prima facie evidence of cognitive slovenliness or moral lassitude. To correct this imbalance, we call attention to the concept of a belief repertoire, putting a positive normative spin on value pluralism.

19. Ironically, now there is apparently a political taboo on explicitly justifying sovereignty on linguistic or ethnic grounds. See National Executive Council of the Parti Québécois, *Quebec in a New World: The P.Q.'s Plan for Sovereignty,* trans. Robert Chodos (Toronto: James Lorimer, 1994).

20. Our argument here has obvious similarities with the arguments that Axelrod (*The Evolution of Cooperation*) presented for the tit-for-tat strategy for generating long-term cooperation. The strategy runs into serious difficulties, however (as Axelrod is aware) when we allow for "misperception" (what one side sees as cooperation, the other side either does not acknowledge or, worse, sees as defection). Because the tit-for-tat rule touches on our deepest intuitions about fair play, there is a great temptation for opportunistic elites to compete for the status of most vigilant defender of in-group rights and detector of out-group violations. Our argument also bears some ominous similarities to the emerging literature on identity politics and subnational fragmentation in places where democratic norms are far

less well established than in Canada (places such as the former Yugoslavia and the former Soviet Union). Here again we find an emphasis on the capacity of opportunistic elites to mobilize resentment toward out-groups who are held guilty of real or imagined slights against members of in-groups. For a review of this literature, see Tetlock, "Social Psychology and World Politics."

21. Dahl, *Who Governs?,* 316.

Appendix

1. Constructing a national sampling frame given the variation in provincial population—for example, Ontario contains 36 percent of the Canadian population, Prince Edward Island only .3 percent—was a complex task. Our sample was designed to provide samples of Quebec, Ontario, and British Columbia, while treating New Brunswick, Nova Scotia, Newfoundland, and Prince Edward Island as one Atlantic region and Alberta, Manitoba, and Saskatchewan as a Prairie region. Weights are used in the analysis to compensate for differences in the sampling fractions across provinces.

2. For a review on the generation of Random Digit Dialing samples in Canada, see Victor Tremblay and H. Hofman, "The Random Generation of Telephone Numbers" (Ottawa: Statistics Canada, 1983).

3. A systematic sample of police officers from the RCMP, the two provincial forces (OPP and QPP), and four major metropolitan police forces were also interviewed (N = 223), but the results from this component of the study are not examined here.

4. For an overview of this approach, see Thomas Piazza, Paul M. Sniderman, and Philip E. Tetlock (1989), "Analysis of the Dynamics of Political Reasoning: A General Purpose Computer-Assisted Methodology," in James Stimson (ed.), *Political Analysis,* vol. 1 (Ann Arbor: University of Michigan Press), 99–120.

Bibliography

Abelson, Robert P. 1959. "Modes of Resolution of Belief Dilemmas." *Journal of Conflict Resolution* 3:334–352.

Abelson, Robert P., Eliot Aronson, William J. McGuire, Theodore M. Newcomb, M. J. Rosenberg, and Percy H. Tannenbaum, eds. 1968. *Theories of Cognitive Consistency: A Sourcebook.* Chicago: Rand McNally.

Adorno, T. W., Else Frenkel-Brunswik, Daniel J. Levinson, and R. Nevitt Sanford. 1950. *The Authoritarian Personality.* New York: Harper and Brothers.

Altemeyer, Bob. 1988. *Enemies of Freedom. Understanding Right Wing Authoritarianism.* San Francisco: Jossey-Bass.

Axelrod, Robert M. 1984. *The Evolution of Cooperation.* New York: Basic Books.

Berlin, Isaiah. 1969. "Two Concepts of Liberty." In *Four Essays on Liberty.* New York: Oxford University Press.

Borovoy, A. Allan. 1988. *When Freedoms Collide.* Toronto: Lester and Orpen Dennys, Ltd.

Cairns, Alan C. 1989. "Political Science, Ethnicity, and the Canadian Constitution." In David Shugarman and Reg Whitaker, eds. *Federalism and the Question of Political Community.* Peterborough, Ontario: Broadview Press.

Commission of Inquiry Concerning Certain Activities of the Royal Canadian Mounted Police (McDonald Commission). 1981. *Second Report: Freedom and Security under the Law.* Ottawa: Queen's Printer.

Dahl, Robert A. 1956. *A Preface to Democratic Theory.* Chicago: University of Chicago Press.

———. 1961. *Who Governs?* New Haven: Yale University Press.

DiPalma, Giuseppe, and Herbert McClosky. 1970. "Personality and Conformity: The Learning of Political Attitudes." *American Political Science Review* 64:1054–73.

Dworkin, Ronald. 1991. "Two Concepts of Liberty." In Sidney Morgenbesser and Jonathan Lieberson, eds. *Isaiah Berlin: A Celebration*. Chicago: University of Chicago Press.

Dye, Thomas R., and Harmon Zeigler. 1987. *The Irony of Democracy*. 7th ed. Monterey, Calif.: Brooks/Cole.

Engelstad, Diane, and John Bird, eds. 1992. *Nation to Nation: Aboriginal Sovereignty and the Future of Canada*, Concord, Ont.: Anansi.

Environics Research Group. *Focus Canada Report 1991–1993*.

Feldman, Stanley, and John Zaller. 1992. "The Political Culture of Ambivalence: Ideological Responses to the Welfare State." *American Journal of Political Science* 36:268–307.

Festinger, L. 1957. *A Theory of Cognitive Dissonance*. Evanston, Ill.: Row, Peterson.

Fletcher, Joseph F. 1989. "Mass and Elite Attitudes about Wiretapping: Implications for Democratic Theory and Politics." *Public Opinion Quarterly* 53: 225–45.

———. 1990a. "Participation and Attitudes toward Civil Liberties: Is There an Educative Effect?" *International Political Science Review* 11:439–59.

———. 1990b. "Policing, Police Culture and Race: Police Attitudes in the Canadian Cultural Context." Unpublished report to the Solicitor General of Canada.

———. 1992. "Canadian Attitudes toward Competitiveness and Entrepreneurship." Ottawa: Industry, Science and Technology Canada.

Fletcher, Joseph F., and Marie-Christine Chalmers. 1991. "Attitudes of Canadians toward Affirmative Action: Opposition, Value Pluralism and Nonattitudes." *Political Behavior* 13:67–95.

Forbes, H. D. 1987. "Hartz-Horowitz at Twenty: Nationalism, Toryism and Socialism in Canada and the United States." *Canadian Journal of Political Science* 20:287–315.

Freiman, Mark J. 1983. "Consumer Sovereignty and National Sovereignty in Domestic and International Broadcasting Regulation." In *Cultures in Collision: The Interaction of Canadian and U.S. Television Broadcast Policies—A Canadian-U.S. Conference on Communications Policy*. New York: Praeger.

Gibson, James L. 1986. "Pluralistic Intolerance in America." *American Politics Quarterly* 14:267–93.

———. 1988. "Political Intolerance and Political Repression during the McCarthy Red Scare." *American Political Science Review* 82:511–29.

Greene, Ian. 1989. *The Charter of Rights*. Toronto: James Lorimer and Company.

Henkin, Louis, and Albert Rosenthal, eds. 1990. *Constitutionalism and Rights: The Influence of the United States Constitution Abroad*. New York: Columbia University Press.

Hewitt, Christopher. 1994. "The Dog That Didn't Bark: The Political Consequences of Separatist Violence in Quebec, 1963–70." *Conflict Quarterly*
14:9–29.

Hirschman, Albert O. 1970. *Exit, Voice, and Loyalty.* Cambridge: Harvard University Press.

Hochschild, Jennifer. 1981. *What's Fair? American Beliefs about Distributive Justice.* Cambridge: Harvard University Press.

Hogg, Peter W. 1992. *Constitutional Law of Canada.* 3d ed. Toronto: Carswell.

Hook, Sidney. 1962. *The Paradoxes of Freedom.* Berkeley: University of California
Press.

Horowitz, Gad. 1966. "Conservatism, Liberalism, and Socialism in Canada: An
Interpretation." *Canadian Journal of Economics and Political Science* 32:141–71.

Jackman, Robert W. 1972. "Political Elites, Mass Publics, and Support for Democratic Principles." *Journal of Politics* 34:753–73.

Johnston, Richard, André Blais, Jean Crete, and Henry Brady. 1992. *Letting the
People Decide.* Montreal and Kingston: McGill-Queens University Press and
Stanford: Stanford University Press.

Key, V. O., Jr. 1961. *Public Opinion and American Democracy.* New York: Knopf.

Kirkpatrick, Jeane J. 1976. *The New Presidential Elite.* New York: Basic Books.

Kish, Leslie. 1949. "A Procedure for Objective Respondent Selection within the
Household." *Journal of the American Statistical Association* 44:380–87.

Knopff, Rainer, and F. L. Morton. 1992. *Charter Politics.* Scarborough, Ont.:
Nelson.

Kymlicka, Will. 1989. *Liberalism, Community and Culture.* Oxford: Oxford University Press.

Lipset, Seymour Martin. 1990. *Continental Divide: The Values and Institutions of
the United States and Canada.* New York: Routledge.

———. 1994. "The Social Requisites of Democracy Revisited." *American Socio-
logical Review* 59:1–22.

MacKinnon, Catharine A. 1993. *Only Words.* Cambridge: Harvard University
Press.

Mandel, Michael. 1989. *The Charter of Rights and the Legalization of Politics in
Canada.* Toronto: Wall and Thomson.

Mason, Andrew. 1993. *Explaining Political Disagreement.* Cambridge: Cambridge
University Press.

McClosky, Herbert. 1964. "Consensus and Ideology in American Politics."
American Political Science Review 58:361–82.

McClosky, Herbert, and Alida Brill. 1983. *Dimensions of Tolerance: What Americans Believe about Civil Liberties.* New York: Russell Sage Foundation.

McClosky, Herbert, and John Zaller. 1985. *The American Ethos: Public Attitudes
toward Capitalism and Democracy.* Cambridge: Cambridge University Press.

McClosky, Herbert, Paul J. Hoffman, and Rosemary O'Hara. 1960. "Issue Conflict and Consensus among Party Leaders and Followers." *American Political
Science Review* 54:406–27.

Meisel, John. 1986. "Escaping Extinction: Cultural Defence of an Undefended Border." *Canadian Journal of Political and Social Thought* 10:248–65.

Mill, John Stuart. 1975. *On Liberty*. New York: Norton.

Miller, Warren E., and M. Kent Jennings. 1986. *Parties in Transition: A Longitudinal Study of Party Elites and Party Supporters*. New York: Russell Sage.

Miller, William L., ed. 1995. *Alternatives to Freedom*. London: Longman.

Morton, F. L., Peter H. Russell, and Troy Riddell. 1994 "The Canadian Charter of Rights and Freedoms: A Descriptive Analysis of the First Decade 1982–92." *National Journal of Constitutional Law* 5:1–60.

Morton, F. L., Peter H. Russell, and Michael J. Withey. 1992. "The Supreme Court's First One Hundred Charter of Rights Decisions: A Statistical Analysis." *Osgoode Law Journal* 30:1–56.

Nunn, Clyde Z., Harry J. Crockett, Jr., and J. Allen Williams, Jr. 1978. *Tolerance for Nonconformity*. San Francisco: Jossey-Bass.

Parti Québécois. 1964. *Quebec in a New World: The P.Q.'s Plan for Sovereignty*, trans. Robert Chodos. Toronto: James Lorimer.

Piazza, Thomas, Paul M. Sniderman, and Philip E. Tetlock. 1989. "Analysis of the Dynamics of Political Reasoning: A General Purpose Computer-Assisted Methodology." In James Stimson, ed., *Political Analysis* 1:99–120. Ann Arbor: University of Michigan Press.

Pole, J. R. 1993. *The Pursuit of Equality in American History*. Rev. ed. Berkeley: University of California Press.

Polsby, Nelson W. 1980. *Community Power and Political Theory*. 2d ed. New Haven: Yale University Press.

Prothro, James W., and Charles W. Grigg. 1961. "Fundamental Principles of Democracy: Bases of Agreement." *Journal of Politics* 22:276–94.

Quine, W. V. 1969. "Natural Kinds." In *Ontological Relativity and Other Essays*. New York: Columbia University Press.

Rae, Douglas, and Douglas Yates. 1981. *Equalities*. Cambridge: Harvard University Press.

Rawls, John. 1971. *A Theory of Justice*. Cambridge: Harvard University Press.

———. 1993. *Political Liberalism*. New York: Columbia University Press.

Rokeach, Milton. 1960. *The Open and Closed Mind*. New York: Basic Books.

Rosch, Eleanor. 1973. "Natural Categories." *Cognitive Psychology* 4:328–50.

Russell, Peter H. 1983. "The Political Purposes of the Canadian Charter of Rights and Freedoms." *Canadian Bar Review* 61:30–54.

———. 1991. "Standing Up for Notwithstanding." *Alberta Law Review* 29: 293–309..

———. 1993. *Constitutional Odyssey: Can Canadians Be a Sovereign People?* 2d ed. Toronto: University of Toronto Press.

Schattschneider, E. E. 1960. *The Semi-Sovereign People*. New York: Holt, Rinehart and Winston.

Schuman, Howard, Charlotte Steeh, and Lawrence Bobo. 1985. *Racial Attitudes in America: Trends and Interpretations*. Cambridge: Harvard University Press.

Schumpeter, Joseph. 1962. *Capitalism, Socialism, and Democracy*. New York: Harper and Row.

Sears, David O. 1993. "Symbolic Politics: A Socio-Psychological Theory." In Shanto Iyengar and William James McGuire, eds. *Explorations in Political Psychology*: 113–49. Durham, N.C.: Duke University Press.

Selznick, Gertrude, and Stephen Steinberg. 1969. *The Tenacity of Prejudice*. New York: Harper and Row.

Shanks, J. Merrill, Maria Sanchez, and Betsy Morton. 1983. Alternative Approaches to Survey Data Collection for the National Election Studies: A Report on the 1982 NES Method Comparison Project." Prepared for the National Election Studies.

Sniderman, Paul M. 1975. *Personality and Democratic Politics*. Berkeley: University of California Press.

———. 1993. "The New Look in Public Opinion Research." In Ada W. Finifter, ed. *Political Science: The State of the Discipline II*, 219–46. Washington, D.C.: American Political Science Association.

Sniderman, Paul M., and Thomas Piazza. 1993. *The Scar of Race*. Cambridge: Harvard University Press.

Sniderman, Paul M., and Philip E. Tetlock. 1986a. "Symbolic Racism: Problems of Motive Attribution in Political Analysis." *Journal of Social Issues* 42: 129–50.

———. 1986b. "Reflections on American Racism." *Journal of Social Issues* 42:173–87.

Sniderman, Paul M., Philip E. Tetlock, James M. Glaser, Donald P. Green, and Michael Hout. 1989a. "Principled Tolerance and Mass Publics." *British Journal of Political Science* 19:25–45.

Sniderman, Paul M., Joseph F. Fletcher, Peter H. Russell, and Philip E. Tetlock. 1989b. "Political Culture and the Problem of Double Standards: Mass and Elite Attitudes toward Language Rights in the Canadian Charter of Rights and Freedoms." *Canadian Journal of Political Science* 22:259–84.

———. 1990. "Strategic Calculation and Political Values: The Dynamics of Language Rights." *Canadian Journal of Political Science*. 23:537–44.

———. 1991. "The Fallacy of Democratic Elitism: Elite Competition and Commitment to Civil Liberties." *British Journal of Political Science* 21:349–70.

Sniderman, Paul M., Barbara Kaye Wolfinger, Diana C. Mutz, and James E. Wiley. 1991. "Values under Pressure: AIDS and Civil Liberties." In Paul M. Sniderman, Richard A. Brody, and Philip E. Tetlock, eds. *Reasoning and Choice: Explorations in Political Psychology*. Cambridge: Cambridge University Press.

Sniderman, Paul M., David A. Northrup, Joseph F. Fletcher, Peter H. Russell, and Philip E. Tetlock. 1993. "Psychological and Cultural Foundations of Prejudice: The Case of Anti-Semitism in Quebec." *Canadian Review of Sociology and Anthropology* 30:242–70.

Stouffer, Samuel. 1955. *Communism, Conformity and Civil Liberties*. New York: Doubleday.

Sullivan, John L., James Piereson, and George E. Marcus. 1978. "An Alternative Conceptualization of Political Tolerance." *American Political Science Review* 73:781–94.

———. 1982. *Political Tolerance and American Democracy.* Chicago: University of Chicago Press.

Sullivan, John L., et al. 1993. "Why Politicians Are More Tolerant: Selective Recruitment and Socialization among Political Elites in Britain, Israel, New Zealand and the United States." *British Journal of Political Science* 23:51–76.

Taylor, Charles. 1993. In Guy Laforest, ed. *Reconciling the Solitudes: Essays on Canadian Federalism and Nationalism.* Montreal and Kingston: McGill-Queens.

Tetlock, Philip E. 1984. "Cognitive Style and Political Belief Systems in the British House of Commons." *Journal of Personality and Social Psychology* 46:365–75.

———. 1986. "A Value Pluralism Model of Ideological Reasoning." *Journal of Personality and Social Psychology* 50:819–27.

———. 1996. "Social Psychology and World Politics." In *Handbook of Social Psychology,* 4th ed., edited by D. Gilbert, S. Fiske, and G. Lindzey. New York: McGraw-Hill.

Tetlock, Philip E., and Gregory Mitchell. 1993. "Liberal and Conservative Approaches to Justice: Conflicting Psychological Portraits." In Barbara A. Mellers and Jonathan Baron, eds., *Psychological Perspectives on Justice: Theory and Applications.* New York: Cambridge University Press.

Tetlock, Philip E., Randall S. Peterson, and Jennifer Lerner. 1995. "Revising the Value Pluralism Model of Ideological Reasoning: Incorporating Social Content and Context Postulates." In Clive Seligman, James M. Olson, and Mark Zanna, eds. *The Ontario Symposium on Social and Personality Psychology: Values.* Hillsdale, N.J.: Erlbaum.

Tocqueville, Alexis de. 1969. *Democracy in America.* J. P. Mayer, ed. Garden City, N.Y.: Anchor.

Tourangeau, Roger, and Kenneth Rasinski. 1988. "Cognitive Processes Underlying Context Effects in Attitude Measurement." *Psychological Bulletin* 103:299–314.

Tremblay, Victor, and H. Hofman. 1983. "The Random Generation of Telephone Numbers." Ottawa: Statistics Canada.

Tversky, Amos. 1977. "Features of Similarity." *Psychological Review* 84:327–52.

Walzer, Michael. 1983. *Spheres of Justice: A Defense of Pluralism and Equality.* New York: Basic Books.

Wheare, Kenneth C. 1964. *Federal Government.* 4th ed. Oxford: Oxford University Press.

Whyte, John D. 1990. "On Not Standing for Notwithstanding." *Alberta Law Review* 28:347–57.

Wolfinger, Raymond E. 1974. *The Politics of Progress.* New York: Prentice-Hall.

INDEX

dissensus: on override clause, 189–
90; theories of, 236
Duke, David, 57. *See also* racists

economic inequality. *See* equality, as
economic value
education, and language rights, 204–
10
education, public funding of religious, 215–23
egalitarianism, 101–12, 245. *See also*
individualism
electoral competition: as definition
of democratic method, 24–26;
between elites, 45–48, 51,
246–47
elites: in Charter study, 8–9; as custodians of democratic values, 11,
17–19, 23, 34, 41–142, 45, 77–
78, 209; danger of, 13; divergence of, 209; and failure of
democratic elitism theory, 36, 47,
59, 242–43; and issues of national security, 26–36. *See also*
democratic elitism theory; *individual elite types*
elites, administrative, 83, 118, 180,
186, 199–200; and bilingualism,
208
elites, conservative, 47
elites, legal, 43, 81, 118, 180, 186,
189–90; and bilingualism, 199–
200, 208; on equality, 83
elites, legislative, 109, 187, 189–90;
and language rights, 208; and
wiretapping, 28
elites, partisan, 36, 37, 49–51; and
affirmative action, 250; and antihate legislation, 66–67; and bilingualism issue, 197–99; and
Charter of Rights and Freedoms,
173–74, 176–77; consensus on
immigrants, 110–14; divergence
between, 25–26, 36, 38, 43, 123–

27, 173–74, 177; and electoral
competition, 24–25, 45–48, 51;
on equality, 83, 85, 118–19, 244;
and Indian rights, 136–37, 145–
46; on inequality, 95; on judicial
review, 166–67; on means-tested
benefits, 129–30; and national
identity, 180; on pornography,
73–75; on profit system, 90; role
of, 40, 241; support for language
rights, 207–10; and tolerance,
106. *See also names of individual
political parties;* political parties;
public opinion
entitlement, 19, 96–98, 246
equality: contestability of, 12, 244–
50; as economic value, 87–95,
244–45; hierarchy of conceptions
of, 129, 149; of income, 94–95,
245; minorities and, 114–19;
norm of, 109–10; of opportunity,
148; of outcome, 148, 151–152;
as political weapon, 129; politics
of, 12, 80; reconception of, 121–
122; of status, 103–19; as symbolic value, 82–87, 244; usages
of, 81. *See also* individualism
equal rights. *See* equality
equal rights legislation, support for,
117–18
error thesis, 53, 236–38
espionage, and government surveillance, 30–33
esteem, politics of, 168–69

fairness, conceptions of, 122, 154,
227–28, 249
federalism, 6, 172
feminists, 72
Filmon, Gary, 231
freedom of expression, 53; contestability of, 61–162; as political
right, 21–122; and pornography,
70–78; support of, 59–60